The Crisis in
economic theory

DATE			

The Crisis in Economic Theory

EDITED BY

Daniel Bell and Irving Kristol

Basic Books, Inc., Publishers

NEW YORK

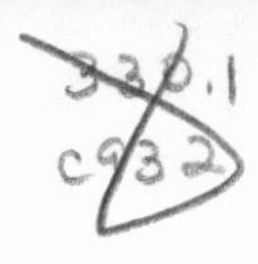

Library of Congress Catalog Card Number: 80–70392
ISBN: 0–465–01476–3
Printed in the United States of America
10 9 8 7 6 5 4 3 2 1

CONTENTS

Introduction

> . . . if [my] ideas are correct . . . it would be a mistake, I predict, to dispute their potency over a period of time. . . . the ideas of economists and political philosophers, both when they are right and when they are wrong, are more powerful than is commonly understood. Indeed, the world is ruled by little else. Practical men, who believe themselves to be quite exempt from any intellectual influences, are usually the slaves of some defunct economist. Madmen in authority, who hear voices in the air, are distilling their frenzy from some academic scribbler of a few years back. I am sure that the power of vested interests is vastly exaggerated compared with the encroachment of ideas. Not, indeed, immediately, but after a certain interval; for in the field of economics and political philosophy there are not many who are influenced by new theories after they are twenty-five or thirty years of age, so that the ideas which civil servants and politicians and even agitators apply to current events are not likely to be the newest. But sooner or later, it is ideas, not vested interests, which are dangerous for good or evil.

These frequently quoted words of John Maynard Keynes, the concluding lines of *The General Theory,* carry a double irony today. Keynes thought it would be some time before his ideas took hold, yet they spread with a rapidity that is astonishing even in contemporary intellectual and political history.* The other irony, of course, is that Keynes's own ideas have become the orthodoxy of academic economists and politicians, with dissenters now regarding them as the *mortmain* that must be lifted if economic theory is to rise to the tasks of the day.

Keynes's *General Theory* was a polemic against the "classical econ-

* The explanation for this rapidity—the book went through eleven reprintings in the twenty years after its publication in 1936—lies outside this discussion, but two facts are relevant. One is the state of bewilderment among political authorities over what to do about the depression other than to let it run its course. The second is Joseph Schumpeter's sociological observation that "many of the men who entered the field of teaching or research in the twenties and thirties had renounced allegiance to the bourgeois scheme of life, the bourgeois scheme of values. . . . But so far as they did not embrace straight socialism, they still had to pay their respect to saving. . . . But Keynes broke their fetters: here at last was a theoretical doctrine that not only obliterated the personal element of private thrift but also smashed the pillar [of inequality] into the dust . . ."

omists"—a term invented by Marx to cover Ricardo and James Mill and their predecessors. Keynes extended the term to cover Ricardo's followers, including John Stuart Mill, Alfred Marshall, and A. C. Pigou. The argument was directed especially against Jean-Baptiste Say who, early in the 19th century, had promulgated a "law" that "supply creates its own demand"—a belief shared by Ricardo and all the classical economists. This belief is equivalent to saying that in a free market economy there is no obstacle to full employment. Even today practically all economists agree that Say's Law applies to a barter economy, in which commodities are considered only in relation to each other—a Ricardian theme that Piero Sraffa revived in contemporary economics. The question is: How valid is the principle in a money and credit economy? How does one account for "general gluts" (that is, depressions), which Say's Law denies? Keynes offered a theory that explained the phenomenon—the failure of savings to pass over into investment—and a policy to cope with it, but *his* theory then could not cope with "stagflation," the coexistence of economic stagnation and inflation, which is a Keynesian impossibility.

Clearly, the contemporary economic theory, specifically the "neo-Keynesian synthesis" forged by Sir John Hicks and Paul Samuelson that combines the neoclassical tradition of microeconomics with Keynes's macroeconomics, is in difficulty. One can say that the world has changed; while undoubtedly true, it is irrelevant, for a good theory provides the means for its own modification under new conditions. Whether the neo-Keynesian synthesis can do so or not is one of the issues now in debate. The broader question, and the starting point for this volume, is: Why should Keynes's theory now be in trouble; and what are the new modes of reorientation in our economic thinking?

To celebrate its fifteenth anniversary issue, *The Public Interest* devoted a special issue—printed here in its entirety—to this question. We emphasize that the discussion focuses on economic theory, not economic policy. But it is hard to separate the two, for most controversies in economic theory involve a clash of assumptions about the structure of economic reality. We need not introduce here all the issues covered in *The Crisis in Economic Theory*, yet it might be useful to single out some of the crucial themes.

The "grand neoclassical synthesis" had sought to integrate microeconomics—as reformulated in a new "general equilibrium" theory by Kenneth Arrow and Frank Hahn—with the reformulation of Keynes's macroeconomics (involving the saving-investment relation and the demand for money) by Sir John Hicks. From this synthesis came the policy conclusions of Paul Samuelson on how fiscal and monetary policy could join to maintain both full employment and economic growth.

It is not only the frustrations of economic policy in the last decade that have caused Samuelson's conclusions to be called into question, although some economists, such as Assar Lindbeck, contend that the theory is correct and the politicians are at fault. Critical intellectual examination of the structure of the model has raised doubts about its very assumptions. One central challenge is to the idea of "equilibrium" itself—the assumption about the way prices adjust to each other so as to "clear all markets." Within the Keynesian camp, "revisionist" theorists such as Robert Clower and Axel Leijönhufvud have argued that Keynesian economics is best understood as a general theory about "disequilibria," or the failure of a variety of adjustment mechanisms. For them, Keynesian economics is about incomplete and costly information, about sluggish price adjustments, and about quantity rather than price adjustments in markets. Why presume, then, that the adjusting mechanisms of the price system will eliminate shortages and surpluses in markets and lead to full employment? To this extent, Clower and Leijönhufvud are pursuing a thread of Keynes's later thought, as laid out in his answer to critics a year after the appearance of *The General Theory*. There he attributed the underemployment of resources and the disequilibria in the economic system not just to sticky interest or wage rates, but to the very uncertainties in any calculations about the future.

The "neo-Austrian" economists, following von Mises and Hayek, challenge the equilibrium assumption from a different perspective. They argue that market prices are not "approximations" to some theoretical set of equilibrium prices, but represent instead unequal exchange ratios between different factors and products. Price variations originate with profit-seeking entrepreneurs whose very alertness to these differences as representing opportunities, creates profit.

Challenges to the idea of equilibrium raise questions about the role of *time, risk, uncertainty,* and *expectations* as major variables that economic theory would have to take into account. For Keynes, psychological factors were the "ultimate independent variables" that determined output and employment: the "propensity to consume" (habits he assumed to be relatively stable over time); attitudes to liquidity (that is, the decision either to hold money instruments or goods); and the expectations about future yields from capital. Keynes considered the latter two volatile, as a result of the inflexibility of interest rates and wages, both of which had become "sticky" or ineffective as switching signals for decision makers.*

If psychological variables are overriding, one needs a theory of economic behavior that rests more on assumptions about expectations and uncertainty. On these matters neoclassical theory is particularly deficient: It treats separately risk-taking under conditions of uncertainty, does not integrate into its schema the expanded role of expectations, and, indeed, has no place for—or even the concept of—the entrepreneur in its system.†

Much of economic theory and policy in the last forty years has centered on macroeconomics, on the role of aggregates, such as GNP, or on aggregate behavior. Yet the rethinking of fundamental assumptions has raised questions about how useful such concentration on aggregates is. The neo-Austrian economists, in fact, dispute the approach altogether; Hayek, for example, allied philosophically with Karl Popper in the doctrine of "methodological individualism," argues that all behavior is understandable only in individual terms, and that there are no such collective entities as the "community" or "society" or "government" whose properties are different from those of individuals. And for that reason economic theory ought to focus, properly, on the microeconomic level.

In a different vein, the brilliant "games" of Tom Schelling (in his *Micromotives and Macrobehavior*) demonstrate the uneasy link between the two levels. In his illustrations, be they concerned with traffic congestion or with the "tipping" of racially-mixed residential neighborhoods, Schelling shows that what each individual wants for

* As G. L. Shackle points out:

> The *General Theory of Employment, Interest and Money* is the most paradoxical of books. Constructed on a purely static and equilibrium frame of formal argument, it clothes this frame in a rich and suggestive mantle of ideas about expectations and their precarious basis and extreme unstable sensitiveness to "the news." . . . Keynes saw in the business world a succession of highly unstable equilibria. In his formal construction he described the equilibria of each situation; in his powerful gloss upon this formal argument he explained their almost explosive instability. . . . But Kalecki, Kaldor, Samuelson and Hicks have in succession opted for a "business cycle machine" complete in itself, to which regular and therefore predictable oscillation is as natural as the tides or the seasons. These latter models give no place at all to expectation and have no use for expectational time, but exemplify in the purest form the concept of a historical pattern seen "from without" by a detached observer in whose mind it exists as a simultaneously valid whole. [G. L. Shackle, *A Scheme of Economic Theory* (Cambridge University Press, 1965), pp. 5–6]

† These questions have been central to the work of Joseph Schumpeter, Frank Knight, and G. L. Shackle, and are often discussed in a descriptive way, but they do not appear in the formal models of neoclassical theory.

himself can in the aggregate become a situation no one wants; in short, one cannot simply add up individual decisions and assume the total to be the simple sum of all the decisions, for at a certain threshold the aggregate consequences may negate the individual's intentions.

If the relationship between micro- and macroeconomic theory frames one set of questions, definitions of rationality and optimization frame another. Neoclassical theory and Austrian economics assume a *homo economicus,* the individual acting rationally to find the most efficient means to realize his ends, or "ordering" his preferences on a scale of utilities. Yet Herbert Simon has argued that "satisficing" rather than optimizing best describes the actual behavior of firms. And an increasing number of philosophers have questioned the practice of equating rationality with functional efficiency.

These are some of the questions and challenges. In the last several years, an extraordinary variety of "answers" have been proposed, embracing the widest spectrum of political and philosophical views. Despite this intellectual ferment, no single publication has sought to reexamine the underlying assumptions of economic theory, or to assemble different spokespersons for revisionist points of view to present their arguments, as we have attempted to do in this volume.

The twelve theorists represented here accept the fact that the consensus on economic theory has been broken. Each attempts a different task. The opening chapters are primarily historical and analytical. In the first, Peter Drucker (an Austrian by birth, but not a complete one in economic outlook), proposes a new way to look at the economy, using productivity and capital as a theory of value. James Dean (chapter 2) reviews the history of the Keynesian consensus and focuses on the newer paths of disequilibrium theory. Daniel Bell (chapter 4) goes back to the logical postulates of neoclassical theory, traces their successive redefinitions by Alfred Marshall, Leon Walras, and John Maynard Keynes, and asks whether these models can "mirror" reality or must remain as fictions, or ideal types, against which to judge the empirical events.

The central group of essays presents the viewpoints of the different schools of thought, each marching off to one of the different corners of the quadrants of the economic universe. Allan Meltzer (chapter 3) makes a case for monetarism, Mark Willes (chapter 5) for the new school of "rational expectations," Israel Kirzner (chapter 7) for the neo-Austrian view of the unrealistic character of equilibrium theory and competition. Harvey Leibenstein (chapter 6) deals with the unsatisfactory character of optimization theory in microeconomics. Paul Davidson, representing the so-called Post Keynesians, argues that the unequal distribution of income and market power are the central determinants of economic activity. Edward J. Nell (chapter 11) sketches the neo-Marxist reconsiderations of the labor theory of value. The two essays by Frank Hahn and Kenneth Arrow, respectively, restate the case for general equilibrium theory and point to new, non-Walrasian equilibrium concepts. The concluding essay by Irving Kristol raises questions about the ability of economics to be a "science," its possibly excessive rationalism, and the need to acknowledge the "bedrock truths" about human desires that were enunciated by Adam Smith in *The Wealth of Nations.*

Though the essays do not represent each and every dissenting perspective that has emerged (or reemerged) in recent years, they embrace the major lines of argument.* If we are witnessing the dissolution of an intellectual establishment, and its fragmentation into conflicting schools, what this eventually leads to—if one reads the history of any intellectual discipline—is the development of a new, comprehensive framework. Although it is far too early to say just what this will look like, we suspect it will incorporate, in varying degrees, elements from the arguments presented here.

One other word of caution is necessary. Economic theory, if it is to be viable, must propose rational solutions to problems. And for that reason, theory cannot exist without practical wisdom. As Michael Oakeshott once observed, no one learned to ride a bicycle by studying its design, though such study might help one design a better bicycle. Or, as Frank Hahn and Martin Hollis point out (in their reader on *Philosophy and Economic Theory*):

> Aero-dynamics, for instance, is a tightly constructed, highly developed theory yet it is quite impossible to design an aeroplane on paper and then go straight into production. The design will need testing with mock-ups and wind-tunnels and may require *ad hoc,* imperfectly understood modifications. Theories have to simplify and then have to patch. The most it is worth insisting on in advance is agreed rules of evidence and argument.

* The absence of an article on what is called "supply-side economics" simply reflects the fact that its import bears more directly on economic policy than on economic theory. Its critique of Keynesianism, for instance, is very much along the lines of "neo-Austrian" theory. To some degree, Irving Kristol's essay reflects the general approach to economic theory shared by those who have been advocating "supply-side" policies.

Keynes, it is once said, urged economists to be "like dentists." Although he did not take the advice himself (as Hahn and Hollis note), it may not be a bad prescription.

DANIEL BELL
IRVING KRISTOL

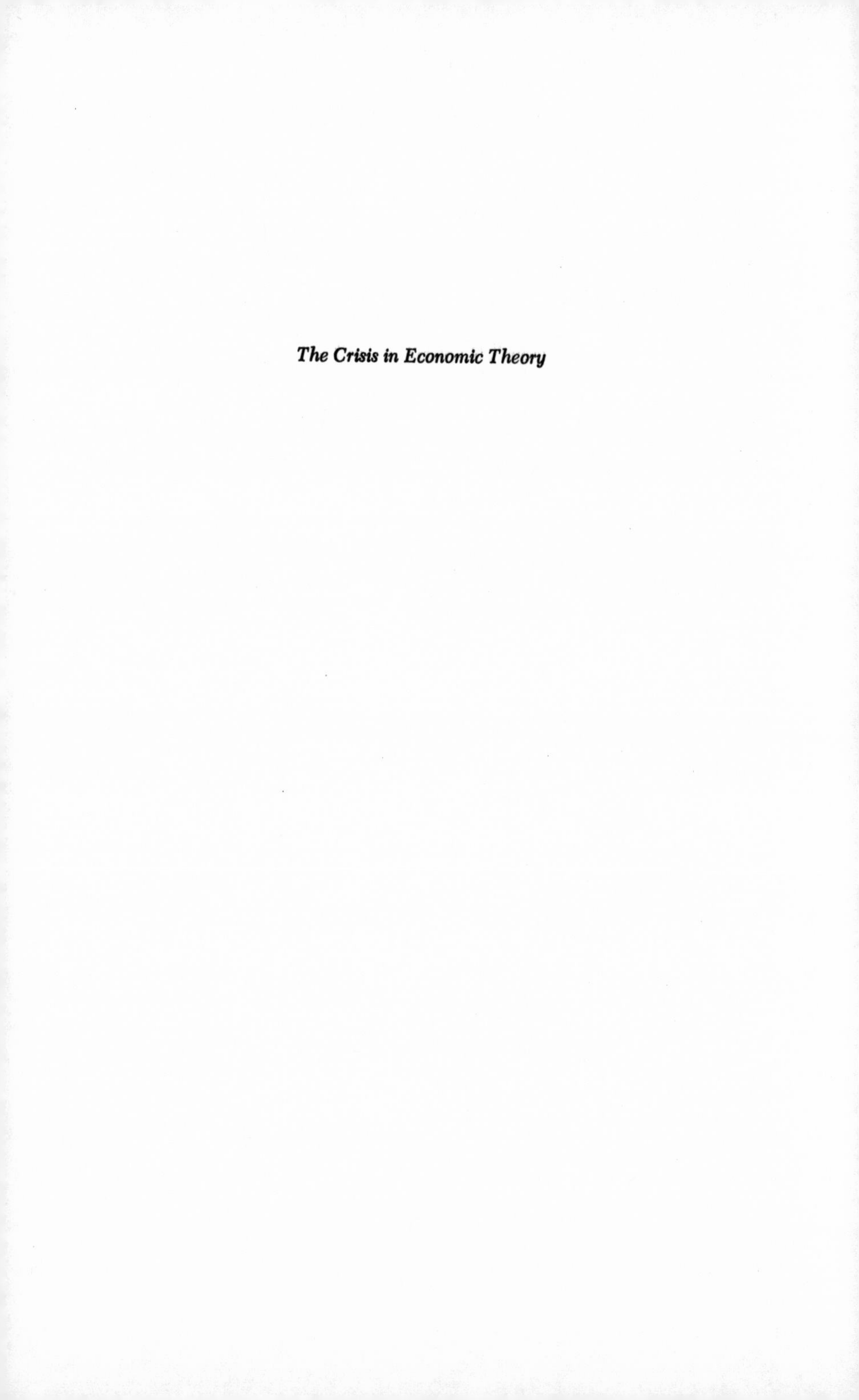

The Crisis in Economic Theory

CONTRIBUTORS

Peter Drucker is Clarke Professor of Social Science and Management at Claremont Graduate School and Professor Emeritus of Management at the Graduate Business School of New York University. His latest book is *Managing in Turbulent Times* (Harper & Row, 1980). . . . James W. Dean is Associate Professor of Money, Banking, and Macroeconomics at Simon Fraser University in Vancouver, Canada, and Visiting Associate Professor of International Banking at Columbia University in New York. . . . Allan H. Meltzer is John M. Olin Professor of Political Economy and Public Policy at Carnegie-Mellon University. . . . Daniel Bell is Henry Ford II Professor of Social Sciences at Harvard University. His new book, *The Winding Passage: Essays and Sociological Journeys, 1960-1980,* has been published this fall by Abt Books. . . . Mark H. Willes was president of the Federal Reserve Bank of Minneapolis from April 1977 until July of this year, when he became executive vice president, chief financial officer, and a member of the management policy committee at General Mills, Inc., Minneapolis. . . . Harvey Leibenstein is Andelot Professor of Economics and Population at Harvard University. . . . Israel M. Kirzner is Professor of Economics at New York University. His most recent book is *Perception, Opportunity and Profit: Studies in the Theory of Entrepreneurship* (University of Chicago Press, 1979). . . . Frank Hahn is Professor of Economics at Cambridge University in England, and is co-author with Kenneth J. Arrow of *General Competitive Analysis* (Holden, 1971). . . . Kenneth J. Arrow is Joan Kenney Professor of Economics and Professor of Operations Research at Stanford University. He is former president of the American Economic Association. . . . Paul Davidson is Professor of Economics at Rutgers University and co-editor of the *Journal of Post Keynesian Economics*. . . . Edward J. Nell is Professor of Economics on the Graduate Faculty at the New School for Social Research in New York. He is the author with Martin Hollis of *Rational Economic Man* (Cambridge, 1975) and *Growth, Profits and Property: Essays on the Revival of Political Economy* (Cambridge, 1980). . . . Irving Kristol is Professor of Social Thought at the Graduate Business School of New York University.

1

Toward the next economics

PETER F. DRUCKER

In its 400-year history, economics has passed through four major changes in its world view, its concerns, its "paradigms." It is now in the throes of another, its fifth "scientific revolution."

Economics today is very largely "The House That Keynes Built." True, even in the English-speaking world, only a minority of economists are Keynesians in their specific theories. But the great majority, perhaps even in the Communist countries, are Keynesians in their "mind set," in what they see and consider important in their concerns and in their basic assumptions. They tend to define themselves largely through their relationship to Keynesian economics, as "near-Keynesians," or "non-Keynesians," or "anti-Keynesians." Their terminology—gross national product, for instance, or "money supply"—assumes the economic aggregates on which Keynesian economics is based. The views of economic activity, economic policy, and economic theory which Keynes propounded—or at least codified—around 1930 have, 50 years later, become the familiar environment, the home-ground of economists, regardless of persuasion. The Keynesians may not muster the biggest battalions. But they have occupied the commanding heights and thereby define the issues.

Yet both as economic theory and as economic policy Keynesian economics is in disarray. It is unable to tackle the central policy problems of the developed economies—productivity and capital formation; indeed, Keynesian economics must deny that these problems could even exist. Nor is it able to provide a theory that can encompass, let alone explain, observed economic reality and experience.

Indeed, the two theoretical approaches which alone during these last 10 or 15 years have shown consistent predictive power are both incompatible with the Keynesian model: the theories of the Canadian-born Columbia University economist, Robert Mundell, and those of the "rational expectations" school. Mundell, after thorough empirical studies, concluded more than 10 years ago that Keynesian policies do not work in the international economy. He correctly predicted the failure of currency devaluation to correct the balance of payments, stem inflation, and improve competitive position. The "rational expectations" school goes even further; it postulates that governmental, that is macroeconomic, intervention might not just be deleterious; it is futile and ineffectual.

But these new approaches are equally incompatible with pre-Keynesian theories, whether neoclassical or Marxist. What makes the present "crisis of economics" a genuine "scientific revolution" is our inability to go back to the economic world view which Keynes overturned. To be sure, most of the economic theorems, economic methodologies, and economic terms found in the textbooks today will be found in the textbooks tomorrow. They will be reinterpreted—the way Quantum Physics reinterprets Newton's Optics. After all, Keynes did not discard a single theorem of classical economics. He even retained "Say's Law," according to which savings always equal investments; it became a "special case." And one of the most advanced tools of modern economics, input-output analysis, goes back to the first attempt at economic analysis, the Physiocrats' *Tableau Economique* more than two centuries ago. But as economic world view, or as economic system, the earlier theories—such as the disciplined orthodoxy of the "Austrians"—will not do. What made Keynes so compelling 50 years ago even to a doubter (as I must confess myself to have been even then) was the new vision he forced on us; we suddenly had to see a whole new reality—and that reality is still with us and will not disappear. The next economics will be "meta-Keynesian." It cannot ignore Keynes but it will have to transcend him.

Of course, there may be no "economics" in the future. Totalitarian regimes, while greatly concerned with the economy, do not tolerate the postulate on which any discipline of economics must base itself: Economic activity, though constrained and limited by non-economic rationality, concerns, and values, constitutes a discrete and separate sphere. Totalitarian regimes cannot accept economic activity as autonomous, internally consistent, and "*zweckrational*" within its boundaries. In a totalitarian regime, economics inexorably becomes a branch of accounting.

But if there is a future economics, it will differ fundamentally from the present one. We do not yet know what the economic theories of tomorrow will be. But we do know what the main problems, the main concerns, the main challenges will be. We do not know the next economics; but we can outline its specifications.

Four "scientific revolutions"

To do this, we have to look paradigmatically—that is, as methodologists rather than as economists—at the economic world views underlying the four "scientific revolutions" in economics that preceded the one in which we find ourselves, and especially at the basic world view and at the assumptions of the last, the Keynesian system.

Economics began with the Cameralists and Mercantilists of France in the first half of the 17th century. They were the first to see the economy as autonomous. Earlier there was no economics, however great the concern with trade and livelihoods, with wealth, coinage, and taxes. As a system, a world view, Mercantilism was macroeconomic and its universe was a political unit, the territory controlled by the Prince. Indeed the definition of the "national state," as it emerged at the end of the 16th century, was essentially an economic one: the unit controlled by the Prince through his control of coinage and foreign trade. Mercantilism was supply-focused economics. To produce the largest possible export surplus, and with it the hard currency needed to pay professional soldiers, was its central concern.

Despite its preoccupation with supply, Mercantilism failed, however, to produce it. Mercantilism collapsed as a system in what we would today call a "productivity crisis." The more the French Government promoted manufacture for export and for the generation of specie, the poorer the country became—especially by contrast with the non-mercantilist, unsystematic, and unscientific English across the Channel. At the same time, Mercantilism also failed to spur capital formation. There were few statistics in those days other than foreign-trade figures, the price of bread, and tax receipts; but there is no doubt that the French savings rate dropped sharply while savings in non-Mercantilist England steadily went up.

The Physiocrats started their "scientific revolution" with the paradox that under Mercantilism Europe's "richest country," France, had become one of its poorest ones, and was becoming the more wretched the more specie it earned. They solved the paradox by applying Gallic logic to Anglo-Saxon pragmatism. Their system remained as much supply-focused as was that of the Mercantilists. But they turned microeconomist, with the individual piece of land and its cultivator the economic unit. This, then, forced them into the first economic theory of value—that is, the first theory that did not square "wealth" with "money." The Physiocrats' source of value was nature in its economic manifestation, that is, land as producer of human sustenance. With this, economics had become genuinely autonomous, had become a "discipline."

Classical economics—the third of the economic world systems—took from the Physiocrats both the concern with supply and the focus on microeconomics. But it shifted the theory of value from "nature" to "man." With the Labor Theory of Value, economics became a "moral science." It is to this, as much as to its success in producing wealth, that classical economics owed its victory and its rapid rise as the star among the new disciplines. But very soon, by the time of the mature John Stuart Mill in 1850 or so, the Labor Theory of Value became an impediment and the cause of serious theoretical turbulence.

This underlay the third of the scientific revolutions, the one that occurred in the second half of the 19th century: the shift from classical to neoclassical economics, from the disciples of Ricardo to Leon Walras in Belgium and the Austrian pioneers of marginal utility. The shift was primarily philosophical. The neoclassics shifted from "value" to "utility." They shifted from human needs to human wants. They shifted from economic structure to economic analysis. To a noneconomist this may not seem like a major shift, and may hardly deserve the name "scientific revolution." But it introduced a new spirit that has animated economics and economists alike to this day.

This third "scientific revolution" also split economics. Marx and the Marxists refused to abandon the Labor Theory of Value. This then forced them to spurn economic analysis. And they were forced also to subordinate economics to noneconomic "historical forces."

The classics' microeconomics with its built-in "equilibrium," they asserted, would work only if and when meta-economic obstacles to labor's obtaining its full share of the social product were removed through political upheavals generated by the system's "economic contradictions"—or, as Lenin later redefined it, by the system's "political contradictions." Then the state would wither away, then microeconomics would take over, then there would be true equilibrium.

Seen against the paradigmatic background of economics, Keynes was indeed right in the claim he voiced in his Cambridge seminar in the 1930's, that his economics represented a far more radical break with tradition than Marx and Marxism. Keynes not only went back to the Mercantilists in being macroeconomic. He stood all earlier systems on their heads by being demand-centered rather than supply-centered. In all earlier economics demand is a function of supply. In Keynesian economics supply is a function of demand and controlled by it. Above all—the greatest innovation—Keynes redefined economic reality. Instead of goods, services, and work—realities of the physical world and "things"—Keynes' economic realities are symbols: money and credit. To the Mercantilists, too, money gave control—but political rather than economic control. Keynes was the first to postulate that money and credit give complete *economic* control.

The relationship between the "real" economy of goods, work, and services, and the "symbol" economy of money and credit had been a problem since earliest times. Few economists were satisfied with the way the Classics (following the Physiocrats) dismissed money as the "veil of reality." Well before Keynes, economists of stature, such as MacCulloch who was otherwise a devout Ricardian, or in the generation before Keynes, the Swede Karl Gustav Cassell and the German Georg Friedrich Knapp, had attempted to replace a thing-based economics with a symbol-based one. But it was Keynes' observation, that in the recession of the 1920's the English labor unions treated money wages as "real" and as "income" even when this actually resulted in lower purchasing power for their members, that then produced a genuine "scientific revolution." In Keynesian economics commodities, production, and work are the "veil of reality." Or, rather, these *things* are determined by monetary events: money supply, credit, interest rates, and governmental surpluses or deficits. Goods, services, production, productivity, demand, employment, and finally prices, are all dependent variables of the macroeconomic events of the monetary, symbol economy. Philosophically speaking, Keynes became an extreme nominalist—it was perhaps not entirely coincidence that he and Wittgenstein were contemporaries at Cambridge.*

To classics, neoclassics, and Marxists, the Great Depression of the 1930's originated in the "real economy," in the impoverishment of Europe in the First World War, further aggravated by reparations and by a sharp drop in the productivity of European agriculture and industry. To a Keynesian, however, including Milton Friedman, the Great Depression was the result of the Stock Exchange crash of 1929, of "speculation," or of a contraction in the money supply—that is, of events in the symbol economy.

The origins of the present crisis

The present "crisis in economics" is a failure of the basic assumptions, of the paradigm, of the "system," rather than of this or that theory. Keynesian economics has run into the most severe productivity crisis since that of 18th-century France which discredited Mercantilism. This productivity crisis in all developed countries—and worst in the two most faithfully Keynesian countries, Great Britain and the United States—invalidates the Keynesian theorem of the demand-control of supply. The crisis in capital formation which we are facing at the same time—again at its worst in Great Britain and the U.S.—could not, within Keynesian economics, have happened at all; it is theoretically impossible within the Keynesian paradigms.

Keynes was fully aware of the importance of productivity. But he was also convinced that productivity is a function of demand and determined by it. In the early 1930's, the great years of the Keynes seminar in Cambridge, one heard again and again of Keynes being asked by one of the first-rate minds in the seminar—Joan Robinson perhaps, or Roy Harrod, or Abba Lerner—"What about

* Looked at paradigmatically, Milton Friedman is as much a "Keynesian" as the Master himself, rather than the "anti-Keynesian" he is commonly depicted as Friedman accepts without reservation the Keynesian world view. His economics is pure macroeconomics, with the national government as the one unit, the one dynamic force, controlling the economy through the money supply. Friedman's economics are completely demand-focused. Money and credit are the pervasive, and indeed the only, economic reality. That Friedman sees money supply as original and interest rates as derivative, is not much more than minor gloss on the Keynesian scriptures. It is "fine-tuning" Keynes. And what has made Friedman stand out is not so much his monetary theory as his insistence on economic activity as being autonomous, on economic values as the hinge on which economic policy and behavior must turn, and on the free market—on all of which Keynes himself would have been in full agreement.

productivity?" He always answered: "We can take productivity for granted, provided that employment and demand remain high."

The classics had not taken productivity for granted. On the contrary, central to classical economics is the "law" of the diminishing return of all resources. Marx had based his forecast of the imminent demise of the "bourgeois system" (the term "capitalism" was not widely used until after Marx's death) on this axiom. What made Marx different was only his meta-economic, semi-religious belief that the end of "alienation" would release such enormous human energy as to reverse the diminishing return on resources in an outburst of "creativity." But just when Marx, in the last unfinished volume of *Das Kapital,* most confidently predicted the demise of the "system" because of its inherent productivity crisis, productivity began to go up sharply. In part this was the result of the systematic approach to work, first developed by Frederick W. Taylor in his "Task Study" (only later misnamed "Scientific Management"), which showed that human work can be made infinitely more productive, not by "working harder" but by "working smarter." In part this was the result of the great age of innovation, as a result of which resources were systematically shifted from older and less productive into newer and more productive employments. In large part, the rise in productivity was the result of steady work on making resources—especially capital—more productive. The greatest productivity increase in the last hundred years has probably not been in the factory, but in commercial banking, where one dollar of assets today supports at least a hundred times the volume of transaction it supported a hundred years ago—and without any release of "creativity" or any great innovation. At that time—that is, in the decades around 1900—the developed countries learned to use capital not to replace labor, but to upgrade it and to make it more productive, as Simon Kuznets has shown in his pioneering studies. Altogether, the reversal between 1900 and 1920 of the theory of productivity from one that postulated a built-in tendency towards diminishing returns to one that postulated a steady increase, was a major factor in the Keynesian "scientific revolution." It made possible, in large measure, the shift from supply-focus to demand-focus—that is, to the belief that production tends inherently to surplus rather than to scarcity.

It was thus not totally frivolous to assume, as Keynes did 50 years ago, that productivity would take care of itself and would continue to increase slowly but steadily, if only economic confidence prevailed for both businessmen and workingmen, and if only demand stayed high and unemployment low. In the early 1930's Keynes' was a rational—albeit optimistic—view (though even then Joseph Schumpeter and Lionel Robbins could not accept it).

But surely this can no longer be maintained. And yet within the Keynesian system there is no room for productivity, no way to stimulate or spur it, no means to make an economy more productive. With productivity emerging as a central economic need and problem, especially in the most highly developed countries—and a need alike in manufacturing, in services, and in agriculture—the Keynesian inability to handle productivity within the theoretical structure or within economic policy is as serious a flaw as was the inability of Ptolemaic astronomy around the time of Copernicus to explain the motion of stars and planets.

For economic theory the decline in capital formation in the developed countries, and especially in the countries of the Keynesian true believers—the United States and Great Britain—is even more serious. Within Keynesian economics the decline cannot be explained, cannot have happened.

Capital is the future. It is the provision for the risks, the uncertainties, the changes, and the jobs of tomorrow. It is not "present" cost—but it is certain cost. An economy that does not form enough capital to cover its future costs is an economy that condemns itself to decline and continuing crisis, the crisis of "stagflation."

The essence of Keynesian economic theory, as every undergraduate is being taught, was the repudiation of "Say's Law," according to which savings always equal investment, so that an economy always forms enough capital for its future needs. Keynes postulated instead a tendency toward "over-saving" for developed economies. "Under-saving"—that is, a shortfall in capital formation—cannot possibly occur in a developed economy according to the Keynesian postulate. From the beginning this was seen as a serious flaw in Keynesian economics by such thoughtful (and sympathetic) critics as Joseph Schumpeter. Surely, once it is accepted that savings and investment need not be identical, "under-saving" is just as likely as "over-saving." And what we have had in the last 30 years in the English-speaking, developed, Keynesian, countries—since well before the energy crisis—is "under-saving" on a massive scale. The basic assumption underlying the Keynesian paradigm can therefore no longer be held or defended. Nor within the Keynesian economic universe can capital formation be dealt with. For Keynesian economics explicitly excludes the possibility of under-saving, and thereby of inadequate capital formation. And if capital is a true "cost" of the economy—and even Keynes never doubted this—demand-based macroeconomics cannot adequately deal with economic theory or economic policy.

Even more serious may be the failure of the basic postulate underlying Keynesian economic *policy*: the "economist-king," the objective, independent expert who makes effective decisions based solely on objective, quantitative, unambiguous evidence, and free of both political ambitions and of political pressures on him. Even in the 1930's, a good many people found it difficult to accept this. To the Continental Europeans in particular, with their memories of the post-war inflations, the "economist-king" was sheer *hubris*—which in large measure explains why Keynes has had so few followers on the Continent until the last 10 or 15 years. By now, however, few would take seriously the postulate of the non-political economist who, at the same time, controls crucial political decisions. Like all "enlightened despots," the Keynesian "economist-king" has proven to be a delusion, and indeed a contradiction in terms. If there is one thing taught by the inflations of the last decade—as it was taught by the inflations of the 1920's in Europe—it is that the economist in power either becomes himself a politician and expedient (if not irresponsible), or he ceases to have power and influence. It is simply not true, as is often asserted, that economists do not know how to stop inflation. Every economist since the late 16th century has known how to do it: Cut government expenses and with them the creation of money. What economists lack is not theoretical knowledge, it is political will or political power. And so far all inflations have been ended by politicians who had the will rather than by economists who had the knowledge.

Without the "economist-king," Keynesian economics ceases to be operational. It can play the role of critic, which Keynes played in the 1920's, and which Milton Friedman plays today. In opposition, the Keynesian economist, being powerless, can also be politics-free. But it is an opposition that cannot become effective government. The Keynesian paradigm is thus likely to be around a long time as a critique and as a guide to what not to do. But it is fast losing its credibility as a foundation for economic theory and as a guide to policy and action.

The next economics

The next "scientific revolution," the overturning of the paradigms that underlay economic theory and economic policy these last 30 years, may start with productivity or with capital formation. There are beginnings in both areas. But that there is both a productivity crisis and a capital-formation crisis makes certain that the next economics will have to be again microeconomic and centered on supply. Both productivity and capital formation are events of the microeconomy. Both also deal with the factors of *production* rather than being functions of demand.

We know a good deal about productivity and capital formation. A vast amount of empirical and theoretical work has been done in both areas in the last 30 years. Productivity, we know, means both the economic yield from every one of the factors of production (the human resource, capital, physical resources, and time) and the overall yield of the joint resources in combination. Capital formation, we know, has to be at least equal to the cost of capital. And in a growing economy, the costs of the future to be covered by today's capital formation are substantially higher even than the cost of capital. In a growing economy, tomorrow's jobs, by definition, will require substantially higher capital investment than today's jobs, and will thus require substantially greater capital formation than the replacement of capital represented by the prevailing return rate for capital. And we know how to determine the rate of capital formation needed for the uncertainties of the future within a margin of error that is no greater than that which pertains to such accepted costs of the present in the accounting model as depreciation or credit risks.

We also know quite a bit about the factors and forces which encourage both greater productivity and greater capital formation. None of them, it should be said, is a factor of the "symbol economy" of money and credit. Events in the symbol economy can discourage, but are unlikely significantly to encourage, either productivity or a higher rate of capital formation.

But while we have both the concepts and the data, we do not have, so far, a microeconomic model that embraces productivity and capital formation. Even the terms are largely unknown to available theories, such as the "Theory of the Firm," which is the microeconomics most commonly taught in our college courses. Instead of productivity and capital formation, the Theory of the Firm talks of "profit maximization." But we have known for at least 50 years that "profit maximization" is a meaningless term if applied to anything other than a unique, non-recurrent trading transaction on the part of an individual and in a single commodity—that is, to an exceptional, rare, and quite unrepresentative incident. The next economics in its microeconomics will, almost certainly, discard altogether the concept of "profit." It assumes a static, unchanging, closed economy. In a moving, changing, open-ended economy, in which there is risk, uncertainty, and change, there is no "profit," except—as Schumpeter taught 70 years ago—the temporary profit of the genuine innovator. For any other economic activity there is only cost—the costs of past and present, which are embodied in the accounting model, and the costs of the future expressed in the cost of capital. Indeed no business is known to apply "profit maximization" to its planning or to its decisions on capital investment or pricing. Instead the theories and concepts that govern the actual, as against the theoretical, behavior of firms are theories of the cost of capital, of market optimization, and of the long-range cost gains (the "learning curve") from maximizing the volume of production rather than from maximizing profitability.

The next economics will thus require radically different micro-economics as its foundation. It will require a theory that aims at optimizing productivity; for a balance of several partially dependent functions is, of necessity, an optimization rather than a maximization. Capital formation requires a minimum concept: the coverage of the cost of capital. It requires a theory that aims at "satisficing" rather than at maximizing profit (though the minimum cost of capital will, paradoxically, be found to be substantially higher than what most present-day economists and most business executives consider the available maximum profitability—which is, of course, why there is a "capital formation crisis"). The next micro-economics, unlike the present one, will be dynamic and assume risk, uncertainty, and change in technology, business conditions, and markets. Yet it should be equilibrium economics, integrating a provision for an uncertain and changing future into present and testable behavior. Much of the spadework for this has already been done—in part, 50 years ago, by the Chicago economist Frank Knight; in part, by the contemporary English economist, G. L. S. Shackle. The next micro-economic theory should thus be able to resolve the dilemma that has plagued economists since Ricardo, almost 200 years ago: Economic analysis is possible only if it excludes uncertainty and change, and economic policy is possible only in contemplation of uncertainty and change. In the next microeconomics, we should be able to integrate both analysis and policy in one dynamic equilibrium through productivity and capital formation.

If productivity and capital formation are its focal points, a micro-economic theory can also do what never before could be done in economics: to tie together microeconomics and macroeconomics, if not make them into one. While productivity and capital formation are events of the microeconomy, they are—unlike profit—meaningful terms of the macroeconomy as well, and measurable macroeconomic aggregates. "Profit," by definition, applies only to one legal entity, the "entrepreneur" or the "firm." But it makes sense to speak of the productivity of a country or of capital formation in the world economy.

In the past, economic theory was either microeconomic or macroeconomic. Alfred Marshall, the last classical economist, tried in the early years of this century to combine the two; but no one, including Marshall himself, thought that he had succeeded. It was Marshall's failure, in large part, that made Keynes opt for a purely macroeconomic system. The next economics will not, it is reasonably certain, have the luxury of choosing between microeconomics and macroeconomics. It will have to accomplish what Marshall tried and failed to do: integrate both. Macroeconomics has proven itself—for the second time—to be unable to handle supply, that is, productivity and capital formation. Yet microeconomics alone is not adequate either for economic theory or for economic policy in a world of mixed economies, multinational corporations, non-convertible currencies, and governments that redistribute half their nations' incomes. But what the term "macroeconomy" will actually mean in the next economics is anything but clear and will be highly controversial.

For 400 years the term automatically meant the "national economy." The Germans, to this day, call the discipline of "economics" "*National*oekonomie" or "*Volks*wirtschaft." But the one theory today which attempts to integrate microeconomics and macroeconomics, that of Robert Mundell, all but dismisses national government as a factor. Mundell's macroeconomy is the world economy. National governments, in Mundell's economics, are effective only insofar as they are agents of the world economy, anticipating its structural trends and shaping their own domestic economies to conform; the examples are Japan and Germany in the years of their most rapid growth in the 1960's. And the countries that attempted to behave like true "macroeconomies" during the post-World War II period—especially the Keynesian countries, Great Britain and the United States—are, as Mundell shows, also countries that had the least control over their national economies at the highest cost.

This, by the way, was the conclusion Keynes himself reached for towards the end of his life. Around 1942 Keynes ceased to be a "Keynesian" and abandoned the nation-state as the macroeconomy.

Instead he proposed to build the post-war economy around "Bancor," a transnational money that would be independent of national governments and national currencies and managed by non-political economists acting as transnational civil servants. "Bancor" was shot down at the Bretton Woods Conference by the American Keynesians, who suspected it of being an attempt to maintain the pound sterling as the world's "key currency," but who also were confident of the ability of the American dollar to be the world's "key currency," and of the wisdom of American economists in managing the dollar and in keeping it free from domestic political pressures. But today even the Americans are pushing the "Special Drawing Rights" (SDR) of the International Monetary Fund as the transnational and non-national money of the world economy. Even the Americans have accepted that there can be no "key currency"—that is, that no nation-state can aspire to genuine economic sovereignty. And the major holders of liquid funds in the world economy—the OPEC countries, the Central Banks, and the very large multinationals based in balance-of-payments surplus countries such as Germany, Japan, or Switzerland—are fast putting their cash into transnational money, such as the SDR's, a "market basket" of national currencies, money of account indexed to purchasing power, or gold.

And yet it makes sense to speak of a "Brazilian economy" or a "British economy." The nation-state is a reality. It is not *the* economic reality, the way traditional macroeconomics has it. But it is also not an "extraneous factor" which can limit economic activity but cannot determine or direct it. The next economics will have to account for this reality. For the national state is surely, for the foreseeable future, the one political institution around.

Predictably, therefore, the next economics will, at its center, have a spirited debate over the place of national government in economic theory. One approach might follow Mundell and consider the national government, at least in developed countries, to be no more than a gear in the system rather than its engine. Another approach, predictably, will attempt to maintain the nation-state and its government as the center of the economic universe, with both the macroeconomy and the world economy, so to speak, planets in orbit around it. There may even be two parallel theorems of such a "Ptolemaic," "nation-centered" economic system, an Anglo-American and neo-Keynesian one, and a French and Cameralist one. One approach would attempt to maintain control and uniqueness of the national economy through money and credit, and the other one control through what the French call "indicative planning"—that is, through allocation of capital, labor, and physical resources. There may be—methodologically there almost has to be—a further approach which tries to organize the three centers in one system, the microeconomics of the individual and the firm, the intermediate economics of the nation-state, and the macroeconomics of the world economy. This, I would think, might be the only model adequate for developing countries, and especially for rapidly industrializing ones. In any event, the next economics will surely again be "political economy," with the question of the relationship between the economic realities of the world economy and microeconomy, and political realities of the nation-state, both central to economic theory and highly controversial.

Equally central, and perhaps even more controversial, will be the relationship between the "real economy" of things—commodities, resources, work—and the "symbol economy" of money and credit. There is no returning to the old dismissal of the symbol economy as the "veil of reality." But there is no holding on to the recent orthodoxy in which the symbol economy is the real and true economy, with things (commodities, services, and work) only "functions," and indeed totally dependent functions, of the "symbol economy."

We may have to be content, however, with something analogous to the physicist's "Uncertainty Principle," in which the only meaningful statements in respect to certain events—for instance, productivity, capital formation, the allocation of resources, and so on—are statements in terms of the "real economy," with events in the "symbol economy" no more than a restraint and a boundary. But other and equally "real" events can perhaps only be discussed, analyzed, and even described in terms of the "symbol economy," with the "real economy" of things being a restraint on them. This would not be a particularly satisfactory outcome—but it may be the best we can achieve.

The new theory of value

The next economics may even attempt to be again both "humanity" and "science."

An anecdote popular among the younger members of Keynes' Cambridge seminar had one of the disciples ask the Master why there was no theory of value in his *General Theory*. Keynes answered: "Because the only available theory of value is the labor theory and it is totally discredited." The next economics should again have a theory of value. It may base itself on the postulate that productivity—that is, knowledge applied to resources through human work—is the source of all economic value.

Productivity as the source of value is both *a priori* and operational, and thus satisfies the specifications for a first principle. It would be both descriptive and normative, both analyze what is and why, and indicate what ought to be and why. Marx, the "Revisionists" of Socialism around 1900 argued, was never fully satisfied with the Labor Theory of Value but groped for a substitute. None of the great non-Marxist economists of the last hundred years, Alfred Marshall, Joseph Schumpeter, or John Maynard Keynes, was in turn comfortable with an economics that lacked a theory of value altogether. But, as the Keynes anecdote illustrates, they saw no alternative. Productivity as the source of all economic value would serve. It would explain. It would direct vision. It would give guidance to analysis, to policy, and to behavior. Productivity is both man and things; both structural and analytical. A productivity-based economics might thus become what all the great economists have striven for: both a "humanity," a "moral philosophy," a "*Geisteswissenschaft*"; and, rigorous "science."

2

The dissolution of the Keynesian consensus

JAMES W. DEAN

On December 13, 1979, the government of Canada fell. For just six months the Conservatives had governed with a parliamentary minority, and they were defeated on a vote of no confidence. The issue was their first budget —a budget that rejected Keynesian economic policies, replacing them with radically different recommendations. Unemployment and slow growth were to be fought not by increasing the federal deficit but by reducing it.

This was a turnabout in what the Conservatives themselves had recommended when sitting in opposition just the year before. Their turnabout mirrored that of much of the economics profession throughout the English-speaking world. It was the decade's last dramatic reflection of a dissolving Keynesian consensus. This paper traces how that dissolution came about.

The late 1940's saw, more or less simultaneously, the invention of the electronic computer, the publication of Paul Samuelson's *Foundations of Economic Analysis,* and the dawning of the Keynesian era. Computers diverted the profession's attention to statistics and econometrics, Samuelson to mathematical economics, and the new Keynesian wisdom to homogeneous vision. Samuelson, in another context, abrogated controversy by inventing in his best-selling introductory textbooks the "neoclassical synthesis," in which Keynesian theory was, he said, consistent with the Marshallian neoclassical tradition that had served so well for the previous half-century. The controversy that had inflamed economic theory for the decade following Keynes' 1936 *General Theory of Employment, Interest and Money* rapidly dissipated. Keynesian theory was deemed, at least on this side of the Atlantic, merely an extension of neoclassicism; many economists busied themselves engineering its application, while others toyed with econometrics and mathematical economics.

As codified for the millions over three decades by Samuelson's textbook and its many imitators, Keynesian theory (or rather *neo*-Keynesian conventional wisdom) emphasized that markets could be relied upon to function much as neoclassical theory promised, *as long as aggregate demand was sustained.* Unemployment could be reduced to some hardcore rate—say 3 percent for the United States—by injecting the economy with appropriate fiscal stimuli via government spending. The Employment Act of 1946 committed the federal government, at least on paper, to inject these stimuli.

After the War, it quickly became apparent that economies were now as susceptible to inflation as to unemployment, but economists simply reminded one another of the implicit symmetry of Keynesian theory: When aggregate demand outstrips the economy's capacity to produce—that is, beyond full employment—inflation rates increase *pari passu* with aggregate demand. Their policy prescription was simple: Fine-tune aggregate demand, increasing government spending relative to taxes when below full employment, the reverse when above.

In 1958, a new twist—or rather, curve—was added to the economist's grabbag by Professor A.W. Phillips, a New Zealander then employed at the London School of Economics. The "Phillips curve" quickly gained lexicographic currency as the inevitable trade-off between inflation and employment. To get less of one, economies must suffer more of the other. Calvinistic reminders that the good things in life (low inflation) can only be obtained at great sacrifice and pain (unemployment) are invariably welcomed by economists, whose ulcerous comments like "there's no such thing as a free lunch" occur particularly during lunch. Thus the Phillips curve was readily absorbed into neo-Keynesian doctrine, interpreted as a necessary specification of the constraint on fine-tuners' ability to inflate or to deflate.

The aura of noncontroversy was underwritten by an era of bening prosperity. By the mid-1960's not only was the level of affluence unprecedented in human history, but business cycles seemed to have been licked: Every year, times were better; downturns seemed consigned to history. Economists proclaimed themselves high priests of social engineering, claiming in their Keynesian wisdom credit for the sustained boom; but there was little about a profession which specialized in fine-tuning the economy to ignite controversy. A few moralists—John Kenneth Galbraith, Barbara Ward Jackson, Gunnar Myrdal—preached the evils of domestic and international income inequality, but by and large the community of economists was rather congenial, though something of a bore.

The roots of dissent

This is not to say that the roots of dissent were absent. Since the 1950's, mainstream Keynesianism has been under attack from at least three quarters. Two represent minority interpretations of Keynes, the third a direct challenge. For purposes of this essay I will call the dissenters Revolutionaries, Evolutionaries, and Reactionaries.[1]

Revolutionaries believe that Keynes sowed the seeds for a paradigm with a potential to be revolutionary. Their prime target is the "neoclassical synthesis" of Keynesian and pre-Keynesian thought due to Samuelson and John Hicks,[2] and their objective a return to (their reading of) the Bible, Keynes' *General Theory*. Prominent Revolutionaries include Cantabrigians Nicholas Kaldor and Joan Robinson, and the University of Pennsylvania's Sidney Weintraub. For most of the postwar period, these fundamentalist Keynesians made little or no impact on the mainstream, though in the late 1970's they were to gain ground and come to be known as "post-Keynesians."

Two Keynesian themes that Revolutionaries claim to be crucial yet largely ignored are *expectations* and *wage-costs*. Throughout

[1] These titles are intended to be descriptive, not pejorative. In particular, "Reactionaries" should not take offence: I merely want to suggest that their response to Keynes has been a return to *pre*-Keynesian ideas. Also, "Evolutionaries" in the sense of this paper are unrelated to the institutionalist economists who comprise the Association for Evolutionary Economics.

[2] Ironically, neither Samuelson nor Hicks is a doctrinaire neoclassicist. The Revolutionaries' emphasis on wage-sourced inflation, for example, is a theme that Samuelson recognizes and that Hicks in the last decade or two has repeatedly emphasized. Hicks in fact has modified his ideas considerably in recent years, stressing the importance of "fix-price" markets in modern economies, and even repudiating his 1937 "ISLM" framework, which has aways been the standard tool of neo-Keynesian analysis in the spirit of the neoclassical synthesis.

the *General Theory* Keynes outlined the implications for income and employment of volatility in entrepreneurs' sales expectations: These latter he christened at one point "animal spirits." Heavy emphasis on the unknowable future has iconoclastic implications for neoclassical theory, and *ipso facto* for mainstream neo-Keynesianism. Mainstream theorists have tended to sidetrack "animal spirits" because of the concept's seemingly intractable primordiality.

The wage-cost theme extrapolates from Keynes' practice throughout the *General Theory* of denominating his model in "wage units." Since such units are exogenous to the model, neo-Keynesians have often found it convenient to assume fixed wages and prices. Or, when they do recognize *rising* wages and prices (i.e., inflation) they drop Keynes' focus on the wage unit and deal with prices instead. This has led them to analyze inflation largely from the demand side rather than from the supply side, which is dominated by wages. Inflation which is "cost-push" in origin, but diagnosed as "demand-pull," will be fought by cutting demand, and the effect will be to reduce output and employment but not prices. This misdiagnosis, say the Revolutionaries, has been typical of postwar policy makers, has led to "stagflation," and is the result of misreading Keynes.

The wage-cost sermon has been preached by Sidney Weintraub since the 1950's, but came into its own in the stagflationary 1970's. It is still a minority message, but the last half dozen years have drawn more adherents, including such doyens of American neo-Keynesianism as Arthur Okun, Abba Lerner, and James Tobin. Weintraub, Okun, Lerner and, to some extent, Tobin, favor incomes policies to control inflation. As alternatives to the draconian inefficiency of wage/price controls, they have devised tax- and market-based incentive and disincentive schemes which try to translate the social costs of inflation into private penalties for the individual firms and labor unions that raise wages and prices, and the social benefits of restraint into private benefits for those who practice it. (Weintraub, for example, advocates "TIP," Tax-Based Incomes Policy, and Lerner advocates "MAP," Market Anti-Inflation Plan.) The "real wage insurance" considered by Congress last session was in this spirit.

In the last decade the Revolutionaries christened themselves "post-Keynesians," and in 1978 Weintraub and Paul Davidson began the *Journal of Post Keynesian Economics.*[3] Between the *JPKE*

[3] The hyphen was deliberately omitted in naming the *Journal*, a somewhat subtle effort to imply a range of interests beyond post-Keynesianism *per se.* Nevertheless the *Journal* has thus far devoted a heavy proportion of its space to "cost-push" inflation and to alternative (particularly tax-based) incomes policies.

and *Challenge* magazine, which carried a "post-Keynesian" series in 1978-79, it is safe to say that the rudiments of Revolutionary ideas are much better publicized in the profession now than a few years ago. But it is not safe to say that the Revolutionaries can take primary responsibility for dissolution of the Keynesian consensus.

Evolutionaries cannot either. But in the late 1960's it was they who seemed to threaten mainstream Keynesians most profoundly. Evolutionaries became concerned, not that neo-Keynesian thought had elided revolutionary themes in its attempt to achieve synthesis with neoclassicism, but that it had done the reverse. Neo-Keynesian macro theory, they noted, was inconsistent at points with the sacred neoclassical axiom of universal maximization at the micro level by individuals, households, and firms. And since universal maximization was conventionally associated with equilibrium over all markets, neo-Keynesian theory seemed also to violate another sacred axiom, "Walras' law," which presumes general equilibrium. Evolutionaries were concerned to validate Keynes' place in the continuously evolving mainstream by providing him with solid microeconomic underpinnings.

Robert Clower fired the opening volley in 1965 when he wrote: "[E]ither Walras' law is incompatible with Keynesian economics, or Keynes had nothing fundamentally new to add to orthodox economic theory. Thus we are caught on the horns of a dilemma." Clower then proposed generalizing Walras' law to allow states of market *dis*equilibrium, concluding that failure to recognize such states had led to "a fundamental misunderstanding of the formal basis of the Keynesian revolution."

Clower's concern sprang from noting that Keynes' key macrobehavioral relationship, the "consumption function," was inconsistent with micro-level maximization. The consumption function—the effects on consumption of changes in income—is critical to Keynesian macroeconomics because without it fiscal "multiplier" theory and policy goes down the drain. But the Keynesian consumption function, Clower pointed out, makes consumption follow from *given* levels of income, and is inconsistent with maximization by the individual as *worker* because he would simultaneously vary consumption and *hours worked,* i.e., income. The individual who accepted his income as given would not in general be maximizing his utility, which depends on leisure time as well as consumption.

Clower's solution was to invent the "dual decision hypothesis." Maximization by individual consumers might still give rise to the

Keynesian consumption function if income was beyond their control—constrained for example by insufficient effective demand for goods and services, as in a recession or depression. Thus, though unconstrained behavior would lead to what Clower called "notional" consumption, constrained behavior would lead to "effective" consumption. So decisions to consume were dual in nature.[4]

Non-notional or "effective" consumption was consistent with maximizing behavior in *dis*equilibrium—that is, a state in which notional demand and supply differ because some price has not adjusted. The key price is labor's wage. If, in response to the decline in demand for goods and labor services, wages fell, labor would remain employed, incomes would remain unconstrained and consumers would not depart from notional behavior.

Why don't wages fall? One answer was offered by Clower's student, Axel Leijonhufvud. In 1968 he published *On Keynesian Economics and the Economics of Keynes.* The economics of Keynes, said Leijonhufvud, depends crucially at the micro level on price expectations: What goes up is expected to return to normal, and vice versa. Thus wage setters (e.g., employers and employees) will respond to business cycle fluctuation by maintaining wages, giving rise to temporary, non-notional, disequilibrium behavior.

For the decade following Clower's article, many macroeconomic theorists sought the future of Keynesian theory in disequilibrium analysis. Independently of Clower, Don Patinkin had devised an analogous method of analyzing voluntary versus involuntary unemployment in labor markets, and in 1971 Robert Barro and Herschel Grossman synthesized Clower and Patinkin.

Establishment Keynesians greeted the Evolutionaries' work with polite interest and a minimum of chagrin. Evolutionary ideas did not seem to threaten existing theory; in fact, to the average economist they seemed somewhat arcane, and the policy implications obscure. Moreover, the mathematics of disequilibrium analysis was not straightforward, and the concept of disequilibrium itself proved difficult to define.

But what really diverted attention from disequilibrium theory was monetarism, the roots of which were reactionary in the sense of being a return to pre-Keynesian theory.

Reactionaries. In 1956, Milton Friedman published "The Quan-

[4] The problems inherent in the axiom of universal maximization have of course received attention outside the Keynesian context. Herbert Simon has introduced the concept of "satisficing," and Harvey Leibenstein prefers to drop the maximization assumption altogether.

tity Theory of Money—A Restatement." The "Restatement" elegantly cast the pre-Keynesian quantity theory of money in modern price theoretic terms, and clearly signaled counter-Keynesian revolutionary intent. Friedman challenged, head on, Keynes' notion of an unstable "liquidity preference"—the idea that if more money were put into circulation it might be hoarded rather than spent. Instead, in the quantity-theory tradition, he postulated a stable demand for money, with the pre-Keynesian implication that "money matters." Too much money would prove inflationary, or too little, recessionary. The Depression, he argued elsewhere, could have been avoided had the Fed pumped out enough money in time.

Then, in his 1959 *Program for Monetary Stability,* Friedman complemented his theoretical resuscitation of money with a policy stance: the fixed monetary growth rule. This idea harked back to Henry Simons, whose influence at Chicago in the 1930's was enormous. Behind the Simons-Friedman rule is a fundamental premise of pre-Keynesian laissez faire economics, namely that the private sector is self-stabilizing. Real-world instability results primarily from the fiscal, monetary, and regulatory actions of government. Keynes, of course, suggested just the opposite.

Testing the inherent stability of real-world mixed economies is problematic, given automatic government stabilizers like unemployment insurance and progressive tax rates which are deeply entrenched politically. But testing the stability of money demand is more tractable. From Chicago and elsewhere poured reams of evidence, cumulating to a consensus in the late 1960's that money is considerably more important than early Keynesians had claimed. A landmark debate between Friedman and the distinguished neo-Keynesian Franco Modigliani, over whether money demand or the consumption function was more stable empirically, ended in 1965 with a standoff. In 1968, Karl Brunner christened the neo-quantity theory emanating from Chicago, "monetarism."

Monetarism takes off

Toward the end of the 1960's the major strands of the decade's benign growth began coming unglued. Rather than confront the political problems of raised taxes, or bond issues and higher interest rates, Lyndon Johnson financed his war deficits with new money. Monetary growth proved excessive—i.e., inflationary—and the monetarists' concerns seemed suddenly relevant. Moreover, in 1968 Johnson's attempt to combat inflation with traditional Keynesian tax tools failed. And despite increased inflation, unemployment was rising too, the reverse of the relationship predicted by that neo-Keynesian favorite, the Phillips curve. Not only was inflation not responding to Keynesian fiscalism it was no longer "buying off" unemployment. Events had outstripped theory.

Thus it was that Friedman's 1967 presidential address to the American Economics Association, in which he unveiled a "new" Phillips curve, was timed to be seminal. The logic behind the new Phillips curve, developed almost simultaneously by Edmund Phelps, suggested that unemployment in the long run would settle at its "natural" rate, irrespective of the steady-state rate of inflation: a formalization of the pre-Keynesian laissez faire premise of a self-stabilizing economy. To this was appended, particularly by Friedman, the monetarist tenet that reduced monetary growth is the *sine qua non* of the reduced aggregate demand. Less money, therefore, would eliminate inflation, and in the long run without higher unemployment. Conversely, more money would generate inflation without in the long run reducing unemployment below its natural rate. In contrast, the traditional Phillips curve had promised that higher inflation would permanently reduce unemployment, or vice versa.

Though the new Phillips curve did not, in and of itself, imply simultaneously rising unemployment and inflation, it did lend itself to rationalizing the stagflation phenomenon. Since employment in the long run was determined by supply considerations, independent of aggregate demand, events like baby-boom teenagers or liberated women hitting the labor force might well raise "natural" unemployment, particularly in the face of market imperfections like the government-legislated minimum wage or unemployment insurance. In addition, misguided Keynesian attempts to maintain unemployment at the old, lower natural rate would result in higher and higher rates of inflation.[5]

What was so startling about Friedman's argument was that it denied the efficacy of the Keynesians' most basic policy description —stimulating demand to reduce unemployment. *Friedman was suggesting that fiscal, monetary, or any other form of demand stimulus could not sustain unemployment below its natural rate. In the long run, demand stimulus (unless ever-increasing) would mean higher steady-state inflation, but nothing more.* Moreover, estimates of nat-

---

[5] Friedman himself, however, is not content to rationalize stagflation in such an *ad hoc* manner. In fact the subject of his 1976 Nobel Prize address was an attempt to rationalize the *positively*-sloped Phillips curve that has been observable internationally since the late 1960's. The 1967 "new" Phillips curve merely rationalizes verticality.

ural unemployment, which have since been generated using the Friedman/Phelps model, fall for the last decade disturbingly near *actual* unemployment. The age of policy nihilism had begun.

The crux of Friedman's argument was that workers are slower to react to demand stimulus than producers. In the absence of immediate increased production, added demand (coming either from more private sector spending or from more government spending) bids up the rate at which prices increase. Labor, however, is slow to raise wage demands because at first it fails to adjust its expectations to the higher rate of inflation. That is, workers either do not realize the extent to which prices are rising faster, or do not extrapolate this higher rate of inflation into the future. Workers do not fully realize that their future purchasing power has deteriorated, and see no call to contract for appropriately higher wages. Their "real" wage declines. Firms, on the other hand, behave differently. They may or may not realize that prices in general are rising faster, but general price inflation does not matter to them. What does matter is that the prices of the products they sell are rising faster, and this they will surely recognize. With higher prices for their products and the same wage rates, they stand to increase their profits by hiring more labor and expanding output. Unemployment therefore declines, but *only temporarily,* along a "short run," negatively-sloped Phillips curve. As workers' inflationary expectations catch up with reality, they voluntarily withdraw their extra services at reduced real wages, and contract for higher wages. Unemployment rises back to its previous level, and with it the real wage. We are back to square one, but in the process of getting there the inflation has risen. Better to have left matters alone.

Notice that the temporary reduction in unemployment, *as well as the return to the natural level,* is modeled as *entirely voluntary.* Changes in unemployment result from voluntary responses to changes in the real wage. As we shall see, this treatment of unemployment and changes in unemployment as entirely voluntary is an Achilles' heel for natural rate models. A further implication of these models is that attempts to reduce unemployment below its natural rate rely on *deception,* since their success relies on labor's misperceptions of the true real wage. Rational expectations theorists, discussed in the next section, have replaced the Keynesian goal of "full employment output" with one "full information output."

Though the essential policy implication of the Friedman/Phelps model is noninterventionist, some have interpreted the model's retention of a *short-run* unemployment/inflation tradeoff as a mandate for continued fine tuning. This loophole in the anti-stabilization logic was quickly closed by a group of young theorists using John Muth's logic of "rational expectations," known now to the cognoscenti as "ratex" (with vermin-killing connotations sure to bait sensitive Keynesians).

Friedman's 1967 short-run unemployment/inflation tradeoff stemmed from "adaptive" price expectations lagging behind rising inflation rates. Muth's logic denied that rational economic units would form such expectations, since if they did they would be systematically in error. In the early 1970's theorists like Robert Lucas, Thomas Sargent, and Neil Wallace replaced Friedman's "adaptive" with Muth's "rational" expectations assumption, thereby denying even the short-run unemployment/inflation tradeoff when economic units have all relevant information. Among believers, the policy implication is extreme: no activism, even in the short run, unless the policy authority is acting on information unavailable to the private sector.

A corollary is that the government ought to disseminate all economically relevant information as quickly and fully as possible: economic "sunshine laws." Then a sophisticated 20th century invisible hand, covering not only the present but the future via rational expectations, will guide individual economic actors to seek and obtain their "full-information" rates of output and employment. "Full information" is the new criterion for optimality.

Closely related to the Friedman/Phelps and "rational expectations" ideas is the notion that unemployment is best modeled as *voluntary*. The logic of the new Phillips curve implies that most or all of the unemployed are simply making a free and voluntary choice based on the real wage available to them. This line of reasoning understandably provokes much controversy and even moral indignation, since it seems to belittle a grave economic and social problem.

At the August 1978 American Economic Association meetings, I asked 15 prominent economists whether the United States was currently at, above, or below its natural unemployment rate. A majority answered "at or below," implying that aggregate demand should either be left alone or geared down to avoid rising inflation. At that time, the unemployment rate in this country sat at 5.9 percent of the labor force, or about 6 million women and men.

At the bottom of the controversy is a philosophical question: *What constitutes free choice?* If the "naturally" unemployed were willing to change occupations or areas of residence, or work for wages approximating what they receive from welfare or unemployment insurance, many could find work. Indeed, a particularly popular theme among economists these days is that unemployment insurance significantly raises natural unemployment, both because it dissuades active job search (and perhaps even induces "phoney" entrants to the labor force) and because it raises the effective wage to employers, who must pay a share of the premiums. Unemployment of this kind is surely "voluntary" only as the state cooperates. A good portion of the "naturally" unemployed, moreover, are mere youngsters who will find jobs in a few years when they grow up. Some are not heads of households—that is, there's a spouse in the background bringing in an income. Do youths or wives seek work less compulsively than their elders or their spouses? And who decides which spouse is the household head?

Economists from the depleted liberal ranks argue that their conservative colleagues of the 1970's, in their preoccupation with the nihilistically connotative concept of the natural rate, have performed a serious social disservice. The concept masks what economists in the 1960's called "structural" unemployment—arising from the failure of job openings to mesh with available skills and proclivities, and exacerbated by a culture of rapidly changing tastes and technology. Economists nowadays prefer to think of unemployment as the result of an extended, voluntary "search" for work. For instance, the last decade has seen a marked increase in women's "taste" for the labor force; appropriate jobs have not opened fast enough, thus women "search" longer.

The new economists

There is little question that in the last decade economists have swung markedly to the right. And this swing encompasses more than just monetarism or rational expectations. A generation of economists under 40—christened by *Newsweek* "the new economists"—have explicitly rejected the Keynesian canons which suckled them in the 1960's. A prime example is Robert Barro, who has foresworn the Evolutionary attempts of his youth to resuscitate Keynes via disequilibrium analysis, and become a leading advocate of ratex. But an older generation has also moved to the right. Most of the 15 doyens I interviewed in 1978 said they had retreated from activism, crediting their latterly wisdom to an inextricable mix of old age, events inconsistent with Keynesianism, and even the immutable advance of logic.

Although the unemployment/inflation tradeoff issue is its most cogent manifestation, the retreat is far more fundamental. At the 1978 American Economic Association meetings, the prestigious Ely lecture was delivered by Alfred Kahn, who as Chairman of the Civil Aeronautics Board had just dramatically deregulated the airlines. Kahn—something of a performer—was roundly applauded. To those I interviewed afterward, the lesson was unambiguous and general: Sweeping deregulation throughout the U.S. economy would work wonders.

Frequently, economists' new love affair with noninterventionism is founded less in ideological commitment to individual freedom and full information than in pragmatism. Not all the "new economists" are dogmatic monetarists, let alone worshippers of ratex. But there is a growing recognition that government often just doesn't deliver, or, worse, incurs unconscionable costs. The reasons for this growing recognition are complex.

Some of the new professional nihilism reflects simply the general disillusionment with big government and its concomitant tax load presently felt by Americans in all walks of life. Alternatively, economists' new-found conservatism may reflect the peculiar circumstances of their own labor market. Perhaps it has to do with the Ph.D. glut and its overflow into employment by business, or with a tendency under Democratic presidents for the liberal intelligentsia to be co-opted by government, with the conservative intelligentsia freed for critical articulation. A somewhat longer-run view might mention the steady gains made by Chicago-style economic philosophy, roughly coincident with the progress of Milton Friedman's career, and the far friendlier reception of his ideas since inflation has become of major and worldwide concern.

A third view might emphasize the pragmatic. There are two aspects to this. One is that experience seems to be teaching us that big government incurs enormous dead-weight costs. In part, these result from the disincentive effects of both spending programs and taxes. Martin Feldstein favors reduced unemployment insurance and social security payments, not out of anti-interventionist principle, but because empirical studies suggest that unemployment would fall and the savings rate would rise. And Arthur Laffer, darling of the *Wall Street Journal,* has become famous for the increasingly plausible notion that rising tax rates discourage and distort work effort, to an extent that total tax revenues end up reduced. Additional dead-weight costs are imposed by government regulation: Recent estimates of total regulatory costs run to $100 billion annually for the federal government alone, and few would believe that the benefits exceed that amount. Currently in vogue "supply-side economics" emphasizes tax reduction and deregulation to stimulate employment and productivity, in contrast to yesteryear's Keynesian concern with stimulating demand. Though high taxes are by no means a logical consequence of Keynesian theory, Keynesian economists in practice have typically advocated demand stimulus via government spending (financed partly by higher taxes), rather than via reduced taxes on consumption or investment spending. Moreover, it is arguable that the "fine-tuning" mentality of Keynesian economists has fostered a general climate of interventionism and thus government regulation.

The second aspect of the new economists' pragmatism is that it avoids sticky philosophical issues which arise when economists confront their ideological roots. Two centuries ago, Adam Smith articulated precepts that underlay 19th century liberalism and have remained doctrine for much of the profession, these days nowhere in more pristine form than at the University of Chicago. A crude characterization of these precepts is that personal liberty is a fundamental goal of economic organization and that it is most nearly approached by means of free markets. Free markets and the pursuit of private gain, said Adam Smith, also maximize the community output, subject of course to the constraint that free people will voluntarily forgo output inasmuch as they choose leisure.

Keynes questioned this belief as a practical matter; free markets, he taught, do not necessarily maximize output because they do not necessarily maximize employment. The "neoclassical synthesis" seemed to reconcile the issue by promising the optimality of free markets once government had intervened to provide sufficient aggregate demand. Keynes himself once described aggregate demand management as "the one kind of compulsion of which the effect is to enlarge liberty." For years economists accepted this compromise, but now they're not so sure.

Dissolution of the Keynesian consensus has meant disillusionment with government intervention even at the aggregate level. Ratex theorists argue that stimulatory demand management has spent its potential because private-sector rational expectations of the inflationary consequences have come to preclude the "deception" which is a *sine qua non* of increased employment according to natural rate models. But for most economists it is the unworkability of fiscal "fine tuning" in practice, rather than principle, that has led to disillusionment. Is Chicago Gospel the only alternative?

Undiluted faith in free enterprise presents problems of political philosophy, a fact of which most economists are at least dimly aware. Values like justice and equality may be compromised under unmitigated free enterprise, rooted as it is in an ethic of absolute personal liberty. Such doubts about Smithian liberalism are shared by 20th century liberals and traditional conservatives. (Edmund Burke wrote, "Liberty too must be limited in order to be possessed.") Yet there's an Adam Smith in every economist; faith in free markets runs deep. And Americans in particular frequently find Burkean philosophy unpalatable, embracing as they do in their Declaration of Independence Thomas Jefferson's absolutist conception of the individual's "unalienable Rights . . . Life, Liberty, and the pursuit of Happiness."

Perhaps, then, mainstream economists in their present disillusioned state embrace a new conservatism because it does not demand philosophical purity. And perhaps it is American economists especially who have welcomed a retreat from the ideological contradictions inherent in interventionism, even the Keynesian interventionism that once seemed so innocuous.

A look to the future

Nevertheless it seems unlikely that the neo-Keynesian consensus will be replaced with an enduring "neoconservative" consensus. First, fundamental theoretical issues remain unresolved. Second, ideological issues are still at stake. For much of the economics profession is at a pragmatic way station until dust from the Keynesian/monetarist conflict settles.

Revolutionaries, of course, in their new mien as post-Keynesians, prosper and even wax, rallying for the Second Coming of Lord Maynard, or at least his True Church. Reactionaries in turn reject messianic claims for Keynes, and, as monetarists and ratex theorists, resolutely elaborate the pre-Keynesian Talmud of neoclassical theory. But though post-Keynesianism and monetarism are currently in vogue, macroeconomic theory's future probably lies with the Evolutionaries. Why so?

Revolutionaries have established a distressing track record of aversion to modern mathematical model-building. This stems in part from Joan Robinson's repeated accusation that the neoclassical and neo-Keynesian mainstream has elided irreversible "historical" time in favor of the mathematicians' world of reversible "logical" time. Unfortunately, acting on this accusation has left an analytical vacuum.

Many of today's post-Keynesians are aware of this vacuum: The *Journal of Post Keynesian Economics* is an attempt to remedy it. And the important post-Keynesian theme of wage-push inflation is certainly plausible if supplemented by careful analysis of the causal connection between rising wages and an expanding money supply. Economists such as Paul Davidson and Basil Moore, who understand real-world financial markets better than most, are making headway on that causal connection. The wage-push theme is, however, improperly placed in a strict Keynesian context: Keynes' allusions to it were sporadic and tentative. Analysis of wage-push inflation is not the monopoly preserve of post-Keynesian Revolutionaries. And Revolutionaries suffer from the additional problem that they are, rightly or wrongly, associated with the politics and ideology of interventionism, an ideology that is definitely out of favor.

As for Reactionaries, their pristine analytic and ideological purity weighs heavy. The natural rate hypothesis is a sophisticated return to the pre-Keynesian notion that economies automatically tend to full employment. It leads to implausible or even counter-factual claims—for example, that workers are unemployed because they believe real wages to be lower than do employed workers, or that real wages move counter-cyclically rather than pro-cyclically. Natural rate aficionados are even tempted to define away the unemployment of the 1930's: Witness Michael Darby's 1976 eyecatcher, "Three-and-a-Half Million U.S. Employees Have Been Mislaid," which recalculates the Depression's unemployment by counting workers in FDR's work-relief programs as employed, implying that they could otherwise have worked for the private sector.

Ratex theorists are even harder to believe. Though the assumption of rational expectations *per se* seems benign, it is often accompanied by implications or even assertions about the real world that most economists, including Friedman himself, find difficult to swallow. These have to do with the speed with which information is or can be disseminated, and with which expectations *become* rational once dissemination has taken place. Extreme ratex enthusiasts tend to minimize the duration of adjustment to unforseeable shocks (e.g., oil-price hikes); that is, they down-play the longevity of the associated inflation and unemployment, arguing that intervention will *always* be counterproductive, impeding the required adjustment.

And the extent of Reactionaries' appeal is also limited by ideological extremism. It might be argued that the philosophical flavor of the ratex, full-information-in-place-of-government ideal is quintessentially American. The recent attempt by certain Wall Street money men to obtain disclosure of the Federal Reserve's intentions under the Freedom of Information Act is imaginable only in the United States. But however much maximizing personal freedom may accord with Smithian or Jeffersonian principles, most economists are at least intuitively aware of the tradeoffs involved.

This brings us to the Evolutionaries. Almost by definition they will prevail, because economics is an evolutionary science. Keynes cannot be elevated as the Messiah anymore than he can be crucified as a False Prophet; undoubtedly he was a Great Prophet, no more or less. To establish him in the theoretical continuum he must be given microeconomic underpinnings consistent with the sacred neoclassical axiom of optimizing behavior. Clower, Patinkin, Barro, and Grossman established that Keynesian disequilibrium unemployment is consistent with constrained optimization (though Barro has since defected to ratex). Leijonhufvud recognized that disequilibrium behavior needs a rationale for sticky prices and wages, and provided one. This early work was then overshadowed in the 1970's by the profession's enthusiasm for the elegance of monetarism, the natural rate hypothesis, and ratex.

But disequilibrium behavior remains important—indeed, if one is to model unemployment as involuntary or inflation as unanticipated, disequilibrium analysis is unavoidable. So by the same token is analysis of the "sticky wage." Thus the last half dozen years have seen a "new new" microeconomics of the labor market, distinct from the "new" microeconomics of Friedman/Phelps fame. The new new microeconomics is concerned with rationalizing sticky wages under optimizing assumptions, i.e., why workers and firms voluntarily contract for fixed wages, which eventually lead to unemployment whenever business conditions deteriorate. Major contributors to this literature include Constantine Azariadis, Martin Bailey, Donald Gordon, Robert Gordon, and Robert Solow.

So Keynes' major problem—to explain involuntary unemployment—is far from solved. The neo-Keynesian theoretical consensus dissolved over the last 15 years not specifically because of monetarists or post-Keynesians, but because economists of all schools recognized that macroeconomics lacks micro foundations. *The major theoretical challenge of the 1980's is to explain why markets in the aggregate don't guarantee employment for all who want it despite the fact that full employment in this sense is desired by all individual market participants.* Solve that problem and you simultaneously solve the problem of inflation, for monetary restraint would be costless were the unemployment consequences removed.

3

Monetarism and the crisis in economics

ALLAN H. MELTZER

To the economists responsible for advice and policy decisions in the 1960's, the main problems of stabilization policy seemed to have been solved. Mild recessions might have occurred because businessmen behaved erratically, or because the timing of the response to government policy actions had not been pinned down, or because politicians did not heed their economic advisers. Mild inflation might result from decisions to reduce unemployment and increase output beyond the point required by price stability. Inflation seemed manageable to the economic advisers of that period, and inflation and unemployment still seemed manageable when they wrote their memoirs.

The job of the economic adviser was to predict the future course of economic activity and to recommend economic policies that maintained the proper balance between unemployment and inflation. The policy recommendations—Keynesian policies—are familiar. When private spending declines, a responsive government substitutes its own spending by running a budget deficit, or reduces taxes to stimulate private spending. The additional spending creates jobs for idle workers. Society gets the benefit of output that would have been lost; increased output and employment raises tax revenues and finances the deficit. To reduce inflation, the government runs a budget surplus. The surplus lowers economic activity, and the surplus is eliminated as inflation falls.

Changes in the federal budget deficit and changes in taxes and government spending occur all the time. Three key elements in the program offered by the economic advisers of the 1960's distinguish their advice from earlier, less activist programs. Greater use was made of short-term forecasts of economic activity, prices and interest rates. Greater reliance was placed on economists' ability to trade inflation for unemployment. Greater emphasis was given in official discussions of economic policy to planned budget deficits as a means of implementing an economic plan and achieving target rates of inflation and unemployment annually and perhaps quarterly.

No one, certainly no one in a responsible position, believed that this type of economic planning and control was infallible. To improve control, other programs supplemented budget policy. One program, known as guideposts or guidelines, restricted changes in individual prices and wages. Guidepost policies were based on the rather vague conjecture that large firms and industry-wide unions worsen the tradeoff between inflation and unemployment. Proponents of guideposts regarded their proposals as imperfect devices for slowing inflation during periods of expanding output. In the language of the time, guideposts were said to be useful against "cost-push" inflation. Another program, or series of programs, sought to reduce the United States' balance of payments deficit and sustain the international monetary system based on fixed exchange rates. Many of the steps taken to achieve balance of payments adjustment during the 1960's involved direct controls, such as the tax on interest rates or restrictions on the amount of government and private spending abroad.

Looking back to the 1960's at the start of the 1980's, one is struck by the flimsy base on which the alleged triumph of "Keynesian policies" rested. There were tax cuts in 1964, relatively large increases in government spending in 1966 and 1967, and a tax surcharge—to slow inflation—in 1968. There were numerous attempts to slow inflation by persuasion and pressure. There was a flood of words about the United States' commitment to maintain fixed exchange rates and the price of gold, and to end the deficit in the balance of payments. When the 1970's produced higher inflation, higher unemployment, and a devalued dollar, some journalists and economists who had hailed the previous decade as the age of economists interpreted the failure as a failure of economic theory.

The age of the economists, born with the tax cut of 1964, did not survive the first signs of sustained inflation. In the words of one foreign observer, Keynesian ideas "faltered sometime in the middle Sixties and stumbled into the Seventies."

These, and many similar statements, are hyperbole. There is a connection between the scientific statements properly described as economic theory and many of the policy recommendations of the economic advisers to Presidents Kennedy and Johnson—or for that matter, Presidents Truman, Eisenhower, Nixon, Ford and Carter. It is proper to attribute part of the steady growth of the U.S. economy in the early and middle 1960's to fiscal policy decisions, including decisions to increase depreciation allowances in 1962, to reduce taxes for households and business in 1964, and to hold the growth of federal government spending near its long-term average during the first half of the decade.

Fiscal policy was not the only, and probably not the most important, factor contributing to the growth of world income in the 1950's and 1960's. Growth resulted from population growth and from institutional changes affecting the world economy that permitted the rising labor force to be absorbed at rising incomes. During those decades, the United States, the Common Market, and Japan reduced tariffs, removed barriers to trade, restored convertibility of currencies and permitted capital to move across borders in search of the highest prospective return. These changes increased efficiency, raised real incomes, and encouraged production and trade.

None of these changes depended either on careful forecasts of output and prices in the year or quarter ahead, or on carefully measured tradeoffs between inflation and unemployment. Economists from the time of Adam Smith onward believed that tariff reduction, increased capital mobility, and freer international trade, benefit both exporting and importing countries and increase the wealth of nations. More to the point, conclusions about these gains from trade are well-established principles of economics. These principles worked—and, as the post-war growth of income in the European Common Market and other market economies suggests, they worked well.

The crisis

A crisis is a decisive change of direction. I believe that the ways in which most economists think about economic policy, and the conclusions they draw, are markedly different at the beginning of the 1980's than in the early 1960's. If the change persists, it will have a lasting effect on the conduct of economic policy.

The research economist, working to increase our understanding of some aspect of human behavior, sees little sign of crisis or decisive change. The problems he analyzes and the tools he uses differ from the tools and problems of a decade or a generation ago. With better tools and newer techniques, the subtleties that were once ignored or neglected become part of the accepted principles. There is at least some truth to the commonplace that describes research as a process of learning more and more about less and less. The startling insight that creates a crisis in theory is a rare event that becomes rarer as knowledge increases.

Economic theory is a set of principles about the allocation of scarce resources. The best established parts of the theory have been developed during the past two centuries into a formal body of knowledge that is highly abstract. In addition to these formalized abstractions, economics—and other scientific disciplines—include a number of relationships that have been observed repeatedly but are not closely tied to the formal theory. A considerable part of the research done by working economists is an effort to extend the range of economic theory to include the observed relationships within the formal structure.

Where the researcher sees gradual progress in the development of economic theory, policy makers, journalists, and legislators may see a decisive change in opinion about economic policy. Academic witnesses before congressional committees, consultants, and advisers to presidents and agencies usually do not abuse their patrons by debating subtle differences—or basic differences—in public. Policy makers want much more to know about the probable outcomes of policies, and the chances of success or failure, than about what was ignored and what was assumed to reach a conclusion. In the 1960's, consultants and economic advisers emphasized short-term, and neglected long-term, outcomes. The advisers perhaps believed that they could manage the long-term outcomes if or when they occurred. Neither they, nor their political sponsors, asked how.

Policy recommendations have undergone much more change than economic theory. One explanation of the change in policy recommendations is that the accumulation of knowledge and new research discoveries revealed the errors in the policy recommendations of the past two decades. This is a comforting idea, but it is, I believe, a very small part of the reason that changes occurred. It is true that some research in the 1950's and 1960's seemed to support the activist policies that were proposed and implemented and that later studies cast doubt on the earlier findings. But it is closer to the truth to say that most of the policy errors resulted from the neglect of long-term implications and of principles that were well known more than a century ago.

Economists trained in the heyday of Keynesian economics were responsible for the major policy failures of the 1960's and 1970's. Their advice and recommendations proved to be wrong, not only because their forecasts were inaccurate but because they ignored long-term effects of policies and because many of their beliefs about their ability to fine tune the economy were wrong. Three examples illustrate the relation between some of the mistakes that were made and the beliefs on which policies were based.

1. *The Alleged Tradeoff: Inflation and Unemployment.* The Phillips curve is one of the key relations on which economic advisers relied in the 1960's. The relation, a statistical curiosity discovered by a British economist in the late 1950's, showed that for nearly a century the highest rates of unemployment occurred when wages or prices fell and lowest rates of unemployment occurred when prices rose. Phillips' work seemed to suggest that output and employment increased during periods of inflation.

Nothing in Phillips' work or in subsequent work showed that higher inflation caused lower unemployment, and nothing in economic theory gave anyone reason to believe that the relation Phillips uncovered was either a dependable basis for policy or consistent with economic theory. Nevertheless, Phillips curves jumped quickly from the scholarly journals to the Executive Office of the President. I do not know any other example in which new economic research findings, and not very strong findings at that, became the basis for official statements about public policy in so many countries in so short a time. The unusual speed with which the Phillips curve was accepted is particularly remarkable because the idea that inflation increases output and real income had been discussed for generations. The issue had not been resolved, but the presumption was that the long-term effect of inflation on output or growth was small in magnitude and uncertain in direction.

One of the oldest principles of economics makes the point that output, employment, and standards of living—real variables—do not depend on the price level. Economists recognized long ago that output and employment are no higher when prices are high than when they are low. A main point of Adam Smith's *Wealth of Nations* is that a country's wealth and income depend on the country's real resources and on the way in which production is organized —and *not* on the price level. Some short-term effects of prices on output were observed, but these effects were recognized as the transitory influence of unanticipated changes in demand. Sudden, unexpected increases in demand that raised prices and output, or sudden reductions in demand that lowered prices and output, were not expected to have any lasting effect on either prices or output.

The classical gold-standard mechanism embodied these principles. Unanticipated increases in gold flows from abroad stimulated production, but gradually raised domestic prices relative to foreign prices. The rise in domestic prices reduced exports, and raised imports, lowering domestic production and employment, and eventually lowering prices. The continuous ebb and flow of gold was anticipated, but the timing of the flows could not be predicted accurately. The inability to predict the timing of flows was recognized early as a cause of unanticipated changes in price and output.

Milton Friedman's presidential address to the American Economic Association in 1967 is a forceful statement of the role of anticipations and an important extension of established principles. *Friedman showed that anticipated rates of price change (inflation) have no effect on employment and output. Once people anticipate that prices will rise, Friedman said, they demand higher wages for their labor and higher prices for their products. The increase in employment produced by higher inflation vanishes. The inflation remains. Attempts to reduce unemployment by increasing inflation work only if people are fooled by the changes. Once people learn to anticipate inflation, the tradeoff disappears.* Friedman and others warned that repeated attempts to reduce unemployment by inflation would cause the rate of inflation to rise but would not lower the average rate of unemployment. A series of studies tested Friedman's argument. The results supported Friedman and other critics of the Phillips curve.

The speed with which the case for a tradeoff was accepted as a cornerstone of economic policy contrasts with the slow acceptance of the more substantial body of evidence suggesting that there was no reliable tradeoff. Friedman's reaffirmation and extension of classical principles of monetary theory was widely accepted in the economics profession long before it was accepted as a basis for policy action. As recently as 1978, high officials of the U.S. government openly promoted the notion of a tradeoff. Their German counterparts resisted, for the most part, and succeeded in keeping their rates of inflation far below ours.

2. *Guideposts, Guidelines, Price and Wage Controls.* Guideposts and guidelines are informal, often extra-legal, controls on the prices and wages paid by large firms. These controls, like the more formal price controls for which they substitute, neither prevent nor reduce inflation. At times, controls prevent the effects of inflationary policies from becoming apparent. But even the totalitarian regimes in Eastern Europe do not—and apparently cannot—control all prices permanently. They, too, often experience inflation following periods of relatively high demand.

Economics provides no support for the belief that controls reduce inflation. Any lasting reduction in inflation, achieved while controls are in effect, depends on government policies to reduce total spending. Unless spending is reduced, the average rate of inflation is not reduced. If spending is reduced, inflation eventually falls whether or not controls are used.

When a few selected prices of goods and services are controlled, people who are able to buy the goods and services at lower prices do not buy an unchanged amount and save the difference. Spending shifts to other goods and services. The controlled prices rise less, but other prices rise more, and a properly constructed measure of inflation is unaffected. If the prices of most domestically produced goods and services are controlled, spending shifts to imports, to used cars and second-hand markets, or to products such as fresh produce that are rarely controlled. Countries that rely on price controls face rising pressure to restrict foreign travel, imports, and other substitutes for domestic spending. Controls often lead to other restrictions: on imports, on foreign transactions, and on travel. To make controls work, ration books or waiting lines replace prices as the means of deciding who gets to buy the goods or services. Anyone who waited in line for gasoline in the spring of 1979, or who has seen the lines at stores in Eastern Europe, appreciates how these mechanisms work.

Economists—whether in the Department of Energy, the Council of Economic Advisers, or elsewhere in the government—are familiar with these basic principles. They do not rest their argument for selective or general controls on economic principles. Usually, controls are defended by appeal to non-economic considerations, to notions of equity or distributive justice, or to guesses about favorable effects on anticipations of consumers, unions, or businessmen.

Controls, guideposts, and guidelines have failed to stop inflation in every country that has used them. The failures are not failures of economic theory or evidence that economic theory is in crisis.

On the contrary, they show that political expedients, notions of equity, or guesses about anticipations are less reliable guides to successful policy than economic theory.

3. *The Illusive Output Gap*. The oil shocks reduced income and potential output in all non-OPEC countries by raising the amount we pay for imports and by raising the cost of using machinery relative to the cost of using labor. The higher cost of oil lowers our standard of living. The higher cost of using machinery lowers the amount of output that can be produced efficiently. We are poorer, as are all other non-OPEC countries. If we all work just as hard, we produce less because it is no longer as efficient as before to use machinery to assist labor.

Four or five years after the oil shocks, the President's Council of Economic Advisers had not incorporated the effect of the shocks into their estimates of potential output. The Council's 1978 report dwells on the amount of idle capacity, and estimates the gap between potential and actual output as two to three times greater than estimates that adjusted for the effects of the shocks on productive capacity.

The Council's view in early 1978 was that the economy was capable of achieving a substantial increase in output and a reduction of the unemployment rate to 4.8 percent without increasing the rate of inflation. In the Council's view, the best policy for 1978 was to pump up the economy by encouraging spending. This view prevailed. Monetary and fiscal policies remained expansive in 1978.

We know the result. The Council was wrong, and the critics were right. There was much less idle capacity, much less potential output, and a much smaller gap than the Council's 1978 report suggested.

Rising inflation in 1978 and 1979 was the result of error, not accident. The error was avoidable. As early as 1975, a group of economists from business and universities, known as the Shadow Open Market Committee, called attention to the "distinction between a decline attributable to real shocks and a decline attributable to cyclical forces. A cyclical decline creates an output gap. Real shocks reduce output and capacity." By 1978, several estimates of the loss of potential output had been made. These estimates, based on careful economic analysis, showed the extent to which the Council's policies were based on illusory estimates of potential output.

There are many other examples of economic policies that have, at most, a tenuous relation to economic theory. Regulatory efforts, policies toward pollution and safety, proposals to tax wage increases or price increases or both, most of the President's 1977 energy program, and many other proposed or actual policies have only two connections to economics. Often the policies are designed or administered by economists—people trained in economics. And many of the policies sacrifice efficiency, about which economists have expertise, for equity, a subject on which economics says nothing and economists have no special expertise.

Monetarism

The term "monetarism" was first used by Karl Brunner in 1968 to summarize three conclusions drawn from contemporary work on money and monetary policy. "First, monetary impulses are a major factor accounting for variation in output, employment and prices. Second, movements in the money stock are the most reliable measure of the thrust of monetary impulses. Third, the behavior of the monetary authorities dominates movements of the money stock over business cycles." [1]

Brunner compared "monetarism" to the views held by economists and officials at the Federal Reserve and in the Administration. At the time, and for the next decade, the Federal Reserve attempted to control interest rates and neglected to control the growth of money. Now, after 15 years of inflation, the Federal Reserve has recognized publicly that its procedures were faulty, that attempts to control interest rates produced higher inflation, a devalued dollar, and higher—not lower—interest rates. Each of these points was part of the monetarist critique of Federal Reserve policy. It is hard to avoid the conclusion that the current inflation is, to a considerable extent, the result of errors made by the Federal Reserve.

Many of the errors were avoidable. On March 25, 1968, Federal Reserve Chairman Martin told the Senate Banking Committee:

> We know that, in the short run, expansive monetary policies tend to reduce interest rates and restrictive monetary policy to raise them. But in the long run, in a full employment economy, expansive monetary policies foster greater inflation and encourage borrowers to make even greater demands on the credit markets. Over the long run, therefore, expansive monetary policies may not lower interest rates, in fact they may raise them appreciably. This is the clear lesson of history that has been reconfirmed by the experience of the past several years.

But Chairman Martin's statement did not lead to a change in Fed-

---

[1] Karl Brunner, "The Role of Money and Monetary Policy," *Review*, Federal Reserve Bank of St. Louis, July 1968, pp. 9-24.

eral Reserve procedures. The Federal Reserve continued to use the level of interest rates to judge their policy stance and continued to control interest rates to carry out policy. Money growth continued to rise in periods of prosperity and to fall in recession.

The monetarist critique of government policy did not concentrate solely on procedures. The argument for controlling money was based on some of the oldest and most reliable propositions in economic theory. Sustained growth of money above the rates of growth of output produce inflation. Sudden, unanticipated reductions of money growth cause recessions and unemployment. Both propositions have been repeated, in one form or another, for about 200 years. Recent developments of economic theory strengthened the analytical foundation for these well-established propositions. Recent events have done nothing to undermine their factual basis.

The breakdown of the fixed-exchange-rate standard, the variability of fluctuating exchange rates, the inability of governments to control exchange rates, the flight from currencies with high anticipated rates of inflation to currencies with low anticipated rates of inflation, the inability of countries to control interest rates by monetary means, the development of substitutes for money to circumvent controls on deposit rates, the repeated failures of price and wage guidelines to have any lasting effect on inflation—these and many other propositions, tested and confirmed by experience and by economic research, show that economics is alive and remains useful—indeed, indispensable—for correct prediction and for stabilizing policies.

Why then did policies fail to reduce inflation and unemployment? Was it the result of arrogance or ignorance? I believe neither is the principal reason for policy failures, though both have played a role. Economists, no less than others, are eager to test their ideas—and impose their views—on others.

The inability of engineers, physicists, or astronomers to predict the point at which Skylab would strike the earth does not reveal some undetected, fundamental flaw in the natural sciences. It shows that some events are difficult to predict and control. Engineers and natural scientists were able to put Skylab into space and to control its path while it was in orbit, but unable to control the path on which it returned to earth.

Airplane crashes, swine flu vaccines, and problems with nuclear reactors show that technology is not flawless and that science can bring improvement, not perfection. These problems, even tragedies, do not raise doubts about the scientific bases of physics, biology, and chemistry—or lead to the conclusion that natural science is in a crisis.

Economics is not the science that gives accurate quarterly projections of employment, prices, profits, and other variables. Economists who promised to steer the economy from quarter to quarter or year to year offered more than economics can deliver. Many may now be dispirited by the failures of the policies they advocated, initiated, and administered, and by the cost of their failures. To describe the failures of government policy as failures of economics is the very opposite of the truth.

The fact that policy makers often rely on short-run tactics that have little relation to economic theory, and fail to develop long-term strategies based on economic theory, tells us that there is a large gap between economic theory and policy. The principal failure of economics as a policy science is a failure to recognize that gap.

4

Models and reality in economic discourse

DANIEL BELL

FOR more than 35 years, economic theory—the skein of Cambridge (U.K. and U.S.A.) economics woven by Alfred Marshall, John Maynard Keynes, and Paul Samuelson, has been a powerful force directing economic policy.* Today, there is general agreement that government economic management and policy is in disarray. Many economists argue that prescriptions derived from previous historical situations no longer apply, but there is little consensus as to new prescriptions. Indeed, there is emerging a prior question about the fundamental postulates of this neoclassical economics—about the model of a competitive equilibrium, and about the guiding assumptions as to how individuals, firms, and governments behave (e.g., utility maximization). To a Mohammedan, all Christians are alike, whether foot-washing Baptists or word-splitting Thomists, and while the theoretical differences between a Friedman and a Samuelson are distinct, and the

* I wish to thank Robert M. Solow for reading an early draft and saving me from some egregious errors; needless to say, he is not responsible for any of my formulations. I would also like to acknowledge as a source, Mark Blaug's *Economic Theory in Retrospect,* as my guide through the bramble bush of the history of economic theory.

policy consequences divergent, there is also the question whether the theoretical framework that encompasses both is itself adequate. In short, there is the question not only whether there is a crisis *in* economic theory but also a crisis *of* economic theory itself. For this reason, one has to go back to the history of that theory and retrace its steps.

I
From the moral to the instrumental

Modern economic modes of thinking—those of the last 200 years—depart in two wholly novel ways from all previous modes of thinking about the subset of human activities that it labels "economic"—a word that was not established until Alfred Marshall's *Principles* in 1890; until that time the term used was "political economy." The first departure was to isolate economics from a traditional context of moral activities, and to establish it as a set of activities that could be judged purely in instrumental terms. The second was to conceive of the world of economic exchanges, analytically, as an autonomous, self-consistent realm, a system of structural relations in which an understanding of economic activities could be derived from the postulates of the system.

There were two intellectual reasons for these developments. Related to the first was the association of economics with modern liberalism and its fundamental tenet that human beings were to be regarded as individuals detached from family, clan, class or nation, as independent, self-determining beings, each the judge of his own actions; a corollary of this tenet was that the rules regulating the relations between individuals were to be procedural, not morally substantive. In this respect, what was true of economics was true of law, religion, and culture as well: Art was to be for art's sake, not subject to moral norms; law and morality were regarded as independent realms. Morals were regarded as pertaining to individual, private conduct and law to the formal, general rules of public conduct. In economics, each man properly pursued his own self-interest.

All this is barely 200 years old. When Francis Hutcheson, the teacher of Adam Smith, published his *Short Introduction to Moral Philosophy,* his "Principles of Oeconomics and Politics" opened with chapters on marriage and divorce, the duties of parents and children, and masters and servants—a tradition going back to the Greek conception of "oeconomics" as the principles of management of the household.[1] Adam Smith would write a *Theory of Moral Sentiments* prior to his *Wealth of Nations,* and while some scholars argue that there is an underlying relation between the two, the contents differ in their emphases. In the former, it is on the disinterested judgments of moral actions, in the latter, on the self-interest of individuals.

Subsequently, in its first 75 years, English economic theory developed in a context of utilitarianism which postulated that the happiness of the greatest number was the outcome, if not the object, of independent economic choices. But it was by no means self-evident—as Henry Sidgwick, the great Cambridge moral philosopher, pointed out in his *Ethics*—that Egoism and Utilitarianism were so easily reconcilable ("unless indeed by religion"), or that it was an obvious truth that "the interest of all is the interest of each." Economics after Marshall, however, moved away from its utilitarian schema and became concerned principally with the egoistic interests of each.

The second, intellectually distinct yet historically related, development was the new idea of economics as a science. But the view of science that was prevalent then was the explication of an underlying structure of constants, of invariant relations beneath the flux of turbulent surfaces, and the formulation of a general set of equations governing the interconnections of those constants. The model is that of classical mechanics. Galileo turned from the study of concrete bodies to their abstract properties, such as mass, acceleration, velocity, and their interrelations within a unified field. In a similar sense, a shift occurred from the political economy of historically-located societies to economics as the abstract study of the interrelated variables that would be applicable to any system of production and exchange. In other words, there began the search for those constants that could be identified as the stable, underlying "reality."

In short, economics moved from the moral (or political) and normative to the instrumental and scientific; and the great structure of this achievement was the neoclassical edifice of Alfred Marshall and the mathematical formalization of this set of relations in the "general equilibrium" theory of Leon Walras.

---

[1] One might say that all this was just prescriptive ideology for men did not then, if ever, manage their economic affairs by such rules; the scions of the Renaissance rulers were taught the "education of Christian principles," not Machiavelli's handbook. That may be, but it only begs the question as to the reasons for this "ideology," and why the ideololgy—if it *was that*—changed so radically.

Economic Man

The concerns of the classical economists, from Adam Smith to John Stuart Mill, were with wealth and economic growth. The measure of economic welfare was the quantity of output which, in turn, was a function of the quantity of labor and its productivity. For the classical economists, the "real" measure of goods was their "value," not their utility. The reason goes back to the famous "diamond-water paradox," in which Smith had argued that since useful goods such as water are free, and useless goods such as diamonds are expensive, utility could not be a determinant of price. In the short-run, the price of a commodity might be governed by demand, but in the long-run it was determined by the cost of production. In effect, Smith largely passed over the demand problem and stated that "natural prices" are governed by the outlay of producers on the supply side of the market.

For Smith, the science of economics was the mode of augmenting capital stock and increasing the productivity of labor so as to expand the output of goods, and thus wealth. The economy was a "system," but in a metaphorical not mechanical sense. The premise was that it does not pay an individual to produce himself what he could buy more cheaply from someone else, for "what is prudence in the conduct of every private family, can scarce be folly in that of a great Kingdom." If each person took comparative advantage of his own resources, all men, if unimpeded—"the obvious and simple system of natural liberty"—would maximize aggregate wealth.

What Adam Smith lacked, however, was the "nuance" of decision, namely just how an individual would maximize his own contribution. This calibration was supplied by W. Stanley Jevons and others in the "marginalist revolution" that began in the 1870's. As Philip Wicksteed, one of its later expositors wrote:

> . . . by increasing our supply of anything we reduce its marginal significance and lower the price of an extra unit on our scale of preferences; and suitable additions to our supply will bring it down to any value you please. Thus, whatever the price of any commodity that the housewife finds in the market may be, so long as its marginal significance to her is higher than that price, she will buy; but the very act of putting herself in possession of an increased stock reduces its marginal significance and the more she buys the lower [the significance] becomes. The amount that brings it into coincidence with market price is the amount she will buy.

This assumption, that the utility of a good declines as the stock increases, means that the process described by Wicksteed is an equilibrating one. As the stock of a good changes, the value of additional units change, thus creating a situation where the marginal value is just equal to the price. Thus, while the total utility of water is undoubtedly greater than the total utility of diamonds, the marginal utility of the stones is high because the stock is low, whereas the marginal utility of water is low because the stock is plentiful.

What the marginalists did was to make *relative* price and *relative* scarcity the fulcrums of economic analysis. As reformulated by Lionel Robbins, economics became the science of allocating given quantities of scarce resources among competing claims to obtain the most efficient or optimal use. As William Breit and Roger Ransom wrote:

> The fact of scarcity creates a necessity for choice and a careful comparing of alternatives. Accordingly a new view of human nature came into focus in the writings of neoclassical economists. The individual is imagined in a constant process of delicately balancing his marginal expenditures and marginal utilities. This rational, calculating human who emerges clearly in the pages of Menger's *Grundsatze,* also appears in most of the works of neoclassical writers, including Jevons, Pareto and Wicksteed.

What we have here, in short, is an abstraction now made flesh, the idea of "economic man"—a term first introduced by Pareto.

II
A system of equilibrium

The behavioral assumption of what is called neoclassical theory is that of the individual's utility maximization. The structural context is a theory of markets, the idea that in the criss-crossing of buyers and sellers a rational sorting-out takes place which satisfies all those concerned. And, as Eric Roll has written: "If . . . we regard the economic system as an enormous conglomeration of interdependent markets, the central problem of economic enquiry becomes the explanation of the exchanging process, or, more particularly, the explanation of the formation of price."

The first neoclassical summation of exchange was formulated by Alfred Marshall. Marshall was able to show, with his ingenious diagrams, how the costs of production on the supply side intersected with marginal utility on the demand side to determine relative price. For Marshall, price theory was what economics was all about. From price theory, he derived the demand curve, the elasticities of demand and supply, the nature of consumer's surplus, the use of long-run and short-run analysis, partial equilibrium, and the other components of the "analytical engine" which he fashioned to understand the terms of trade.

With Marshall, too, came the first nuanced analysis of the character of economic equilibrium. The classical framework had been Say's Law of Markets which, crudely put, stated that "supply creates its own demand." Inadequate demand as a cause of unemployment was unlikely since human wants were deemed to be insatiable, and supply would generate the demand through the circular flow of payments from suppliers to consumers or investors and back to suppliers. Temporary gluts or shortfalls might always occur, but these would adjust themselves through the movements of wages and prices in each market.

Neoclassical economics, following Marshall, refined Say's Law by using marginal analysis to determine the level of real output. A producer would never seek to offer a worker a wage greater than the value of the added output his labor could produce, so that the number of workers hired by a firm would be set at the point where cost of the marginal worker would equal the value of his output. And, by the same reasoning, John Bates Clark sought to show in his *Distribution of Wealth* (1899) that the same principle would apply not only to wages, but to the markets for all the factors of production, to rents and returns on capital (interest and profit) as well. Clark concluded that under perfect competition each factor would receive a return precisely equal to its own contribution, a return equal to the value of the marginal product. In this fashion Clark re-introduced a normative principle of a "just return" to labor and capital as factors in production.

Given these millions of transactions in hundreds of different kinds of markets, where the aggregate of prices in a product market must match the aggregate of prices in a factor market, and where the prices paid out equal the incomes received, how is all this to be accomplished? As Mark Blaug puts it:

> . . . What reason do we have for thinking that the whole process hangs together? Business firms enter product markets as suppliers, but they enter factor markets as buyers; households on the other hand, are buyers in product markets but suppliers in factor markets. Is equilibrium in product markets necessarily consistent with equilibrium in factor markets? Does the market mechanism guarantee convergence on a general equilibrium solution? If so, is this solution unique, or are there several configurations of prices that will satisfy a solution?

> Even if a unique general equilibrium exists, will it be stable in the sense that a departure from equilibrium sets up automatic forces that bring the system back into equilibrium?

The first full set of theoretical answers had been given by the French economist Leon Walras, in his *Elements of Pure Economics* (1874): The product prices and factor prices are determined simultaneously, and by solving the simultaneous equations, one can determine the general equilibrium. As Schumpeter declared, Walras' *Elements* is nothing less than the Magna Carta of exact economics.

Yet if there was a general equilibrium, was there some other criterion which would tell us whether the equilibrium was optimal? Walras' system was elaborated by his successor at Lausanne, the Italian engineer-economist Vilfredo Pareto. Pareto provided a more elaborate mathematical presentation of the Walrasian general equilibrium scheme and added an additional criterion which introduced a new normative consideration. As against the notion of the greatest good for the greatest number (which depends upon comparing quantities of unlike things), or seeking to compare interpersonal utilities, Pareto abandoned the idea of a unique social optimum and introduced the idea of compensating payments, or what we call today a "trade-off." Thus a welfare trade-off, or "Pareto-optimality," would be that point when no person would be less well off and at least one person would be better off. The theorem was neglected for many years until resurrected by Abba Lerner in 1934. It is today the foundation of welfare economics.

Seduced by the idea of a general equilibrium for all economic transactions, Pareto sought to generalize the idea to the entire range of social phenomena. Arguing that economics was but one type of human action, namely logical or rational action, Pareto attempted in his *Treatise on General Sociology* to set forth a comprehensive scheme that would embrace non-logical actions as well. He hoped, for example, to show that the "circulation of elites," which he held to be the fundamental character of politics, could be charted with the same accuracy as the circulation of goods.

The rational and the real

Let us leave aside, for the moment, the problem of a unified theory of social actions and restrict ourselves to the economic—the logical and rational—as deriving from self-interest.

The development of neoclassical economics as a positive science raises two epistemological questions. The 19th century view of science, drawing from traditional philosophy, held that beneath the surface of appearance was an underlying structure of reality. Thus, for Marx, beneath the "anarchy" of the market was a structure of social relations; for Freud, below the rationalizations of behavior, the impulses of the unconscious; for Pareto, underneath the intellectual justifications, the residues of sentiments. Neoclassical economics posits its master key as well, the structure of a general equilibrium in markets.

But this raises a second question—which goes to the heart of the character of the social sciences as science—whether the general equilibrium that one can define, in theory, is a *fiction*, a normative standard, perhaps, against which to judge an actual economy, or a *description* of how economic exchanges (if unhampered) take place in accordance with the "laws" of economics. Can the theory "model" reality? For the economist, the starting point is the distinction between "real" and "nominal" magnitudes.

The everyday world is one of sharp fluctuations in price, of gluts and shortages, of changing ratios between values, and the like. To measure these, one must have a standard of measure that itself is invariable. Common sense makes a distinction between the listed price of a good or of one's dollar income and its purchasing power over time, corrected for the changing value of money. For the economist, the first are nominal magnitudes, but underneath are the real relations established in the long-run by the equilibrating forces of relative prices which clear all markets and bring the entire system into balance. The questions that have dominated contemporary economic theory are whether these equilibrating forces do act, in practice, to bring the economy back to the "real"—some would say "natural"—relations.

When Adam Smith in his *Wealth of Nations,* wrote "Of the Real and Nominal Price of Commodities, or of Their Price in Labour, and Their Price in Money," he was not seeking to distinguish between purchasing power and the value of money, but to define economic welfare, to see whether an individual was better off or not over time. The contemporary assumption is that such a concept revolves around an increase in real income, in the standard of living defined as to the things we can buy. For Smith, however, the improvement in welfare was identified with the reduction of the "toil and trouble" involved in irksome labor. It was for this reason that when Smith corrected nominal (money) values he did it, not in relation to the changes in price level, but in relation to money wage rates.

Adam Smith was a believer in the free market, but not for the reasons of modern positivist economics. For Smith, the *effect* of the market, its higgling and bargaining, was to iron out or equalize the disutilities of work by the "trade-off" of wages, but the *virtue* of the market was not its presumed mechanism of allocative efficiency. It was rather that, by comparative advantage, specialization, and the division of labor, it would extend the scope and scale of economizing (i.e., productivity) and thus increase the wealth and welfare of mankind. For Adam Smith, the prod of self-interest was not such that it would create a "natural harmony" of society (he was too much of a Scot ever to accept that pap) but that it would reduce irksome toil through the phenomenon of economic growth.[2]

Alfred Marshall was quite aware—as Talcott Parsons pointed out almost 45 years ago in his *Structure of Social Action*—of the diverse motivations and wants of man and, as a good Victorian of probity and responsibility, he wanted to foster improvement in the human lot. But as a child of his time, Marshall wanted also to advance economic science, which he defined as the discovery and measurement of regularities in behavior. And, while man often acts irrationally in many spheres, actions in economic life are more easily plotted because they are constrained by cost calculations, reinforced by a psychological hedonism (e.g., diminishing utility), and are measurable in prices. Thus, for Marshall—as distinct from Smith (or Marx)—the scope of economic analysis became coterminous with price theory.

With Walras the move from determinacy of price in one market to equilibria in all markets rounded out the boundaries of the system. Walras' solution was the picturesque theory of *tâtonnement* (literally "tapping") in which buyers and sellers grope along until a set of equilibrating prices (which match the "underlying" set

[2] For Smith, as is clear in the book on moral sentiments, it is not economic motivation that prompts a man to work, but status, respect, esteem, moral mettle, qualities which would allow him to be a man of worth and dignity. Smith believed man to be a *socius* whose actions are taken always with an eye to the judgment of his fellows. His theory of society is a theory of sympathy, not as Hume thought of pleasure in a system of utility, but as a measure for gentlemanly conduct in social relations. The primary virtue is justice and, as he wrote in *The Theory of Moral Sentiments*, "we feel ourselves to be under a stricter obligation to act according to justice than agreeably to friendship, charity or generosity; that the practice of these last-mentioned virtues seems to be left to some measure to our own choice, but that, somehow or other, we feel ourselves to be in a peculiar manner tied, bound, and obliged to the observation of justice."

In this respect, Smith was still a pupil of Francis Hutcheson and a practitioner of Aristotle's *oeconomics*.

of "real" prices as established in the equations) are reached. Walras made two assumptions: one of perfect competition in all markets; the other, an absence of advances in technical knowledge, since these would change the parameters of the equations. That theory is completely static. But within its premises, what economists could now do was to define precise functional relations between quantifiable variables and to construct geometric, and later algebraic, models of economic behavior.

Since Walras, general equilibrium theory has been polished and perfected in its mathematical elegance by writers such as Arrow, Debreu, and Hahn. When put together with the neoclassical reformulations of Hicks and Samuelson, we have a general system of theory to explain the relative prices of goods and services and of the factors of production, the allocation of these factors to various uses, the levels of employment, and the level of prices. More precisely, economics developed two general systems of theory, one for relative prices and allocations (microeconomics), the other for levels of employment and price (macroeconomics). It was this rigor, as Keynes wrote in a memoir of Marshall, that led to "a whole Copernican system by which all the elements of the economic universe are kept in their places by mutual counterpoise and interaction."

A confusion of realms

In the history of economic theory, these developments are looked upon as advances in scientific knowledge and technical sophistication (especially when mathematics is employed), and as a mark of cumulative growth. But what is almost completely ignored—yet the consequences are crucial if theory is to be directive of policy—is that these "paradigms" (I use the word to mark off distinctive modes of defining reality) each make different assumptions about their subject matter. The words "nature," "natural rates," "economic laws," "economic science," occur in almost all these schemata, yet the assumptions vary so radically as to alert one to the fact that four different philosophical and epistemological modes are present, and have become confused with one another.

When Adam Smith is using the word *nature*, his idiom and context are classical (i.e., ancient) philosophy. Nature implies a *telos*, a purpose immanent in the form of the object, which is the task of men to realize. Natural liberty is not the state of nature of Hobbes, a mechanistic world driven by appetite, murderous self-interest, and aggrandizement. It is a world—otherwise *The Theory of Moral Sentiments* makes no sense—where men strive for disinterested moral judgments (what Aristotle called *phronimos*) by seeking for those general standards that comprise "sympathy." The Smithian world is individualistic (because conscience rescues a man from the bonds of conformity) but not egoistic. There is, in the phrase coined by him, "the Great Society." Economics, as an aspect of it, is inextricably normative and moral.

With Marshall, the moral impulses are also evident. His *Principles* are shot through with concerns to improve the well-being of men. He proposes, even, a measure of welfare, the "consumer's surplus," or the difference between what a consumer actually pays for a product, as against what he would have been willing to pay, and this becomes an index of well-being over time.

But with Marshall, morals and money are sundered. Since science is "inductive," economics must limit its scope to phenomena that have a price measurement. And economic laws are those generalizations—regularities—about human behavior which could be measured in terms of money, as men moved about "the ordinary business of life," seeking the best advantages for themselves. Given the scaling of utilities that Marshall now thought possible, regularities of behavior could be observed and measured, and predictions made about future events.[3]

Economics, then, deals with the maximization of utilities, and the different ordering scales whereby individuals rank their wants. Utility, thus, becomes equated with welfare. But such a conception begs four questions: 1) that the distinction between "needs" and "wants"—needs which are common to all men, wants that are idiosyncratic and psychological—can be erased and all demands treated as wants; 2) that the social welfare is defined only in terms of the welfare of individuals; 3) that every individual is the best judge of his own welfare; and 4) that the welfare of individuals may not

[3] Quite remarkably, in fact, Marshall sought to convert all phenomena to utilities, from qualities to quantities, so to speak. As he writes on "Utility and Demand" in his *Principles*:

> Men cannot create material things. In the mental and moral world indeed we may produce new ideas; but when he is said to produce material things, he really only produces utilities; or, in other words, his efforts and sacrifices result in changing the form or arrangement of matter to adapt it better for the satisfaction of wants.
>
> Utility is taken to be correlative to Desire or Want. . . . There is an endless variety of wants, but there is a limit to each separate want. This familiar tendency of human nature may be stated in *the law of satiable wants* or of *diminishing utility*. . . .

be compared. Yet, if money and morals are sundered, it does not therefore follow that traditional moral questions can be set aside.

Walras' idea of *tâtonnement,* of the groping of individuals in response to signals from an external environment is, unconsciously but perfectly, an image of the Darwinian world. Here society is like nature, in which adaptation is the natural process by which selection takes place. No single group of persons can control the entire process, for the number of wants and desires are so diverse that no one can plan to match these consciously, as through some giant switchboard or computer.

The sociological and philosophical framework for this image of *tâtonnement* was proved by the Austrian economist Karl Menger, one of the multiple discoverers of marginal utility with Jevons, and a founder of the so-called "Austrian economics." For Menger, society is an evolutionary system in which "spontaneous order" arises out of the mutual adaptation of individuals, and the whole is functionally integrated by natural processes, exactly similar to biological processes. Human calculation simply cannot anticipate and provide for the diversity which is the characteristic, and the strength, of creative natural forces, so that planning is inherently restrictive and self-defeating, limiting the ability of individuals to make their own adaptive responses.

In contemporary thought, the argument has been expanded most vigorously by Friedrich Hayek, who claims that not only is there no such thing as "social" justice outside of individual desert, but that individual liberty is the necessary condition for individuals to respond to the unforseeable and unpredictable onset of multifarious events, if a society is to maintain that capacity for spontaneous adaptation which would keep a social order viable. Economics, for Hayek, while integral to freedom, has little relation to virtue. It is a view almost diametrical to those of the ancient philosophers.

The "general equilibrium" model, as perfected by Arrow, Debreu, Koopmans, et al., is a jewelled set of movements, a celestial clockwork, to use the old image of Laplace, in which perfect competition and optimal allocations operate as an Invisible Hand, except that the Invisible Hand is neither God, the principle of benevolence, nor the spontaneous adaptation of Nature, but a Mathematical Theorem, a set of "coefficients of transformations" sublimely indifferent —as Barone earlier, and Lange and Lerner later pointed out—to the private ownership of the means of production or a decentralized price system of market socialism. It is a work of art, so compelling that one thinks of the celebrated pictures of Apelles who painted a cluster of grapes so realistic that the birds would come and pick at them. But is the model "real"?

Walras had thought of his model as actually describing how competitive markets would come into equilibrium. He thought that the trading prices in actual markets would be the same, eventually, as those which would solve the system of simultaneous equations. Yet the problem of disequilibrium in different kinds of markets—such as labor markets—is too obviously a real-world problem. The conclusion is inescapable. There is no empirical guarantee that the blind "groping" of the market produces a set of "clearing prices" that are identical with the underlying set of equations. If the model, as elaborated by Arrow, et al., has validity, it is only as a "fiction"—logical, elegant, self-contained, but a fiction nonetheless.

III
Four bridges to reality

The luster of neoclassical theory in the last 35 years obscures the fact that in the first three decades of this century, especially in the U.S., it had fallen to a low state of esteem. It was regarded as "academic" (in the pejorative sense of the word), as "theoretical" (again pejorative), abstract, ahistorical, hypothetical-deductive, etc. The new hope was for institutional economics, as exemplified by John R. Commons, who drew on historical and sociological concepts, or "evolutionary economics," as illustrated by Thorstein Veblen, who drew upon anthropology for his usages regarding habit, custom, emulation and the like. What gave new life to neoclassical theory was two developments. One was the initiation of statistical studies, such as those of Wesley Clair Mitchell and such subsequent students at Columbia as Arthur F. Burns, Simon Kuznets, and Milton Friedman. These sought to look at actual economic behavior and to construct various indices—the formation of index numbers itself was a major achievement—chart magnitudes over time, as business cycles, and create systems of national accounts. Yet many of these are atheoretical: the system of national accounts, for example, patient and ingenious as is the construction, which is "simply" the construction of structural identities of output and income. But the statistics were to provide the coefficients for the theoretical variables.[4]

[4] The history of statistical theory—the work of R.A. Fisher, Neyman and Pearson, Yule and Kendall, Wald and Hotelling—is curiously neglected, in fact often omitted, in standard histories of economic theory.

The second were a number of "bridges" from theory to actuality. Competitive equilibrium was the theoretical fiction of neoclassical economics, but empirical men had to find ways of relating the abstract image to the buzzing confusions of the everyday, workaday world. In relation to the debates on the viability of neoclassical theory, I wish to single out and discuss four such bridges.

1) *The quantity theory of money.* Wealth, we assume, is land, machinery, goods. But is money also wealth? For traditionalist Catholic writers, as for the young Marx, money was a stealthy means of expropriating productive labor or the use-values it creates. For John Law, the paper-money mercantilist of 1705, as for the later American populists, "money stimulates trade," and cheap money is the road to prosperity.

The quantity theory of money, from John Locke down to Milton Friedman, is an effort to correct both these views by arguing that money can only reflect, or distort, real relationships. Writing in the 1690's, Locke stated that prices vary in definite proportion to the quantity of money, and that the abundance of money makes everything dear; and Hume a half century later sought to demonstrate a causal relationship between money and prices. As Milton Friedman has written:

> There is perhaps no other empirical relation in economics that has been observed to recur so uniformly under so wide a variety of circumstances as the relation between substantial changes over short periods in the stock of money and prices; the one is invariably linked with the other and is in the same direction; this uniformity is, I suspect, of the same order as many of the uniformities that form the basis of the physical sciences.

The framework of the argument is simple. The price level itself—the general price level—is a ceiling determined by the quantity of money in circulation. The prices for individual commodities (i.e., relative prices) might fluctuate for natural or exogenous reasons (such as droughts for food prices or cartels for oil). But so long as the total quantity of money was steady, the general price level could not rise, though individual prices would adjust to each other as demand shifted. Thus, having to spend more for fuel oil would force one to cut spending for other products. For the same reason, Friedman believed that trade unions could not force up the *general level* of wages (so that "wage-push inflation" was an impossibility), so long as the total money supply was constant. Unions could only affect the "relative shares" of wages among industries, or between capital or labor—but not the general price level.

This neoclassicist view, of course, made a fundamental distinction between the real value of money and its nominal value. The real value expresses the tangibles money can command; the nominal, the existing amount expressed in a monetary unit. (To be a millionaire may not mean much if it costs a million marks to buy a cup of coffee, as in Germany in the 1920's.) Quantity theorists said that people act to maintain some level of *real* balances (i.e., real purchasing power). If the relation between the nominal and real balances moved out of line, people would seek to adjust their nominal money balances to equal the customary or desired level of *real* balances.

The neoclassical economists understood that there were often sharp price fluctuations in the real world, and that purely monetary or nominal events, such as a big gold strike, let alone a war financed by printing press money, could have real effects in the short run. But they believed that such economic fluctuations were transient, or that monetary distortions after a while would leach away, since underneath these "top of the wave" turbulences was the "real economy" of capital equipment and labor. The logic of market-oriented equilibrium economics was thus, if perturbations occurred, to let them run their course, since adjustments (even if at times painful ones) would, in the long run, wring out the nominal excesses.

In neoclassical theory, a cut in money wages was the same as a cut in real wages, if prices were flexible. If a money wage was too high, competitive pressure would drive that wage down to the price where the employer would be able to hire again. If money wages were "sticky," an employer would not hire workers so that, under those conditions, unemployment would be the "partial equilibrium" (i.e., the trade-off), but the general price level would fall.

The picture for wage and product markets was rounded out for capital markets by the Swedish economist Knut Wicksell who sought to show how the quantity of money—and credit—influenced interest rates which, in turn, influenced the flow of savings into investment. In Wicksell's scheme, the interest rate became the equilibrating instrument for the supply of, and demand for, capital.

In short, there was macroeconomics before Keynes, because the neoclassical quantity theory of money was, in fact, what we now call macroeconomics.

2) *The theory of monopolistic competition.* Neoclassical economics recognized only two market structures—competition and monopoly—as ideal types. If markets are interdependent, entry of firms

easy, and substitution of products possible, then the pressures to keep each firm producing at its most efficient level would be the result. Clearly, however, this did not reflect the actualities of the business world. The man who coped with this fact was Edward H. Chamberlin of Harvard, who first approached the question in his Ph.D. thesis in 1927, and published the results in 1933.

The phrase, "monopolistic competition," is an oxymoron. The idea is simple, though the ramifications for neoclassical theory complex. Chamberlin focussed on a firm's control of a *product* rather than price. What he called into question were the postulates of homogeneous products and interdependent markets that underlay the theorem of competitive equilibrium. His work opened the way to a new theory of the firm and of industrial organization. It questioned the assumptions of price theory, which is the core of Marshall's conception of economics. He opened the way to a revolution in microeconomics in the way that one speaks of a Keynesian revolution in macroeconomics.

Marshall had described the price behavior of commodities within an industry. But he had not really looked at the behavior of an individual firm, or identified a commodity in other than a generic way (e.g., "textiles" or "tobacco"). But a firm which can establish product differentiation, by "branding" its product, gains a quasi-monopolistic advantage over its competitor and thus creates a special market enclave. Given branded products, consumers do not behave as if all similar products are alike.

By treating a product as relatively unique, Chamberlin showed that a firm could—with the help of advertising—affect the demand curve and establish "market power." Other firms in the same "industry" might compete, but the competition would be less on price than on their own product identification.

For economic theory, Chamberlin's demonstrations of a firm's behavior in price and cost diagrams were revealing. Given the new kind of competition, each firm produces less than under conditions of perfect competition. Price does not equal marginal cost, and price and output are sloped along monopolist lines. Yet because of product competition, profits are lower than they would be under a monopoly. Not only is Adam Smith's market hand invisible; it is just not there. From the view of social beneficence and consumer optimality, there is only a wasteland: Monopolistic competition provides the disadvantages of monopoly (i.e., higher prices than at a price-competitive level) and none of the benefits of competition (since entry into the market, which requires a new brand identification, is not easy). These conclusions of Chamberlin, 50 years ago, are the basis for the more popular Galbraithian critiques of capitalist market practices.

Chamberlin, however, had more than complicated the neoclassical view of competition. He had called into question some of the easy assumptions about price signals as the "switching mechanisms" between products and industries, and, by questioning the interdependence of markets, he was implicitly calling into question the assertion that a "general solution" or multi-market equilibrium was possible. While the "realism" of Chamberlin's description of product markets rather than price markets was quickly established, the more unsettling implications of Chamberlin's arguments, coming as they did in the midst of the Depression, were put aside because of the macroeconomic problems posed by world-wide depression, unemployment, and social unrest.[5]

3) *The Keynesian Revolution.* For a work so widely hailed, yet so rarely read, Keynes' *General Theory* is a bewildering book. A technical discussion of the marginal efficiency of capital is followed by a self-contained chapter on speculation, comparing the stock market to a game of "snap, of Old Maid and Musical Chairs." As Paul Samuelson wrote in a retrospective essay in 1946:

> It is a badly written book, poorly organized; any layman who, beguiled by the author's previous reputation, bought the book was cheated of his five shillings. . . . It abounds in mares' nests of confusions. . . . In it the Keynesian system stands out indistinctly, as if the author were hardly aware of its existence or cognizant of its properties. . . . Flashes of insight and intuition intersperse tedious algebra. An awkward definition suddenly gives way to an unforgettable cadenza. . . . I think I am giving away no secrets when I solemnly aver —upon the basis of vivid personal recollection—that no one else in Cambridge, Massachusetts, really knew what it was all about for some twelve to eighteen months after its publication. Indeed, until the ap-

[5] Some of Chamberlin's work was obscured by the appearance in the same year of Joan Robinson's *Economics of Imperfect Competition.* While the title of Mrs. Robinson's book caught the "gist" of Chamberlin's argument (though not its technical demonstration of a firm's quasi-monopolistic advantage), the two books actually dealt with different problems, and the conflation of the two fuzzed the impact of Chamberlin's argument. Mrs. Robinson's book was a refinement of Marshall's idea of monopoly, using an industry as the analytical unit, and did not, as Chamberlin did, deal with market power of firms. As Mark Blaug writes: "Despite superficial similarities between the two books, it is now perfectly obvious that Chamberlin was the true revolutionary."

The sociological irony is that Chamberlin himself was politically conservative, and on labor quite reactionary, while Mrs. Robinson is the quintessential blue-stocking radical. The most vigorous criticism of Chamberlin has come from the Chicago school, most notably George Stigler, in *Five Lectures on Economic Problems* and Milton Friedman in *Essays on Positive Economics.*

pearance of the mathematical models of Meade, Lange, Hicks and Harrod, there is reason to believe that Keynes himself did not truly understand his own analysis.[6]

Though Keynes is popularly known for the ideas of deficit financing and "pump priming," these were *not* the concerns of the *General Theory*.[7] The *General Theory of Employment, Interest and Money*—to give the book its full title—was an onslaught on Say's Law, the argument that in the long-run the "real forces" of the economic system would tend to full employment equilibrium. Thus Keynes' remark that, in the long-run, we are all dead.

Keynes made two arguments: One, highly technical, that even if Say's Law was valid in a static (i.e., self-contained) model, it could not show that a full-employment equilibrium was dynamically attainable since the process of moving toward an equilibrium *through time* displaces the equilibrium itself.

The second, which received the most attention, was that, in a depression, a static equilibrium was impossible for three reasons: the inelasticity (i.e., unresponsiveness) of interest rates as a means of stimulating investment; a "liquidity trap," or the desire of savers (financial institutions or individuals) to hold ("hoard") money; and the stickiness of money wages and prices. What Keynes was saying was that nominal magnitudes, such as wage rates or interest rates, would not function as price signals, so that "real wages" and "real interest" rates could not come back into balance. With the price levels relatively rigid, nominal magnitudes have a full effect on real quantities. Keynes was seeking to recast economics—away from the quantity theory of money, to an emphasis on income and levels of employment as the determinants of equilibrium, and (the theme is so largely neglected in the popular image of Keynes) on the centrality of investment as the fulcrum of economic policy.

The technical demonstration of Keynes' argument was worked out by Sir John Hicks—the "IS" and "LM" curves (i.e., investment-savings and demand for money) which now appear in all the textbooks, and which show the various equilibria at which different rates of interest, and different demand schedules for money, intersect to achieve different levels of investment.

---

[6] Yet Samuelson, the ironist, concludes: "When finally mastered, its analysis is found to be obvious and at the same time new. In short, it is a work of genius."

[7] They had been prescriptions proposed by Keynes in a paper with Hubert Henderson in 1929. But in and of themselves, they were not new: A. C. Pigou, Keynes' predecessor at Cambridge, had put forth a rationale for public works in 1912.

In neoclassical theory, the rate of interest was a real, not a monetary phenomenon, determined by the demand for capital (at its marginal productivity) and the degree of savings in the community. But for Keynes, the two decisions are independent: The volume of savings is a function of the levels of income, and the degree of investment a function of the rate of interest. In a severe depression, monetary policy is ineffective because of the "liquidity trap" whereby lenders prefer to "hoard" their cash, and, unless the government becomes the leading lender, easy money in and of itself provides little inducement for investment.

The third element in this tripod is wage rates. Keynes assumed that wages are sticky because workers are mesmerized by a "money illusion." They bargain for and react to changes in money wages, because they see only their immediate wage packet and have no means of knowing whether "real wages" (which would have to result from a fall in product prices) would keep pace with the fall in money wages. Thus, the labor supply responds to nominal wages and becomes inelastic. Since wages have become sticky, when business is bad employers lay off workers rather than cut their wages, and aggregate demand falls.

What follows? In the United States, the quick championing of Keynes by Alvin Hansen led to an emphasis on "compensatory finance" in which government intervention, through tax policy or government spending to raise aggregate demand, became the key policy prescription. In England, the expository essay by J. R. Hicks (in 1937) stressed that the unemployment equilibrium was due largely to the disjunctions in the capital markets and in the money markets: The liquidity-preference schedule was seen as too interest-elastic, and the investment schedule was believed to be too interest-*in*elastic, for the interest rate to function effectively to generate investment.

The paradox is that in the Hansen version, Keynes was regarded as a radical, the champion of the necessary role of government as a permanent arbiter of the economy. In the Hicks version, the Keynesian and neoclassical views of aggregate economic behavior were assimilated into a unified economic model which re-established the idea of equilibria as the fulcrum of economic theory.[8]

[8] It is this "Americanization" (one can call it even vulgarization) of Keynes that had led to the persistent misconception that Keynes was a theorist only of demand, not of investment. Thus, in a recent issue of *Business Week* on "The Reindustrialization of America," the editors begin, in the section on erosion of savings: "Ever since World War II, policymakers under the influence of John Maynard Keynes have focused on demand management. The idea was

A concentration on the technical elements of Keynes' theories necessarily slights the larger, historical revolution which Keynes introduced. As against the Marshallian tradition, Keynes made macroeconomic analysis the center of economic theory. As against the conventional concentration on individual decisions of firms and households, Keynes placed in the center of analysis the interrelation of aggregates such as investment and wages. And from the quantity theory emphasis on the money and price level, he shifted the focus to output, income, and employment, as these are coordinated in the markets for commodities, capital, and labor, as the fulcrum of concern.

What remains problematic—and it is the crux of the issue—is the question of equilibrium. Keynes was clear that no automatic adjustment of "real" economic forces toward the full utilization of productive resources was a realistic possibility in a modern differentiated society. But was *disequilibria,* and with it a long-run tendency to secular stagnation, an endemic problem?

When Hicks wrote his reconciliation of Keynes with neoclassical theory—still the *fons et origo* of the standard interpretation, as Mark Blaug put it—Keynes wrote on his personal copy of that essay that he had "next to nothing to say by way of criticism." Yet a year after the publication of the *General Theory,* Keynes wrote an article in the *Quarterly Journal of Economics,* a reply to four critiques by Taussig, Leontief, Robertson, and Viner in which he attributed the chronic cause for the underemployment of resources, and the inherent disequilibria in the economic system, to the inherent uncertainty of knowledge, the inability to know the consequences of our actions, the impossibility of making forecasts, or knowing, therefore, what capital returns or discount rates of capital might be. "About these matters," Keynes wrote, "there is no scientific basis on which to form any calculable probability whatever. We simply do not know."

Marshall had assumed that through rational action and the law of large numbers, wherein individual variations are cancelled out, prediction was the great achievement of economic science. Yet if, as Keynes believed, economic behavior is ruled by uncertainty and indeterminacy, we are all adrift in the open sea.

4) *The Phillips curve.* It may seem strange to group the Phillips

---

to spur consumer spending at the expense of saving to create the huge markets that in turn would generate investment."

But this is to distort Keynes—and his economic prescriptions—since the crucial argument of Keynes was that investment was the key to the reinvigoration of the economy, since its multiplier effects would expand demand.

curve—which began its life as a prosaic statistical relation between wage rates and employment in the United Kingdom from 1862 to 1957, first noted by a New Zealand economist, A. W. Phillips, at the London School of Economics—with such grand concepts as the quantity theory of money, or monopolistic competition, or the Keynesian Revolution, as one of the bridges from the rarefied purlieus of abstract theory to the messy marketplace of haggling and higgling. But the Phillips curve did seem to show a way of threading a course between the maze of persisting (and even rising) rates of unemployment and a rising price level, a situation that to all economists, neoclassical monetarists and neoclassical Keynesians alike, was a logical paradox in theory and a disturbing actuality in the real world. And it did so by positing the validity of nominal magnitudes, a concept dear to the heart of Keynesians. It is little wonder that Paul Samuelson (at a symposium of the American Enterprise Institute in 1967) declared that the Phillips curve is "one of the most important concepts of our times."

Keynes and his immediate successors were not primarily concerned with the theory of inflation. They thought that with unemployment and underutilized capacity, as in a depression, price levels were sticky so that nominal magnitudes then had substantial effects on real quantities. But once full employment and full capacity were reached, the relations between nominal magnitudes and real quantities would diverge, and a rise in nominal expenditures (wage rates or prices) would produce demand-pull inflation, a task for the monetary authorities to control by compressing the nominal levels back to the "real" price levels.

The "missing equation" in this picture was the famous Phillips curve which, as Robert Solow has wryly observed, provided after the publication of the article in 1958 more employment (in this case, for economists) than any public-works enterprise since the construction of the Erie Canal. As Solow has described its import:

> Notice that [Phillips] was comparing the rate of changes of wages, a nominal quantity, with the percentage of the labor force out of work, a real quantity. If there were no long-run connection between real events and nominal events there ought to be no relation between those two time series. If the crude dichotomy in the Keynesian picture were a good description of the world, then the rate of wage inflation ought to be near zero for anything but full employment. And in times of full employment, if there were any to be observed, there ought to be substantial inflation.
>
> What Phillips found was really pretty astonishing. The simple bivariate relation, relating only one real and one nominal variable, held

up very well over a very long time during which the nature of British industry and labor changed drastically. Here was evidence for a strong, and apparently reliable, relation between the nominal world and the real world. It did not appear to be a short-run transient affair, as the mainstream macroeconomics of the 19th and early 20th centuries would have suggested. It seemed not to be a simple dichotomy between less-than-full employment and full employment, as the casual picture of the early 1950's might have suggested. It seemed to say quite clearly that the rate of wage inflation—and probably, therefore, the rate of price inflation—was a smooth function of the tightness of the aggregate economy.

Phillips' study had been a "straight" empirical one. But the theoretical implications for public policy and Keynesian economics were worked out in 1960 by Paul Samuelson and Robert M. Solow.[9] The two M.I.T. economists assembled an analogous time series for the United States, and from it they posited a hypothetical relation between the rate of inflation and the unemployment rate. "This shows the menu of choice between different levels of unemployment and price stability as roughly estimated from the last twenty-five years of American data," they wrote.

The relation known as the Phillips curve, and its generalization by Richard Lipsey, won immediate and widespread acceptance in American economic thinking. It served, as Franco Modigliani of M.I.T. has put it, "to dispose of the rather sterile 'cost-push/demand-pull' controversy. It also managed to reinforce the idea that one could now 'manage' the economy even more decisively because of the 'menu of choice.'" On the theoretical level, it could even be squared with aspects of monetary theory. As Modigliani put it in his 1976 presidential address to the American Economics Association:

> Acceptance of Phillips curve relation implied some significant changes in the Keynesian framework which partly escaped notice until the subsequent monetarists' attacks. Since the rate of change of wages decreased smoothly with the rate of unemployment, there was no longer a unique Full Employment but rather a whole family of possible equilibrium rates, each associated with a different rate of inflation (and requiring, presumably, a different long-run growth of money). It also impaired the notion of a stable underemployment equilibrium. A fall in demand could still cause an initial rise in unemployment but this rise, by reducing the growth of wages, would

[9] As Solow recalls the discovery: "I remember that Paul Samuelson asked me when we were looking at the diagrams for the first time, 'Does that look like a reversible relation to you?' What he meant was, 'Do you really think the economy can move back and forth along a curve like that?' And I answered, 'Yeah, I'm inclined to believe it,' and Paul said, 'Me too.'"

eventually raise the real money supply, tending to return unemployment to the equilibrium rate consistent with the given long-run growth of money.

But at the practical level it did not lessen the case for counteracting lasting demand disturbances through stabilization policies rather than by relying on the slow processes of wage adjustment to do the job, at the cost of protracted unemployment and instability of prices. *Indeed the realm of stabilization policies appeared to expand in the sense that the stabilization authority had the power of choosing the unemployment rate around which employment was to be stabilized, though it then had to accept the associated inflation.*

Most of the discussions of the Phillips curve, however, have obscured two very different kinds of issues. One is a movement *along* the Phillips curve, which posits a "trade-off" between a specific percentage increase in the rate of inflation in exchange for a specific percentage decrease in unemployment (and vice versa). The other is *a shift in the slope of the curve itself,* in which the relation is more nearly "vertical," so that one could have a rise in employment without inflation, or a drop in inflation without cutting jobs.

The experiences of the late 1960's and early 1970's (one can take President Johnson's Committee on Price Stability in 1967 for illustration) showed that macroeconomic policies could move us *along* the curve, but it could not *shift* the curve.[10] The one feeble effort to shift the curve lay in the adoption of wage and price "guidelines" in order to mitigate the price movements. And, to the increasing dismay of economists, in the last few years, the Phillips curves seemed to have gone flat, so that even the menu of choices, the trade-offs up and down *along* the curve, seems to be vanishing.

Again, as Solow reported:

> We know that in the inflation of the 1970's each of the Phillips curves in the family is relatively flat; you have to accept a lot of unemployment to push the economy down any one of those curves.
>
> Most of the serious estimates suggest that an extra 1 percent of unemployment maintained for one year would reduce the rate of inflation by something between 0.16 and 0.5 percent. That trade-off is not very favorable. We also know that the inflationary process involves a great deal of inertia; that is, it takes a long time for the economy to pass from one member of Phillips curves to a lower one,

[10] The explanation given is the old sticking point of wage rigidities. Samuelson still believes that individuals are ruled by a "money illusion," so that market responses are made to the fluctuations in the money (i.e., nominal) values of income and prices, rather than real values.

at least under normal circumstances. For instance, an extra 1 percent of unemployment maintained for three years would reduce the inflation rate by something between 0.5 and 1.75 percent. (An extra point of unemployment for three years costs the economy about $180 billion of production, which makes this a very expensive way to reduce the inflation rate.)

We know those two things, albeit in a tentative and gingerly way. What we don't know . . . is why the inertia is so great, why those Phillips curves are so flat. That is, we do not know what bits of our social and economic structure would have to be changed in order to change those relationships.

IV
Impasse

The "golden age" of economics, from 1947 to 1973, arose from the confluence of empiricism and theory. On the one hand was the towering work of Simon Kuznets who constructed the macroeconomic identities of national income and national output, and the aggregation of their magnitudes, into a system of national accounts. On the other was the synthesis of Keynesian and neoclassical economics into a formal mathematical model and a set of policy tools to manage the economy. The combination of the two produced a new growth industry of econometrics, and a spate of forecasting models to chart the movement of economic activities and predict the direction and magnitude of their interactions.[11]

But there are two fundamental problems—one might even say fallacies—in the utilization of economic models to understand the ups-and-downs of economic activities. One is that economic theory, *pace* Marshall, is not a generalization about human behavior but, following Pareto, derives from an "ideal type" of one kind of action, so-called "logical actions." And these may well be a minority of economically significant actions.

The other is that an economic *system* is not an economy; it is an analytical abstraction, an ideal, closed world where resources flow freely in response to price, where comparative advantage dictates a shift of resource utilization, where labor is not people but units of skill (or lacks thereof), where there are no political

[11] The Brookings model of 1965 had 18 major components, such as labor force, consumer demand, residential construction, etc., in 36 producing sectors and made its forecasts through the use of 300 equations. Project Link, which Lawrence Klein, one of the founders of the Brookings models, has constructed to forecast the world economy, has 1,178 simultaneous non-linear equations in the set of 12 national models, plus several hundred equations to cover trading relationships in the rest of the world.

boundaries, and where machinery, capital, and commodities distribute themselves to the maximum benefit of "mankind." It is a utopia, a utopia imagined by John Locke and Adam Smith, and even by the Manchester liberals such as Richard Cobden and John Bright who thought that the rational advantages of productivity and free trade would make war and exploitation—indeed, even political boundaries—only a memory of the dark past of mankind.[12]

In short, economic theory is a convenient fiction, an "as if," against which to measure the habitual, irrational, logical, egoistic, self-interested, bigoted, altruistic actions of individuals, firms, or governments—but it is not a model of reality. But even as a fictional ideal, it is inherently problematical.

Modern economic theory is based upon two specific assumptions about human behavior and its social setting. One is the idea of "utility maximization" as the motivational foundation for action, the other is a theory of markets as the structural location where transactions take place. The assumptions converge in the thesis that individuals and firms seek to maximize their utilities (preferences, wants) in different markets, at the best price, and that this is the engine that drives all behavior and exchange. It is the foundation for the idea of the comprehensive equilibrium. The "reform" of neoclassical theory has to begin with these two postulates of utility and markets.

The maximization of utility

Paul Samuelson has noted that many economists would "separate economics from sociology on the basis of rational or irrational behavior, where these terms are defined in the penumbra of utility theory." Utility is identified as egoism, or self-interest, and rationality is defined as consistency—that is, that preferences are transitive (if x is preferred to y and y to z, then we would have to assume, in predicting behavior, that x would be preferred to z).

Yet the crucial question is whether the obverse of the rational is the irrational rather than the *non*-rational, and whether or not non-rational motivations can provide a valid assumption for an

[12] In a very real sense, this utopia of John Locke and Adam Smith is a rival to the utopia of Marx, and Marx understood this quite well, especially in those pages of *The Poverty of Philosophy* where he defined the classical economists as the "theoreticians" of the bourgeoisie, just as the "intellectuals" were to be the theoreticians of socialism. The one was a utopia of individualism, the other of collectivism.

understanding of *economic* behavior—i.e., the behavior which seeks to enhance the wealth and welfare of mankind. As Amartya Sen, who has raised the question in an acute form, has written:

> The primary concern . . . is not with the relation of postulated models to the real economic world, but with the accuracy of answers to well-defined questions posed with pre-selected assumptions which severely constrain the nature of the models that can be admitted into the analysis.

As against egoism, for example, Sen proposes the idea of "commitment," which would require the reformation of welfare economics models, particularly in the areas of "public goods." On the basis of "egoism theory" people are expected to try to avoid their share of costs on the expectation that if it is a public benefit, it would in any case be extended to all. Such a theory proceeds from a theorem of Bentham that the "community is a fiction," and that, in effect, there is no such thing as a "social" point of view apart from one's own self-interest. Yet the radical individualism that underlies this assumption, and that has shaped the models of economic behavior, flies in the face of the large variety of traditional and ideological attachments which often do shape an individual's action into collective form.[13]

It is also assumed that not only individuals but firms are "utility maximizers." In fact, it was often assumed that, while individuals, responding to habit, custom, or to impulse, may be "irrational," the firm, subject to the discipline of the "bottom line," acts

[13] Perhaps the most radical effort to recast all the theories of behavior into utility theory has been made by Gary Becker in his book, *The Economic Approach to Human Behavior*. Becker argues that human behavior is not compartmentalized into economic and non-economic behavior, but that individuals do act to maximize their advantages. Thus, Becker has taken microeconomic theory and extended it to marriage, crime, and what would usually be thought of as "non-economic" areas. In an essay, "A Theory of Marriage," he treats marriage as a two-person firm with one or the other of the partners as the entrepreneur, "hiring" the other at a salary, and seeking to increase the "firm's" profits by the investments and expenditures made. Becker's students have applied utility theory to crime by seeing such actions as risk-taking activities which are maximized when the penalties are low. And another student of Becker, George L. Priest, has argued about law, "With respect to the probability of litigation, a legal rule is like any commodity. A change in relative prices (here as between efficient and inefficient rules) will change the distribution of consumption choices toward relatively cheaper and away from more expensive commodities."

The crux of the argument is that where there is the pain of choice forced upon us by scarce resources, we will take the most "pleasurable" route. But this hedonic calculus is itself the most narrowly culturally-bound interpretation of human behavior, ignoring the large areas of traditionalism on the one hand and moral reflection on the other.

in pure "rational" ways, and so becomes the primary agent in "clearing all markets." In recent years, an entire literature has arisen which disputes that simple-minded idea. In this issue, Harvey Leibenstein expounds his theory of X-efficiency, which undercuts some of the traditional assumptions of microeconomics. And Herbert Simon has won the Nobel Prize in economics, in part, for his theory that firms operate not as "profit-maximizing" but as "satisficing" institutions.

Can utility theory explain "wage stickiness"? Is it only a "money illusion" as Keynes thought? In a recent, illuminating discussion, *The Crisis in Keynesian Economics,* Sir John Hicks suggests a very different answer from the Keynesian one. Reviewing the history of British wages for the past 70 or so years, Sir John suggests that (except for a few rather abrupt periods of rapid slide) wages and employment tended to be sticky because neither employers nor unions wanted to disrupt traditional relationships. "The 'stickiness' is not a matter of 'money illusion'; it is a matter of continuity." In looking at the more recent history, Sir John points out that the major factor in the movement of wages is a combination of "expectations" and a sense of "fairness." It is the "social pressure," he writes, that has become dominant, and the sense of comparative fairness which prompts the competitive pressure. "Wages rise, whether or not there is labour scarcity; so they rise in slumps as much, or nearly as much as in booms. Everyone, on some comparison or other, feels left behind. . . ."

So, in this crucial area of utility theory it is sociology ("irrational actions"?) that seems often to provide more adequate basis for explanation than standard economic theory.

And to the degree that government enters the picture, conventional utility theory is at a loss as to how to deal with it. Individuals and households presumably are utility maximizers, firms, partnerships, and corporations are profit maximizers. But what do governments maximize? The older German school of public finance, with typical Teutonic thoroughness, states that governments maximize utility for something called the State. Anglo-American economic theory, since its premises are individualistic, ignores the problem completely. Between the gap of these two views one can drive most of the GNP of the country.

Clearly, the question is the most central one of our time, since governments, even in "market societies," account for between 20 percent and 60 percent of all economic transactions. What does the government maximize?

Much of the discussion in contemporary economic theory of government expenditure, priced in market terms, centers on the question of "public goods." The question was re-opened in 1954 in an essay by Samuelson on "The Pure Theory of Public Expenditure." But the problem is couched in the terms of individualistic economics. It assumes that, where there will be public goods (i.e., goods which are not divisible and would be provided to all), consumers will hide their "preference functions"—i.e., how much they would be willing to pay for it—since they know that it will be available to all. The question of an optimal price, or tax, thus is difficult to answer. Samuelson, with his customary brilliance, constructed a "pseudo-market equilibrium," using an abstract mathematical model—its only difficulty being that it has little relevance to actual behavior.

But none of this provides any insight into the question of how these collective decisions are made or should be made. An economist might reply that this is a matter for political theory, not economics, but when government is so massively involved in the economy, such an answer is surely unsatisfactory.

One has to return to the historical point I made at the beginning of this essay. Modern economic theory derived from classical liberalism. But that liberalism was anti-political; that is the meaning of *laissez-faire.* Adam Smith did not look to government to set the boundaries of individual actions, he looked to civil society, that network of social ties of family, clan and neighborhood, parish and church, to set the general standards of moral conduct. Liberalism sought for the autonomy of realms: not only the distinction between Church and State as temporal powers, but the division between economics and politics as autonomous activities of individuals. The crucial point, as made so brilliantly by Carl Schmitt in *The Concept of the Political,* is that economics treats individuals as *competitors,* while politics divides individuals into *friends and enemies.* One need not accept this extreme formulation of the character of politics, but a qualitative difference in the way individuals behave in these two realms does exist. But the corollary of Schmitt's argument has greater empirical force: Once an economic action becomes political, it becomes inextricably bound with the State and implicitly accepts the power of the State to adjudge the validity of these actions.

But what is the State? Is it an agency, in contemporary Western society, to shore up capitalism, even over and above the interests of individual capitalist firms? Is it a Leviathan, seeking to engorge itself on the economic body of the country for the benefit of the bureaucracy—or the "new class"—that fosters it? Is it an "*ad hoc*" instrument evolved out of the "functional necessity" that some central body manage the interdependence and complexity generated by the new scales of the communications and technological revolutions of modern society? And since it is a political body, having to manage economic institutions, who is it intended to serve? Economic theory, even as a technical instrument to analyze the consequences of such decisions, is highly limited unless it attempts some answers to these questions.[14]

Markets, free and otherwise

The question of markets is one that has threaded economic discussion since the time Adam Smith first observed that merchants habitually came together over a pint of bitters, among other things, to fix the price of the product they were selling. Shop talk is price talk. References to market imperfections or market failures are as frequent in economic literature as the obeisance to the other obligatory caution of *ceteris paribus*. And the sticking point in any empirical theory of equilibrium is why there are persistent disequilibria in certain markets—as in labor markets.

Until recently—and except for Chamberlin's theory of distinct product markets, rather than homogeneous price markets in an industry—there has been a lack of comprehensive theory as to the character of actual market structures in the contemporary economy. Within the last decade, a rough consensus has emerged—though the terms vary. This is what Sir John Hicks has called "fixprice" and "flexprice" markets, or what William Nordhaus of Yale (and the late Arthur Okun) have called "auction" and "administered or customer" markets. As Sir John Hicks put it in his 1973 lectures:

[14] The one economist who did begin some answers was Joseph Schumpeter in a 1918 essay, long neglected until now, entitled "The Crisis of the Tax State." Rejecting the traditional approach of public finance, which sought to measure the incidence of different kinds of taxes, Schumpeter wrote: "Once the state exists as a reality and as a social institution, once it has become the center of the persons who man the governmental machine [its nature] can no longer be understood merely from the fiscal standpoint, and for which finances now become a serving tool. . . . The kind and level of taxes are determined by the social structure, but once taxes exist they become a handle, as it were, which social powers can grip in order to change the structure."

To understand this new phenomena, Schumpeter called for the development of a new field which he called, ironically, "fiscal sociology." For a discussion of these points, see my *Cultural Contradictions of Capitalism*, pp. 227–232.

> The fact surely is that in modern (capitalist) economies there are, at least, two sorts of markets. There are markets where prices are set by producers; and for those markets, which include a large part of the markets for industrial products, the 'fixprice' assumption makes good sense. But there are other markets, 'flexprice' or speculative markets, at which prices are still determined by supply and demand. . . .
>
> A pure flexprice theory . . . is not realistic, though it may be instructive. It is doubtless less realistic than a pure fixprice theory. But a pure fixprice theory is itself not wholly realistic. For speculative markets (such as markets for staple commodities, not to speak of financial markets) do exist.
>
> What we need is a theory which will take into account both sorts of markets, a theory in which both fixprice and flexprice have a place. Why some sorts of commodities should be traded on one sort of market and some on the other is an interesting question. . . .

Why these different kinds of markets have developed, we can leave to the sociological economist. But the evident fact of their existence calls into question the idea of facilitative resource adjustments through market prices—an idea which still underlies all the models of economic behavior.

The consequence of "fixprice" markets is price rigidities, which sometimes may be beneficial, sometimes not. Market power may inhibit flexibility, but it also introduces stability. In periods of shortages (where black markets often develop) it is more often the large corporation that will eschew large price increases for established customers in order to maintain long-term relations. (It is what Max Weber meant by rational capitalism rather than "Levantine" trading.) In periods of unemployment, it is the basis of the "implicit contract" (or what Arthur Okun has called the "invisible handshake") when employers, bound by traditional relationships, or even some residual obligation, hold on to a labor force as long as they can, and thereby induce stickiness into the labor markets.

How far all this traditionalism, these rigidities, these fixprice markets, extend we do not know. But it is clear that price signals are not the switching or shunting mechanisms of standard economic theory which create equilibria, or "optimal" distribution of resources, in the society. And if institutional and political factors may become more important than market determinants, all these raise crucial questions for public policy. One can demand, as old-fashioned populists and new-fangled monetarists do, radical policies (e.g., a more vigorous application of anti-trust law) to bring in more competition and price flexibility in the economy. Or one can ask for more government intervention to shift resources, such as the proposals to help "sunrise" industries (i.e., new technological firms) and kill off "sunset" industries (such as some of the large auto and steel companies). Or we might have tax incentive policies (T.I.P.) as proposed by Henry Wallich, Arthur Okun, and others, to moderate price and wage increases that go beyond official guideline levels. All these are crucial questions of political economy, and the standard models of economic theory give us little help in answering them.

V
Rationality or time?

There is little question that most economies are in trouble. But it is misleading to think that these perplexities are peculiar to capitalist or to market economics. Poland faces problems of capital accumulation, sector imbalances, and price distortions which seem little different from those of many Western economies. The Soviet Union finds its growth rate falling because of planning inflexibilities and low productivity. On the other hand, Japan, Singapore, and Taiwan seem to be doing very well. Perhaps the answers lie in culture and national character, or the historical release of what Keynes called the "animal spirits" that seem to animate some societies at specific times and then exhaust themselves.

It is quixotic to note that at the beginning of the 20th century the central question that concerned sociology, as posed by Max Weber, was: Why did rational capitalism develop in the West, rather than in China or other parts of the non-Western world? And his answer was that capitalism had been abetted by a new set of legitimations (principally religious in orientation) that tore down *traditional* relationships (guilds, parishes, clans), fostered *individualism*, and made all resources (such as land and labor) completely mobile, subject to the market. Yet at the close of the 20th century, the emerging sociological question seems to be why capitalism has been so successful in a Japan which has *maintained* traditional relationships (and even converted the traditional village structures into the factory structures), emphasized communalism and consensus, and provided long-term if not life-time employment for its workers.

The economic theory that developed in the West in the last 200 years is impotent before such questions. It has been ahistorical and abstractly analytical. But that is precisely the rub. Economic theory, by and large, is based on the model of classical mechanics and operates in the image of the natural sciences. The model leads to the idea of an "equilibrium" in which the "natural" forces seek to reassert themselves and restore economic relations to a balance, the fulcrum of which is "perfect competition." The result is a basically mechanistic view of human behavior, and when discordances occur, there ensues a series of desperate and twisted efforts to square the "nominal magnitudes" (i.e., the irrational) with the "real magnitudes" (the rational) that underlie the system. How Hegelian!

But this enterprise ignores a crucial distinction. Classical mechanics is *constitutive* of nature; it seeks to discern the intrinsic order which is hidden in the properties of the system. Economics is *not* constitutive. It is a *constructed* logic, at best an "as if" model of how some resource distributions would be made if individuals acted in a specified "logical" way. But there is no single "underlying structure" to a society. Since men act variously by habit and custom, irrationally or zealously, by conscious design to change institutions or redesign social arrangements, there is no intrinsic order, there are no "economic Laws" constituting the "structure" of *the* economy; there are only different patterns of historical behavior. Thus, economics, and economic theory, cannot be a "closed system." The social sciences necessarily are partial "prisms," selecting out different facets of behavior in order to understand the causes of change and their meanings. And what sets their boundaries is not the "essential" properties of a subject matter, but the different questions they ask, which is why they are so permeable.[15]

Keynes himself, it may be recalled, had raised doubts about the possibility of predicting human behavior, especially when such

[15] The strength of contemporary economic theory, it should be pointed out, derives from the narrowing of the questions and the powerful technical apparatus of mathematical reasoning. In becoming an "analytical science" rather than a descriptive inquiry, the simplifying assumption was that it would treat "capital" and "labor" as homogeneous entities and see all exchanges in relation to price. But all this itself entailed a large cost. The first was to ignore technical advance and even when, in a brilliant article in 1957, Robert Solow sought to estimate the contribution of technology to economic growth, he had to treat it as a "residual," a left-over after other inputs were accounted for—a finding later disputed by Jorgenson and Griliches, who argued that capital inputs alone could explain such advances.

Contemporary economic theory lacks a scheme to account for technology, innovation, demographic factors, or entrepreneurship. All of these are merely "sociological."

behavior is based on variable expectations. To put that issue more formally, as G. L. S. Shackle does in his book, *Epistemics & Economics,* the economic theorist can choose either "rationality" or "time." The theory which rejects time can set forth propositions such as subjective marginalism, partial or general equilibrium. But the introduction of time not only produces uncertainty; it also necessitates understanding the "non-rational" behavior if it is to deal with the choices that human beings make.[16]

An "interpretative" economic theory

What are the roads to reconstruction? What ultimately provides direction for the economy, as Veblen pointed out long ago, is not the price system but the value system of the culture in which the economy is embedded. The price system is a mechanism for the relative allocation of goods and services, not in accordance with human nature (or utility maximization), but within the framework of the existing distribution of income and the cultural patterns of social wants. Accordingly, economic guidance can only be distributive as equitably as the cultural value system which shapes it.

An "interpretative" economic theory[17] might have to consider that its own analysis only makes economic sense when joined to sociology. For the hard-nosed economist, this is a fate feared worse than the pox, yet one finds, pleasantly, that even so rigorous a theorist as Robert M. Solow, in his presidential address to the American Economic Association (December 1979), seeking to formulate a theory of wage stickiness to fill in the chinks in Keynesian theory, resorts to explanations such as "social conventions" and "codes of good behavior enforced by social pressure" to explain the "persistence of disequilibrium in the labor market." And he concludes, "Economic man is a social . . . category." That, too, is a modest start toward the reconstruction of economic theory.

An economic theory has to understand its underpinnings not only in relations to politics, but to political theory. The great paradox of

[16] To recall an earlier point about Say's Law and Keynes: As a "static" feature, a full-employment equilibrium is theoretically possible within a closed and timeless system, but the process of moving toward an equilibrium *through time* displaces the equilibrium point itself, so that one may simply be chasing a will of the wisp.

[17] I use the term "interpretative" in accordance with a growing usage in the social sciences to define a mode of inquiry which is not positivist but defines inquiry in relation to the *meanings* of actions of individuals, rather than just the "observable behavior" itself.

all modern social theory is that political philosophy, going back to Machiavelli, Hobbes, and Rousseau, saw men as being ruled by appetite, passions, or will, while economic theory has defined human actions as rational behavior—albeit such rationality is defined in purely instrumental and functional terms.[18] Only Max Weber, among modern theorists, has sought to sketch a theory of social action that takes into account the rational and the non-rational, and to look at economics and administration, politics and religion, in terms of the two modes.

Within that context, economic theory has to integrate political practice within its body of understandings. Price theory is *distributive*. Resources flow to the most profitable (or least costly) places. Necessarily, some persons lose; what Schumpeter has called "creative destruction," or, more recently, Lester Thurow has called the zero-sum game. But political practice is *redistributive*, responding to the weights (votes, money, power) of the different interest, functional, ethnic, advantaged and disadvantaged groups in the society.

And, finally, economic theory has to return to time (in the logical sense) and to history (in the empirical fact)[19] in order to be responsive to the complex new social arrangements that derive from the widening of scales and new arenas of economic and social actions. The world of Adam Smith was one of thousands of small family firms, of visible merchants and customers, so that Smith could look to civil society, not government, as the arena in which competition would be regulated by custom and ethics, rather than by contract and law. A post-industrial order is one in which eco-

[18] Since economic theory, from the start, has eschewed moral norms, the "ends" of human actions were taken as diverse, or as given, and economics concentrated on efficacious means.

[19] Mancur Olson cites evidence (from the findings of the monetarist Philip Cagan) that the tendency for prices to fall during recessions has diminished steadily over time. And, as he writes, in an unpublished essay, "An Evolutionary Approach to Macroeconomics":

> Obviously something is accumulating or progressing over time such as changing policies, structures or institutions, which is changing the character of the macroeconomic problem. We know, both from the tendency for real output to vary more with changes in aggregate demand and from direct observation of the prices themselves, that stickier prices and wages are crucial to the change that is taking place. But we do not *explain* the change by referring to sticky prices, any more than we explain anything by referring to *ad hoc* assumptions like 'rigid wages' or merely descriptive concepts like Phillips curves. The *cause* of the fact that most wages and prices were less flexible in the interwar years than in the nineteenth century, and still less flexible in these stagflationary times, must be found. That cause, in turn, must play a leading role in our macroeconomic theory.

nomic innovation is ruled by the codification of theoretical knowledge, yet contemporary economic theory, rooted in a world of agriculture and industry, has no means of measuring the "output" of science, or little, even, of technological change.[20] Yet without such understandings, how effective can economic theory be as guidance, let alone as a "model" of the economic reality?

The crux of my argument is an epistemological one. Economic theory, unlike physics, is not constitutive of a single underlying reality. Nor can it be, *pace* Alfred Marshall (and Gary Becker), timeless generalizations about human behavior. In consequence, economics cannot be, as its model in classical mechanics, a "closed system" which ignores change or the effort to discern specific patterns of change.

Does this mean the abandonment of the powerful logical engine of rationality and equilibria, of maximization and markets, to the vagaries of sociology and the unrestrained wiles of politics? Not at all. "At least from the time of the physiocrats and Adam Smith," Paul Samuelson has observed, "there has never been absent from the main body of economic literature the feeling that in some sense perfect competition represented an optimal situation." We have also seen, in recent years, the growth of a large body of literature in welfare economics which, deriving from Pareto-optimality, defines a set of optimal outcomes for allocations of resources and distributions of incomes. But this is a divergence, and a necessary one, from the positivist tradition which has ruled economic theory. The corollary of all this is that economic theory should not be taken as a "model" (or template) of how human beings behave, for these will always be inadequate, but as a "Utopia," a set of ideal standards against which one can debate and judge different policy actions and their consequences. That, it seems to me, is the meaningful role of any social "science" in theorizing about human affairs.

---

[20] The one economist, again, who wrestled with these questions, was Schumpeter. He developed a theory of innovation, although this theory was never integrated into neoclassical analysis.

5

"Rational Expectations" as a counterrevolution

MARK H. WILLES

If there is a crisis in economic theory, it is a crisis in Keynesian economic theory. Most economists, even the Keynesians, seem to agree that there are at least some defects in this theory, although they may disagree passionately about what those defects are and how they should be remedied. Until the early 1970's, the economists who opposed the Keynesians had to be content with pulling a few fish off of their opponents' hooks. But when what has become known as the theory of "rational expectations" began to be developed, these economists found that they could simply dynamite all the fish in the lake. While this may be unsportsmanlike, it does demonstrate an admirable grasp of fundamentals. Today, to continue the metaphor, a fleet of stunned Keynesians is quibbling about which of their few remaining fish are still flopping.

I know how they feel, for I once believed in conventional, Keynesian theory and the economic models based on it. Now, however, I am persuaded that this theory is fundamentally wrong, so wrong that it can never yield adequate models for evaluating policy. Although rational expectations theory is still in its infancy, it has already devastated conventional theory and appears to offer a promising alternative to it.

Rational expectations can be understood as an attempt to apply the principles of classical economics to all economic problems and specifically to macroeconomic policy. These principles have never before been seriously applied to macroeconomic policy making. Rational expectations, then, is a new classical economics.

Classical economics, which dominated economic method in the first part of this century, is built upon two premises. The basic one, seldom disputed, is that individuals optimize. In other words, the model's economic agents—both firms and individuals—seek maximum expected profits or maximum expected utility, within the limitations of their incomes and technologies. The second premise of classical economics, somewhat more controversial, is that markets clear. That is, in each market the amount willingly offered equals the amount willingly bought at a particular price unless legal strictures, discrepancies in information, or government policies prevent it. Equilibrium to a classical economist means that these two premises hold. Equilibrium in each product market means that, at existing prices, the quantities firms want to sell exactly match the quantities consumers want to buy. In labor markets, similarly, at existing wage rates, workers offer as many hours of labor as they want to offer, while firms receive as much labor as they want to hire. Though simple, the classical premises proved remarkably rich for building theory.

All of the early classical models, however, had an important failing. They implied that resources would always be fully employed, that there would never be shortages or unemployment. This failing became obvious during the Great Depression, when millions of people who wanted to work couldn't find jobs and the labor market apparently was not clearing. The classical models of the 1930's could give no explanation for this deep and prolonged depression. They couldn't even account for the existence of ordinary business cycles.

Today, economists have two alternative ways of dealing with this early crisis in economics—they can reject classical premises as the Keynesians have done, or they can seek more coherent and sophisticated versions of the classical premises, as the rational expectations school has done.

The Keynesian revolution

To meet the crisis in economic theory engendered by the Great Depression, John Maynard Keynes deliberately rejected the classical premises about the behavior of individuals and markets. In their place he put premises about the behavior of aggregates, such as the general price level and total unemployment. With these new premises, he was able to build a model of an economy in which involuntary unemployment appeared—an economy with a persistent disequilibrium in the labor market.

Keynes' method of aggregate-level, disequilibrium modelling is the foundation of macroeconomics, the branch of economics that has dictated economic policy since the New Deal. The classical method of individual-level, equilibrium modelling has been relegated exclusively to microeconomics, where it has had small opportunity to influence macroeconomic policy. It is odd that these two branches of economics should be based on incompatible theories and even odder that Keynesians should accept classical theories for microeconomics but not for macroeconomics, but that is the case today.

Although many outstanding economists have continued to work with the classical method, the Keynesian method has prevailed since the 1930's not only for policy making but for economic modelling. Even the monetarist school, which has perceptively criticized macroeconomic policies, uses aggregate-level premises for its models, just like the Keynesian school. Moreover, virtually all of the large-scale macroeconomic models that businesses and governments use for planning, forecasting, and decision making are, at root, Keynesian.

With the help of these models, economists once hoped to improve policy making. In the early 1960's, when rapid advances in computer technology made highly detailed models possible, many economists—I, for one—believed that the government could control business cycles by manipulating fiscal and monetary policies. We didn't question whether government could accomplish this. We only wondered how to do it most effectively. We asked, for instance, if monetary or fiscal policy produced the most economic growth; we asked how long it took for policy actions to have their effects. Despite these questions, though, we had faith that we could do almost magical things once we properly modelled the economy's major relationships.

We believed that a model could be made to simulate the results of whatever policies we were considering. In this way, we could see in advance what our policies would do to the unemployment rate, the price level, or any other variable in the model. Having a perfected model was like having a crystal ball. We could look into it to see the consequences of our policies—or so we thought.

We also believed that we could generate a mathematical rule to tell us how to change policy in response to new information. To do this, we would have to spell out precisely what we were trying to achieve with the variables in the model. We would have to decide, for example, how much more inflation we would accept in return for a bit lower unemployment. With such decisions made, though, we believed that we could turn an economic model into an effective policy maker and that many of our economic worries would then vanish like an egg in a magician's hat.

Such prospects, however naive, motivated a great deal of research to develop economic models for policy making. For example, the Federal Reserve Board of Governors during 1966 and 1967 co-sponsored the development of a large model, the FRB-MIT model, that was designed to be useful for monetary policy making. Universities and private concerns developed other large models of at least a hundred equations representing aggregate behavior for a dozen or more sectors. These models were quickly put to work making forecasts and predicting how the economy would respond to alternative policies.

The failure of the Keynesian models

These economic models flatly failed. As recently as the early 1970's, they uniformly predicted that the United States could push its unemployment rate down to 4 percent if it accepted an inflation rate of about 4 percent. If it accepted a slightly higher inflation rate, according to these models, it could reduce unemployment still further, and with a 5 or 6 percent rate of inflation, it could practically consign unemployment to the history books. Clearly, these predictions were far off the mark. Unemployment did not drop when inflation went up—unemployment went up too. For the last few years, in fact, unemployment and inflation rates have averaged close to 7 or 8 percent.

These mistaken predictions were based on the assumption that there is an exploitable trade-off between inflation and unemployment, a trade-off that is often represented graphically as the Phillips curve. An exploitable trade-off implies that unemployment can be lowered at any time simply by creating a little more inflation, and that high unemployment coinciding with high inflation is an extremely unlikely event. As the crisis in classical economic theory was that it could not explain the vast unemployment of the Depression, so the crisis in Keynesian economic theory is that it cannot explain the debilitating concurrence of high unemployment and high inflation in the 1970's. Keynesian theory by itself provides no explanation for why inflation and unemployment have been rising together.

Even before the rational expectations school developed, economists were beginning to question the foundations of the Keynesian theory, especially its presumption that there is a stable trade-off between inflation and unemployment. In a volume edited by Edmund Phelps in 1969, for example, several economists, recognizing that Keynesian method does not adequately represent individual behavior, tried to construct theories of unemployment and inflation based not on aggregate-level assumptions, but on individual-level assumptions. Again, in 1973, just as the rational expectations school was making its early breakthroughs, Sir John Hicks delivered a series of lectures on *The Crisis in Keynesian Economics* that identified many of the failings of conventional theory.

The rational expectations school, then, is not the only one to see the weaknesses in conventional Keynesian theory, but its criticism of the theory is probably the most basic. According to the rational expectations school, Keynesian method and theory are full of irreparable errors.

Error number 1: irrational expectations. The rational expectations school has demonstrated that all existing macroeconomic models are useless for policy evaluation, because the method used to construct them dooms them to produce forecasts that are incorrect when policy changes. Any macro model is essentially a group of equations that represent how some aggregate measures are related to one another. Some of these equations, in effect, specify which information agents use to make their decisions about production, employment, or consumption. In any reasonable model, the agents consider information about the future, since they presumably make some decisions based on their expectations of the future. Their expectations of future prices, interest rates, and incomes, for instance, influence their current decisions to save or consume.

Although almost everyone agrees that a model must represent expectations about the future, building a model that represents them is tough. Macro-model builders have generally given their agents "adaptive expectations." Agents who have adaptive expectations expect the future to be essentially a continuation of the past. They expect the future value of any variable in the model—prices, incomes, or anything else—to be an average of its past values and to change very slowly. The average is weighted so that the recent past is more important than the more distant past, but it is always based entirely on the past. The model consequently has no way of formulating expectations for a future that is substantially different from the past.

These kinds of expectations make sense only if relationships among the past and future values of aggregate variables are fixed. They make sense, that is, only if agents can reasonably base their expectations exclusively on historical data. But the assumption that these aggregate relationships change very little, and the related assumption that agents expect them to change very little, can produce ludicrous forecasts when policy changes. If Washington doubled the money supply, eliminated the income tax, and named the Ayatollah Khomeini to the Supreme Court, agents in the adaptive expectations scheme would expect very little change in the economy. Even if Washington changed policy in less extreme ways, such as by passing a windfall profits tax, these agents would expect much too little change in the economy. Adaptive expectations thus amount to irrational expectations.

If economic agents optimize, as most economists agree they do, they cannot be this irrational. Irrationality is unnecessarily expensive—it is more expensive than using the available information efficiently. If agents overlook a series of policies that will obviously increase the price level, they are bypassing large opportunities for economic gain. Workers who overlook such policies, for instance, are signing contracts for slowly rising wages, although foreseeable increases in the price level will quickly erode their buying power. Speculators, likewise, are failing to buy low and sell high, simply because they are ignoring pertinent and readily available information. Irrationality, in short, is not optimizing behavior.

Obviously, agents wouldn't throw their money away willingly. So the economists who defend adaptive expectations claim that agents can be tricked into making wrong decisions by a change of policy. Perhaps agents don't foresee that a policy change is coming, or perhaps they don't understand what its effects will be. It is possible that all these people could be tricked like this once or that some of them could be tricked repeatedly. But it is not very likely that everyone in the economy, on average, could be bamboozled again and again by the same old macroeconomic policies, because they would soon learn what these policies do. As Herbert Stein has said, "The lady in the box cannot be fooled by the illusionist who pretends to saw her in half." If people behave this way, they are not optimizing—not seeking the things they want. They should be studied not by economists but by psychiatrists.

The insight of *rational* expectations is that the equation that best represents agents' expectations is not something as irrational as a weighted average, but is rather the entire model. Agents, this implies, don't know exactly what a particular variable—say, the future price level—will be, but they make the best possible predictions with the information at their disposal. Although they may make mistakes, they don't throw out pertinent information.

With the rational expectations scheme replacing the adaptive expectations scheme, agents in the model take policy changes into account. If a change in policy creates opportunities to make extraordinary profits, they do not ignore them as they do under adaptive expectations. In a rational expectations model of the economy, agents change their decisions to take full advantage of whatever opportunities are produced by a new policy.

It is already possible to impose rational expectations on simple conventional macro models. Simply imposing rational expectations on these models shows how much their forecasts depend on their assumptions about expectations, although it doesn't correct all of their problems. Under the assumption of rational expectations, these models give much different predictions for the effect of a policy change. In a Keynesian model with adaptive expectations, an activist policy such as increasing the money supply generally lowers unemployment and raises output, although it also increases inflation somewhat. But in a similar model with rational expectations, activist policy has no effect on unemployment or real output. It merely boosts inflation. Similarly, in the St. Louis model, a seven-equation monetarist model, monetary expansion normally lowers the unemployment rate over several quarters with only a gradual pickup in the rate of inflation. But after rational expectations is imposed, the trade-off predicted by the model nearly vanishes. Monetary expansion now reduces the unemployment rate only slightly, but quickly pushes the inflation rate into the stratosphere.

Such demonstrations show that policy makers cannot be confident about the forecasts of conventional models unless they are confident that these models accurately portray expectations—which they don't. This may seem self-evident, but it is truly a devastating conclusion. It means that hundreds of laws and thousands of dissertations, books, and articles—including some of my own—have been pointless. It means that all the macroeconomic models that businesses and governments rely on for their economic planning are useless except in the narrowest of circumstances. And that's the *good* news for the Keynesians!

There are even deeper problems with conventional macroeconomic modelling. The Keynesian approach to macro modelling is wrong not just because it muffs expectations. It is fundamentally incapable of providing models valid for policy evaluation first, because it is inherently inconsistent and second, because it depends on arbitrary measures of policy success.

Error number 2: inconsistency. Conventional modelling is inconsistent because its premises about aggregate behavior are based on conflicting assumptions about individual behavior. In conventional models, the main equations, which represent aggregate functions like consumption and labor supply, are based only indirectly on individual behavior. For one aggregate function the models may assume that agents make their decisions based only on the current period—that they don't consider future income, future taxes, or future price increases. For another function, though, they may assume that agents plan ahead almost infinitely—that they are much more farsighted.

It is fairly obvious that conflicting assumptions like these will lead to serious inconsistencies. If agents decide how much to consume based partly on how much they work, as economists generally agree, then the consumption function cannot be separated from the labor supply function. The same personal decisions about how much to work determine both total consumption and the total supply of labor. Conventional models, however, often treat consumption and labor as unrelated variables, which implies that agents are inconsistent or even schizoid.

The more sophisticated models nod politely to this reality by using some of the same assumptions about agents for both of these functions. Unfortunately, these models have no mechanism for making sure that the individual decisions implied by changes in the labor supply are consistent with those implied by changes in consumption. In these models, policy can cause labor supply to change independent of consumption—something which does not happen in the model's original assumptions, which cannot happen in economic theory, and which does not happen in real life. Policy, likewise, can cause other aggregates to move independently, violating the model's assumptions. This guarantees that Keynesian models will be logically inconsistent.

Aggregate behavior in Keynesian models thus does not correspond with individual optimizing behavior in all conditions. It is, at best, consistent with individual behavior only under some specific conditions. Simplification is of the essence of good science, but the things Keynes has thrown away have made macro models impotent for evaluating policies.

The rational expectations school maintains that only by formulating in a coherent way the decision problem facing individuals can one begin to develop models capable of evaluating policy correctly. *Because aggregate outcomes are only a sum of individual decisions, the aggregate relationships should have no independent existence,* but they do under the Keynesian approach.

Error number 3: arbitrary measures of success. The third fundamental problem of conventional macroeconomic modelling is that it relies on arbitrary measures of policy success, such as the total unemployment rate and the rate of change in the price level. As measures of a policy's success, these indexes are at best ambiguous, and at worst, misleading.

In classical models or rational expectations models, where agents are assumed to be acting in their own best interests, the success of a policy can be adequately determined. Economists can be confident, for instance, that if they eliminate barriers to trade or decrease uncertainty, they have increased individual welfare. They can know this because all the agents make the decisions that are best for themselves, given their constraints, and because the agents now have fewer constraints. To simplify: Opportunity is almost always good in these models. Optimizing agents will take advantage of new opportunities to make themselves better off in their own terms. Providing more opportunity is a means of increasing people's well-being.

In Keynesian models, in contrast, the success of a policy cannot be clearly determined. Because these models replace individual decisions with aggregate actions, they say nothing about individual welfare. Since these models don't consider people's well-being, the economists have to make guesses about what increases it. Generally, they guess that lower unemployment and greater output increases it. People probably do want these things, but not if the costs—in terms of inflation, lost leisure, economic uncertainty, or anything else—outweigh the benefits. Studies with rational expectations models, in fact, have shown that the costs can easily exceed the benefits. Policies designed to reduce employment fluctuations, even if they succeed, can reduce people's economic welfare over the course of the business cycle.

To simplify again, growth is usually good in Keynesian models, regardless of what it does to individual welfare. Agents are permitted to make themselves better off only in the terms dictated by policy makers, not in their own terms. Economists who rely on these models, then, cannot be sure that they have increased people's well-being, even if their policies actually do what they are supposed to do.

Rational expectations: the counterrevolution

Rational expectations, in sum, avoids the errors of Keynesian economics by applying a few well-established classical principles. It corrects the Keynesian assumption of irrational expectations with the established assumption that agents optimize or, in other words, form the best expectations possible with the information available to them. It avoids Keynesian inconsistencies by building all its theoretical structures on the same foundation, on coherent assumptions about optimizing agents. Finally, it avoids arbitrary Keynesian goals that are only proxies for individual welfare, such as economic growth, by seeking to improve individual welfare in more direct ways.

Taken literally, of course, rational expectations is simply a procedure for economic modelling. On that score it's about as exciting as live bait. But its implications are pure dynamite: Almost everything we thought we knew about macroeconomic policy isn't so. The rational expectations school endorses rational expectations *per se* only as one assumption. A more complete picture is that the school builds on the foundation of classical economics, including the premises that individuals optimize and that markets clear. Using classical premises, it has constructed models that exhibit the main features of business cycles, such as the correlated swings in unemployment and inflation, which the old classical theory couldn't handle. This new classical economics has found cogent grounds for rejecting the Keynesian approach to model building, and it is working to replace it with a new and more consistent approach.

The roots of the rational expectations school were already forming in the 1960's, before the crisis in Keynesian economic theory. The literal notion of rational expectations was introduced in a landmark 1961 paper by John F. Muth, who apparently borrowed the concept from engineering literature. Muth's goal was to model expectations the same way economists model other microeconomic behavior: by assuming that agents optimize and use information efficiently when forming their expectations. He was thus able to construct a theory of expectations that was consistent with an economic theory that most economists agree on.

Muth's breakthrough, though, did not convince a significant number of economists to give up their conventional macro models. This task was not accomplished until the early 1970's, when several economists began what, in retrospect, was an all-out assault on existing macroeconomic models. The three that I am most familiar with are Robert Lucas, Thomas Sargent, and Neil Wallace. Lucas proved that a model based on classical principles could generate a correlation between inflation and employment, a correlation which previously had appeared only in conventional models. He thus showed that classical models were more broadly applicable than many economists had thought. His work stimulated Sargent and Wallace, who began to trace some of the implications of the rational expectations hypothesis. They demonstrated that existing models could not be used to evaluate or design policy.

It is no secret that reactions against the new classical economics have been strong. That's understandable, since the rational expectations school strongly attacks ideas many economists have spent their careers refining and denies the usefulness of the models promoted by well-established commercial interests. The most frequent criticism of the school is that its fundamental assumptions—in particular, rational expectations and equilibrium modelling—are unrealistic.

One version of this charge is that agents in rational expectations models are preternaturally smart. Of course, individuals don't always use available information efficiently, so the rational expectations assumption isn't completely realistic, but neither is the generally accepted assumption that individuals always optimize. The point is that theories cannot be judged by the realism of their assumptions—superficially unrealistic assumptions can produce realistic results. The assumption that agents use information efficiently is a useful simplification precisely because it gives realistic results. The assumption that agents optimize is useful for the same reason. In fact, the assumption that agents use information efficiently is, at heart, just a logical extension of the assumption that they optimize.

Charging rational expectations with being unrealistic, therefore, doesn't bolster the case for conventional models. While models with either rational expectations or adaptive expectations have unrealistic assumptions, models with adaptive expectations have unrealistic results. These models are plainly unrealistic in more important ways—ways that deprive them of any ability to evaluate policy.

Another version of the charge against the rational expectations school is that the premise that markets are continuously clearing—or are in equilibrium—is unrealistic. The alternative, of course, is that markets do not clear or are in disequilibrium. It may well be more realistic to say that some markets do not clear, but again that's not relevant. The relevant issue is what assumptions produce realistic results when used to predict the effects of policies. Existing economic models cannot be used to predict policy effects, and this is in no way changed by resorting to nonclearing markets.

The rational expectations school argues that, for evaluating policy, the economy is best represented by a model that includes continuous equilibrium. Equilibrium modelling is the best strategy available because it is consistent with a useful and fruitful body of economic knowledge. It is linked to the main body of price, value, and welfare theory and is thus able to share the highly refined theorems those fields have already developed. It appears to be able to explain unemployment and the business cycle without discarding what we know about microeconomics.

James Tobin has caricatured this desire to be consistent by commenting: "In other words, if you have lost your purse on a street at night, look for it under the lamppost." He intimates that classical theory, like a lamppost, is applicable only to one area and unable to solve our macroeconomic problems. That really underestimates the capabilities of equilibrium modelling. It is not necessary, after the new advances in classical theory, to resort to disequilibrium models in order to account for unemployment, queues, quantity rationing, or other phenomena that accompany the business cycle. There's no reason, in principle, that these phenomena can't be reproduced by equilibrium modelling—indeed, some of them already have been. Besides, disequilibrium modelling poses enormously complex problems. Efforts to solve these problems would be welcome, but the most promising strategy for devising useful models is clearly equilibrium modelling. The advice of the new classical method is that when you go out at night to look for your lost purse, go with flashlight in hand. Why grope in the dark when a light is available?

Another prominent criticism of rational expectations is that its predictions are valid only under constant policies. Only then, critics argue, could agents know the model well enough to foresee the results of policy. That's really turning things on their heads. Keynesian models, in fact, are the ones limited to constant policies because they do not recognize that people react to a new policy—that if people are faced with a new policy, their decision rules will change.

Rational expectations models may not have solved all of the problems inherent in Keynesian models, but they at least acknowledge that people can and do react to a new policy. Advocates of rational expectations concede that their models have not yet been able to capture fully what happens in the economy when policy changes. But the new method, because it is logically consistent and based firmly on accepted economic principles, has a good chance of producing models that can. The conventional method *in 40 years* has not produced one model that captures what happens when policy changes—*and it is absolutely incapable of doing so.* While Keynesian models can produce very good forecasts as long as policies do not change, they cannot describe how individual agents in the economy make related decisions in response to new policies, as they must if they hope to reproduce the effects of a policy change. An economy in motion is best modelled by having agents change their decisions when the available information changes. This is what rational expectations models try to accomplish—and what Keynesian models forget.

Another false charge is that rational expectations implies that monetary and fiscal policies don't have any real effects on overall employment or production. *Business Week*, for instance, reported: "In essence the rationalists maintain that the government is impotent in the economic sphere" (June 26, 1978). The rational expectations school makes no such claim. In fact, its proponents believe that government has a tremendous influence on economic matters—though it does not have the influence that the Keynesians claim.

A new style of policy making

The rational expectations school has shown that no one knows much about what happens to the economy when economic policy is changed. The methods of evaluating policy that we thought would work don't—and they cannot be patched up. This means that our policies must be much different than they have been in recent years. Specifically, it means that activist macroeconomic policies—those designed to stimulate economic growth by cutting taxes, increasing government spending, increasing the money supply, or increasing the federal deficit—must be curbed.

Activist policies must be curbed, first, because a growing body of evidence, both empirical and theoretical, suggests that existing models cannot succeed in offsetting the normal fluctuations in output, employment, or other aggregates. They may be able to influence economic activity in some circumstances, but they cannot tame the business cycle.

Second, activist policies must be curbed because most of their effects are uncertain. Although we know that they don't work the way they are supposed to, we don't know—even approximately—what they really do. Every economic theory wisely recommends that policy should be more cautious when its effects are less certain, for the obvious reason that a misconceived policy could make matters worse. Policy makers need to move more slowly, with smaller steps. They must not try to stimulate economic growth with such massive measures as they have been using, because no one can be sure what these measures will accomplish.

Third, activist policies must be curbed because even if we knew what their results would be, we wouldn't know whether they were desirable or not. Policy makers who rely on the Keynesian method cannot let individuals in the economy choose which results are good; they are compelled to choose for them. The result is that activist policies may well be making people generally worse off, unless their preferences exactly match those specified by the policy makers.

Some critics of the new classical economics accept, at least for purposes of argument, the premise of rational expectations in macro models, but nevertheless attempt to justify activist policies. Typically, they have modelled situations in which the government knows what is happening in the business cycle better or sooner than agents. The government then exploits this advantage to fool agents into making decisions they would not make if they knew what it knew. But merely to demonstrate the potential to exploit such information does not establish that it is desirable to do so. In particular, it does not even consider whether simply making this privileged information freely available would make agents better off than tricking them. These attempts, in short, do not result in a verdict in favor of activist policies.

Another common way to justify activist policies is to put various rigidities into a model, such as contracts that lock agents into fixed prices or wage rates over long periods regardless of policy changes or higher inflation. Under these conditions activist policy can work, but only by playing favorites. It requires that the agents with inflexible contracts lose while others win. Even if this inherent favoritism could be excused, such policy making would not be feasible for very long. Any repeated attempts to exploit these rigidities would soon become so expensive that agents, if they optimized, would begin to be wary of rigid contracts. They would find some way to avoid being harmed by these contracts when policy was changed—perhaps they would insist on shorter contracts or escalator clauses.

Instead of activist policies, we need stable policies. Which stable policies are the best is still a matter of debate, but a general approach can be surmised. The government should specify the rules for the economic game—that is, the policies and regulations—so that people know what opportunities are available and understand the probable consequences of their decisions. Tax policies, for example, should be set so that people can know if their relative taxes are going up or down from one year to the next. Spending policies should be announced well in advance and explained so that they don't trick people into making harmful decisions. Regulations on financial markets should be systematic and well announced instead of changing from month to month. Even the regulations pertaining to bankruptcy need to be more predictable, so that future Chrysler Corporations will know in advance what to expect.

For the consequences of the rules to be well understood, the rules must not change very often. The government, of course, would want to be able to change some policies, particularly those that are not succeeding, but it has a responsibility to see that people are not intentionally tricked by a new policy. At present, many of our most important economic policies come as surprises for one reason or another. No one will say what happens at a Federal Open Market Committee meeting. No one will say how much the United States spends to prop up the dollar. Congress changes tax laws so fast that labor contracts, wills, and investments often fail to do what people intend. Changes in policy must come more slowly. In the future, perhaps, when our economic knowledge is more sophisticated, we will be able to design fair and well-understood rules for changing policies, but for now we must choose policies that accommodate our ignorance.

An important principle behind this new approach to policy making is that government rules and rule changes should not be based on arbitrary indexes such as the unemployment rate. Rather, they should be based on their ability to improve the general welfare. If a policy can increase efficiency or otherwise make people better off, then use it. But if all it can do is shift some aggregate numbers that may not mean much, why bother? I suspect that this approach to policy making would lead to much less government involvement in the economy than we now have, since it is hard to demonstrate that government involvement has improved welfare. Government may still have a large role as a rule maker, but this is necessarily a passive role. The referee, after all, shouldn't intercept a pass.

Perhaps because of these tentative policy implications, the rational expectations school has sometimes been identified as a conservative branch of economics. "Conservative" is not an entirely accurate term for it, however. It does conserve some classical principles, but it isn't really striving to conserve anything out of a sense of nostalgia or duty to the past. With equal accuracy, in fact, the school might be called radical, for it is attempting to recultivate macroeconomics from the roots up. It might also be called liberal because of its emphasis on individual welfare, rights, and opportunities. Political labels, though, don't quite fit such an academic enterprise. The advocates of rational expectations are seeking a kind of truth, not an ideology. If they persevere and find it, as I believe they will, then the question will be not whether they are left or right, but how much their knowledge can benefit us.

6

Microeconomics and x-efficiency theory: If there is no crisis, there ought to be

HARVEY LEIBENSTEIN

In a recent biography Eleanor Dulles reports on her experience in a New York hairnet factory circa 1920. "The owner of the factory never came out there, he just sat in New York and took the money. . . . The manager was a very sharp type. I told him I could increase production, so I worked out an incentive scheme whereby for a 50 percent increase in production they could make 30 to 40 percent more in wages. . . . The girls really began to put out. They got very much interested in their work, and the good ones were soon earning 16 dollars and more a week."

To her astonishment, the manager didn't like it.

" 'I'm not going to have those girls thinking they are good,' he said. 'I'm going to get rid of the good girls. I didn't pay them to get above themselves.' "

"He deliberately slowed down supplies and made things awkward for the smarter girls, so they just lost spirit and left."

The story is instructive from a number of viewpoints. First, it describes a situation that cannot be explained on the basis of conventional microeconomic theory, since the factory was not minimizing costs, nor maximizing output for the size of the work force. Second, it illustrates the different objectives of the factory owner *vis à vis* the factory manager. *This is unquestionably a case where management was made aware of a way of increasing output and yet chose not to use it.*

While it is rare to find such instances documented so clearly and graphically, this type of situation is not at all atypical. In 1974 in the United Kingdom (as a result of a coal strike), the Conservative government of Prime Minister Heath restricted manufacturing to a three-day week for six weeks. The result was that although labor and capital was utilized no more than 60 percent of the time, output was more than 80 or 90 percent of its normal level.

Neither of these situations is explained by conventional economic theory. In neither case were costs minimized, and in both instances the opportunity to utilize resources could have been improved considerably. This failure of conventional theory points up the need for a theory that enables us to examine, analyze, and predict instances where this type of inefficiency exists.

Conventional microeconomic theory is concerned with allocative or market efficiency. However, there are no markets *inside* productive organizations. We cannot simply assume that such organizations handle their affairs as well as they possibly can, as the conventional cost-minimization assumption implies.

What I have called "X-efficiency theory" is concerned with the type of inefficiency resulting from missed opportunities to utilize existing resources within productive organizations. (Since at an early stage in my research I was unable to find an adequate name for this type of inefficiency, I simply called it "X-inefficiency.") This theory attempts to analyze such inefficiencies and to determine their consequences. It is concerned with all types of non-allocative inefficiency.

Clearly it is more than organizational efficiency we are talking about. It addresses the type of inefficiency that takes place within households, as well as the inefficiency displayed by private enterprises and by governments. *Basically, what is involved are all types of inefficiencies resulting from the complete or partial lack of motivation to use economic opportunities as effectively as they might be used.* To the non-economist it may appear surprising to learn that standard economics does not cover this type of inefficiency. Yet in fact, it is *assumed away* by the maximization postulate, and especially by its corollary, the cost-minimization assumption.

The field of economics is divided into two broad approaches: macroeconomics and microeconomics. Macroeconomics deals with large aggregates: savings, investment, GNP, the money supply, and so on. Most of the grand problems of an economy, such as unemployment and inflation, are treated from a macro viewpoint. Newspaper and television economics, and a great deal of current controversy, is in terms of macro-magnitudes and macroeconomics.

However, most of what economists study, and the *foundations* of economics, falls into the realm of microeconomics. Micro is concerned with individual *markets* and the determination of price in such markets. Central to this is the theory of the supply and demand of particular goods. But behind supply and demand there is a theory of human motivation—a theory of how economic units behave. Essentially the conventional theory says that economic units try to do as well as they possibly can when they make economic decisions—in other words, they "maximize." This assumption means that, for production of goods and services, firms *minimize costs per unit of output* for a given scale of operation. Further, the theory asserts that it makes no difference whether such units are individual consumers, many-person households, one-man firms, or large, many-person enterprises. That is, the existing theory states that demand and supply relations determine what goes on in markets. It goes further to state that demand and supply relations are determined by the standard economic theory of decision making—that is, maximizing profits or utility, and minimizing cost. It is this latter position that we question. *If there is a crisis in microeconomics it is with respect to the decision superstructure and how the superstructure affects our view of economic life.*

Is there a "crisis" in micro theory? Several recent presidents of the American Economic Association and a recent Nobel Laureate have lectured economists on the shortcomings of microtheory. That is, there has been some concern in "high places." Yet this does not prove that the average economist is concerned about the nature and content of microeconomics. Quite the reverse is probably the case. Certainly the content of teaching in this area has not changed much in the last three or four decades. There is little evidence that there is any feeling of crisis.

What I will argue is that if there is no general erosion of confidence in conventional microeconomics, there ought to be. Briefly and bluntly, I feel that as economists:

1. We do not know the extent of our knowledge. We have a theory that appears to apply to everything. It is formal and universal. (By way of contrast, well developed sciences such as physics, chemistry, and microbiology know to a considerable degree where their knowledge is on solid ground and where it is either lacking,

vague, or uncertain.) There is, of course, a great deal that economists do understand about the behavior of the economy. Yet, obviously we do not know everything in microeconomics. Most curiously *we do not know what we know*. That is, with regard to various aspects of economics, economists cannot say "these aspects are what we know to be true, and these aspects we know little or nothing about." If a discipline after two centuries of intellectual activity still does not know what it knows, it cannot be said to be in a good state, or based on a solid foundation. Surely this fact alone should engender a feeling of crisis, or at the very least signs of concern.

2. A great source of difficulty involves the interpretation of the maximization postulate. Some interpret it as a behavioral or factual postulate; others interpret it tautologically. To my mind, the former is the proper interpretation. Yet we know of cases under which it is untrue—circumstances under which people do not maximize. The tautological approach implies that all behavior represents maximization, *whatever* the nature of the behavior. It says people always maximize, but that they may have complex and hidden objectives. This goes counter to the sensible notion that the definition of maximization as a term must admit non-maximization as a possibility. Furthermore it goes counter to the major scientific tenet that assertions can be criticized on the basis of factual or experimental data. The tautological approach immunizes the postulate, and many implications of the theory of which it is a part, from all possible criticism.

3. There is something basic missing from the conventional theory which is found in reality. In reality there exists the possibility of *differential* degrees of motivation. Yet the standard theory implicitly assumes that people are always fully motivated (maximization). Observation of the real world shows us that this is simply not the case. Some people are less motivated than others; and the same people appear to be more motivated in some circumstances than in others. Economic behavior, the amount and nature of effort that people put forth in their economic affairs, is in response to such differential degrees of motivation. Furthermore, different environments create and affect the degree of motivation that exists in different contexts. These elements influence to a significant degree the costs of production and output in the economy. The theory as currently constructed cannot handle "differential motivation." The Dulles hairnet factory story, and the three-day-week experience, are examples that fit a differential motivation postulate and contradict full motivation (i.e., maximization).

X-efficiency theory

All well-formulated theories in science are based on postulates (i.e., assumptions). In formal presentations the most important postulates are specified in advance. Consider two of the critical postulates of traditional microeconomics: 1) maximization and 2) the production function. By maximization (or the rationality postulate) we usually refer to the idea that decision units try to do as well as they possibly can, given their objectives. Thus, it is usually assumed that enterprises try to maximize profits; most important this implies that they attempt to *minimize costs* for a given output. The reader should note that it is the cost minimization postulate that, in a basic way, X-efficiency theory questions.

The production function postulate says that there is a *unique* relationship between inputs and outputs. To some economists it seems obvious that businessmen are sensible, and that sensible businessmen will know what they are doing—hence they will want as much profit as possible, as low costs as possible, and they will know the relation between any particular aggregate of inputs and any particular aggregate of outputs. Is this really so? Should we base our theories on these notions?

Even though these assumptions are sanctified by at least a century of tradition, there is nothing holy about them. In most sciences, especially in response to new findings, new postulates are considered, and new models or "pictures" of the world are developed, to try to account for phenomena that were not well explained on the basis of the previous model. This is the spirit in which I have attempted to develop X-efficiency theory. With this in mind, let us look at one element not well handled by standard theory—the process of production.

Let us go back to the hairnet factory example. Clearly there was *no unique relation* between the number of people hired and output. Furthermore, the management did not choose to minimize costs. Now let us look at the problem of production from a more general viewpoint. Clearly it is not the number of machines, the amount of space, the amount of materials, nor the number of people hired that determines output. What is critical is the amount and nature of the effort that the individuals hired put forth. Yet effort as such is not a variable in standard microtheory. Hence, in X-efficiency theory we focus on effort as a major variable, and relate it to the motivational system within the enterprise. Thus we assume that there is no unique connection between inputs purchased and output produced. Just putting people on the payroll does not by itself produce results. We have to examine what it is that people do within the enterprise and why they work the way they do, in order to understand productivity. Hence a very basic assumption that we will employ is that effort is, to some degree, a *discretionary* variable for all enterprise members. In other words, our theory assumes that to some extent individuals can choose 1) some of their activities; 2) the rate at which they carry out these activities; and, 3) the quality of their effort. The nature of the choice each individual makes will depend on the motivational system.

In contrast to the standard assumption of maximizing behavior, we assume non-maximizing most of the time. Maximization is a special case, in our view. Thus, most individuals are looked upon as non-maximizers most of the time. For example, most students will not study very effectively on most occasions, but their effectiveness increases as soon as there is the external pressure of an important examination. In a similar way, we assume that most individuals will move toward maximizing behavior as external pressure increases. Of course, we must also take into account the internal pressure that is part of an individual's personality. There may be some individuals whose personality is such as to approximate maximization all of the time. However, we will assume that this is the exception rather than the rule.

How does non-maximization work itself out in practice? There are two parts to normal decision making. First, in the flow of events most activities are handled on the basis of habit, routine, or well-entrenched conventions. These terms overlap. The first problem is to determine what changes in circumstances activate decision making. Once explicit decision making is activated, we then have to consider *how* such decisions are made. We cannot capture all of the details or specifics of every individual's decision-making procedures. However, we believe they are likely to fall into three categories. The first we have already mentioned, namely habits, routines, and conventions. The second is decisions according to imperfect and *partial* calculating procedures. Finally, there is a class of procedures which comes close to *complete* calculation. This last approximates maximization.

Most of the time decisions are not activated. When changing circumstances cause external pressure to become sufficiently great, activation takes place. At first, most individuals will fall back on a convention or a habit as a solution to the decision problem. If the pressure of the importance of the decision is sufficiently great, there will be a shift towards partial calculation. The greater the apparent cost (or pressure) of incomplete calculation, the greater the shift towards a more complete procedure. Thus, in general the degree to which any decision procedure deviates from maximization depends on the degree of external pressure.

A concept related to the existence of pressure is that of *inert areas*. The concept of inert areas postulates that only if external pressure (or external cost) is sufficiently high, will behavior change. For instance, many people will continue to smoke cigarettes knowing that it is bad for them, but a slight heart attack will lead some of them to quit. The event increases pressure and activates an explicit decision activity. Something akin to the use of the inert area idea is the suggestion that upper and lower bounds exist within which routine behavior takes place. An extreme example of behavior within an inert area (or inertia) is described in the Russian 19th century novel, *Oblomov*. When we first meet the hero, Oblomov, he is in bed despite the fact that a number of business and social problems require the type of attention that can only be given to them out of bed. Some 300 pages later Oblomov's problems have not diminished yet he has not moved out of bed. (So as not to spoil things for those who have yet to read Goncharov's classic, I will refrain from indicating what happens after page 300.)

The last postulate we consider is the concept of *effort entropy*—a type of organizational entropy. As in physics, entropy is viewed as a measure of disorder. More specifically, we look upon it as representing the degree of insufficient coordination with presumed enterprise objectives. Once again the existence of pressure is central. As more pressure for coordination flows from the top there is likely to be a greater degree of coordination. If a decrease in pressure occurs, then—up to a point—there will be a related increase in effort entropy, and a decrease in X-efficiency.

Implications of X-efficiency theory

The consequences of these assumptions will depend on the environment within which the enterprise operates. The external environment puts pressure on the executives of the enterprise, who in turn transmit pressure to other members of the firm further down the hierarchy. Under a high degree of competition, if sustained over a long period of time, the external pressure may be sufficiently great that the result may approximate cost minimization. However, many markets are imperfect. They provide *shelters* from competitive pressure. Probably the hairnet factory reported on by Eleanor

Dulles was of this type. Of course, firm managers, and owners, desire shelters. It was already noted by Adam Smith, over two centuries ago, that when businessmen get together they frequently attempt to work out agreements on prices or other market conditions —that is, to work out sheltered arrangements.

In sheltered environments there is no necessity for business firms to minimize costs. There is no reason for management to transmit pressure from the top down through the various layers of the hierarchy in order to foster the most effective effort levels. The non-maximization and inert-area postulates imply that once employers choose effort-activity-quality routines that are non-optimal they will continue with such routines. *Hence cost minimization will be the exception rather than the rule.*

Important implications of our postulates have to do with the relations between cost and price. It is frequently stated that if the cost of some input, say labor, increases, the cost of output must increase accordingly. But this does not necessarily follow. If there is a rise in the cost of some input but at the same time the pressure on management to be more effective increases, resulting in more effective effort choices, then this may engender a reduction of X-inefficiency and a decrease in costs. *One thing is clear: There is no necessary relationship between the percentage increase in costs of inputs (labor, raw materials, machinery, etc.) and the percentage increase of the cost of the output.* The cost of the output can turn out to be very much smaller, or not rise at all.

In the Fall 1979 issue of *The Public Interest,* Richard L. Freeman and James L. Medoff argued that while unionization resulted in increased wages, in 75 percent of the cases unionization also resulted in a 20 to 25 percent increase in productivity per man. Here we have a set of fairly clear-cut cases where increases in the cost of the input did not result in an equal increase in the cost of the output. It is possible for no increase in cost to result. The reader will recall that in the hairnet factory example, the cost of the increased wages was less than the increase in productivity.

It is of special interest to note that an increase in the price of a product will not necessarily leave costs unaffected. In the mainline theory, it is assumed that the price of a product and the costs of production are separate matters. In X-efficiency theory, an increase in the product price that comes about as a result of an increase in "sheltering" may be associated with an increase in costs of production.

Professor Primaux of the University of Illinois compared the cost per unit of output of the 49 cities in the United States that have two electric-utility companies with the cost per unit of output of all other cities which have only one. The single electric-utility city is the norm. Electric utilities clearly constitute a sheltered industry. In the two-company cities each company faces competition from the other company. If the standard theory is correct, there should be no difference in cost (after making an adjustment for scale) between the two-company cities and the single company cities. If, on the other hand, X-efficiency theory is correct, the less sheltered case (two companies) should have lower costs. Primaux found that, in fact, the 49 two-company cities had about 11 percent lower costs.

It is conceivable that the retardation in the productivity growth of the American economy which has taken place in recent years is not only a contributor to inflation but to some degree is a consequence of it. An inflationary atmosphere permits business enterprises to pass cost increases on. Higher prices result because there is relatively little fear of a competitive disadvantage, since other firms are in similar circumstances and behave in a similar fashion. In other words, the inflationary atmosphere allows managers to be somewhat less concerned about transmitting pressure within the firm towards cost containment, since the alternative of price increases which pass on X-inefficiency is readily available. A recent television program (*60 Minutes*, NBC, December 9, 1979) discussed the automobile-insurance-fraud rackets, specifically organized frauds caused by false accident reporting. A lawyer involved in some aspect of the problem was asked why the insurance companies did not do more to investigate the possibility of fraud. His reply was that it is easier for the insurance companies to pass through to its customers the costs of fraudulent claims in the form of higher rates. Obviously, there is no pressure to minimize costs.

Our theory argues that in order to understand productivity changes we have to understand how the economic environment operates as an incentive towards more or less effective effort levels. After all, our real standard of living, on the average, depends on productivity per man. This in turn will depend on the organization of markets, the nature of the economic units within these markets, and how the environment influences incentive structures. Mainline theory does not really study such questions because it does not address itself to the non-market production activities within the firm, the impact of sheltered environments on motivation, and the significance of differential motivation. X-efficiency theory focuses on these considerations.

A standard conclusion of conventional theory is the desirability of expanding international trade in accordance with the comparative advantages in production of each country. The general idea is that if a country can specialize in those things which it produces at relatively lower resource costs, and trades them for those things which it produces at higher resource costs, it is better off than if it tries to produce all products on its own. Even if Canadians could grow both apples and bananas, it would require so many more resources to grow bananas than apples that Canada is better off growing apples and trading them with some Central American country for the bananas which grow easily there. This argument for trade, which has been around for several centuries, is valid. However, according to X-efficiency theory a more important gain from trade may also result from the importation of products *similar* to those produced reasonably well in the country in question. Such imports put pressure on local producers to produce at lower costs than would otherwise be the case. Thus Americans may gain from the importation of foreign automobiles since imports put pressure on American manufacturers to maintain higher levels of productivity and/or higher quality standards than would otherwise be the case.

From some viewpoints the impact of X-inefficiency on the retardation of economic growth may be of greater importance than the underutilization of resources at any point in time. Growth depends on the introduction of innovations. Its essence is to go counter to the maintenance of routine procedures. Of course growth takes effort, but it is a special kind of effort—that type which redirects existing effort levels. Thus the atmosphere of a sheltered environment which is conducive to relatively high costs is also likely to reduce the incentives for management and workers to introduce new types of machinery and new techniques. Considerable deviation from maximizing behavior is likely to be inimical to innovation. Furthermore, inertia has to be overcome in order to introduce innovations, and at certain levels of disorganization (effort entropy) it is likely to be extremely difficult to introduce innovations effectively. At this point we do not wish to suggest a theory of innovation; rather, we simply want to indicate how the categories we have developed can be used to analyze environments in which the introduction of innovations is likely to be difficult as against those in which innovating is easier.

Bureaucracy, and especially governmental bureaucracy, is a significant problem area usually ignored by economists. Bureaucracy also exists in private organizations. It is a product of organization, size, and complexity, and is therefore not limited to government. However, keeping in mind that 30 to 40 percent of the gross national product is attributable to the activities of government, it seems appropriate that economists analyze the organization of government's economic activities as we do that of private enterprises.

The principal-agent relationship is especially diffuse in bureaucratic organizations. This single fact is a major element of bureaucracy and helps to account for some of its characteristics. Whom does the governmental bureaucrat really work for—the citizenry? Bureaucrats rarely, if ever, take orders from the citizenry directly. Nor do they attempt to determine their appropriate objectives on the basis of the desires of the citizenry. Clearly bureaucratic careers do not depend on behavior that primarily considers the aims of the principal. Between the true principals and the agents there are a host of elected politicians, political appointees, and civil servants who interpret and reinterpret the nature of the task to be carried out. The environment within which agents have to choose their effort levels is surrounded on the one hand by negative rules of accountability, and on the other by rules and conventions which define the privileges of the civil service. Frequently one gets the impression that the demands of the citizenry play a minor role in influencing the actual performance to "their" agents.

It is most important to keep in mind that governmental activities are completely sheltered from competition. The Post Office and many other agencies even have rules that make competitive activities illegal. Even when the nature of the service is determined by the context, the environment, or legislation (e.g., picking up and delivering mail), the lack of pressure from the environment permits a very wide range of inefficiencies. Calculations of inefficiency are not usually made, but in the few cases in which this has been done, such as in a recent study comparing government versus private garbage collection, it was found that government collection cost, on the average, 61 percent more than private collection.[1] The point is that, normally, if government becomes expensive we cannot shop around elsewhere for competing services.

It is not my intention here simply to delineate various aspects of bureaucracy. Rather it is to suggest that the arguments just stated would follow for bureaucracies in almost any large organization, be it public or private, which are sufficiently sheltered from competition.

[1] See E.S. Savas, *Policy Analysis*, Winter 1977.

How important is X-inefficiency for the economy as a whole? It is hard to say. The ideas are too new and as yet no one has attempted to work out a careful assessment. But there are a lot of partial data floating around from particular studies. While the question might be raised whether they are representative, I feel we do have enough data to make a preliminary "back of the envelope" type of assessment about the order of magnitude of X-inefficiency. If unionization can increase productivity by 20 to 25 percent; if instances of monopoly show cost differences of more than 10 percent; if we presume that the government sector is considerably less X-efficient than the non-government sector—then it is not a wild guess to expect the production sector to be only, say, 70 percent as X-efficient as it could be.

But households are also X-inefficient. To what degree do households spend their money and use their goods less well than they could if they were maximizing? Suppose it is 85 percent of maximum X-efficiency.[2] The X-efficiency of the economy is the product of household X-efficiency and production X-efficiency. For the numbers assumed, this implies that the economy is operating only 60 percent as well as it could be. While these numbers should not be taken too seriously, in my view they are not beyond reason.

A micro-micro approach

We have contrasted the X-efficiency approach with that of the mainline microeconomic approach which assumes that business enterprises minimize costs per unit of output. If firms do not minimize costs, then this is a basic source of inefficiency in the economy, one which is likely to be significantly larger than any other source. The figures suggest that the magnitude of X-inefficiency at any one time in the United States may be between 20 to 40 percent of net national product. Figures developed by T. Y. Shen (University of California, Davis) suggest that X-inefficiency may be even higher in developing countries. Contrary to the conventional theory, firms in developing countries do not merely substitute labor for capital. Shen found that these countries not only used more labor in the same industries for the same products as advanced countries, but also more capital. While using more capital they also use, in some cases, between

[2] A recent paper by three Dutch economists, Arie Kapteyn, Tom Wansbeek, and Jeanine Buyze, "Maximizing or Satisficing?", *The Review of Economics and Statistics* (November 1979), estimates that in Holland consumers purchasing durable goods did only about 75 percent as well as they would have had they been maximizing.

three- to ten-fold more labor than was used in technologically advanced countries. The long-run impact on growth is likely to be of greater importance than the short-run slack.

X-inefficiency also exists in households. If household budgets are not handled optimally, an equal social loss is involved. The total loss due to X-inefficiency, then, will grow rapidly as household or production efficiency decline.

Clearly the magnitudes of X-inefficiency are extremely important. In my view the theory necessary to explain them must deviate from the postulates of profit maximization, utility maximization, and cost minimization—the most strongly held beliefs of a large segment of the economics profession. Reluctance to relax the maximization assumption deprives the profession of a research pathway that can lead to discoveries of significant economic pathologies. There ought to be, to a greater extent than there is, a questioning of the current direction of work.

The implications for research of the approach presented here differ from those of the neoclassical theory. We suggest that a great deal can be learned by going more deeply into the decision procedures and motivations that exist within firms. That is, we recommend a *micro-micro* approach. This means studying in detail what the standard theory simply assumes. In a sense this would take us in the same direction as physics and microbiology—towards the study of smaller and smaller fundamental entities. This approach brings some elements of economics closer to the subject matter of business schools. Economists, however, would continue to look at these matters from a different viewpoint.

Some of our findings are different from the implications of standard theory. According to X-efficiency theory, 1) cost minimization will be the exception rather than the rule; 2) increases in input prices need not result in increases in output costs; and, 3) raising the price of the product may increase cost through the operation of increased effort entropy. Thus inflation may be a cause, in part, as well as a result, of cost increases.

While our findings are different in some cases, they do not always point to different policy directions. The conventional theory views the expansion of international trade as a good thing on comparative advantage grounds. X-efficiency theory also sees it as beneficial because it puts pressure on domestic producers to lower costs. For reasons that are too technical to present here, it seems likely that the X-efficiency improvements would be considerably greater than the comparative advantage benefits. On the other hand, in contrast to the conventional view, X-efficiency theory suggests that profits are not a good indicator of efficiency if production takes place in sheltered environments. Thus, it would probably not be good public policy to control natural monopolies such as electric utilities by controlling the profit rate. X-efficiency holds that incentives must be provided for operators to reduce *costs* toward the minimum.

Finally, the X-efficiency approach is in the spirit of the development of models based on different postulates than those already existing—a conventional procedure in many sciences. Relaxing the maximization postulate would permit the study of different types of economic activities, *including* those undertaken by governments, in terms of a continuum of environments which provide different degrees of motivation toward efficiency of performance. In general, once the cost-minimization postulate is dropped, X-efficiency theory opens the way for the analysis of cost-containment problems and countermeasures.

7

The "Austrian" perspective on the crisis

ISRAEL M. KIRZNER

THE tragedy of "mainstream" economic theory is that its present crisis-like situation appears as the natural outcome of an intellectual process that was, perversely, set in motion by a series of significant theoretical advances. Somehow the dynamics of this history has produced, out of basically sound insights, an elaborate structure of theory, dazzling in its technical sophistication, inspiring in the architectonic quality of its intellectual edifice—but seriously deficient in any genuine understanding of the workings of market capitalism. Such, at any rate, is the "Austrian" perspective on the current state of the dominant Anglo-American "neoclassical" orthodoxy in economic theory.*

Several important aspects of this unique Austrian perspective need to be noted. First, this perspective sees the edifice of modern neoclassical economics as built upon essentially sound foundations. (This is certainly the case insofar as these foundations are compared with the general world view expressed in the classical economics

* The term "Austrian" economics has been used with a number of different meanings. For our purposes the term refers to the work now being done in this country by a group of younger economists who have rediscovered, especially through the work of Mises and Hayek, the value and fruitfulness of certain insights basic to the earlier school of Austrian economics, originating in the 1870's with Karl Menger in Vienna.

which neoclassical economics replaced.) The required task of reconstruction does not, in the Austrian view, call for a radically different set of *fundamental* insights (as would be required, for example, by a Marxist view). On the contrary, the task of reconstruction calls, in part, for consistent attention to precisely those fundamental insights to which the dominant neoclassical tradition owes its beginnings—insights to which its proponents still, on occasion, pay lip service. Indeed, part of the difficulty encountered by Austrians in persuading their colleagues of the need for reconstruction arises out of the circumstance that many of these orthodox colleagues believe themselves to be *already* thoroughly in sympathy with what (to Austrians at least) appear to be the revolutionary insights which form the basis for Austrian economics.

Second, the task of Austrian reconstruction is one which calls for a good deal of attention to the history of economic ideas, especially in the early years of modern economics. If the essentially healthy elements in modern neoclassical economics are to be preserved, if the basically sound ideas fundamental to it are to serve as the inspiration for a hoped-for reconstruction of the edifice, reconstruction dare not be undertaken without thorough familiarity with the sources of earlier mistakes. It is necessary to know where, in its earliest development, neoclassical economics went wrong. Only in this way may we hope to make over the shape of modern economics in a radical manner—yet without sacrificing its positive features.

Third, despite our remarks on the healthy roots of modern neoclassical economics, there should be no doubt about the gulf which separates the mainstream view of market capitalism from that with which Austrian economics proposes to replace it. *In the Austrian view, a thorough training in neoclassical economics simply does not equip one with a sensitive understanding of how the market economy works.* It is this very disturbing circumstance which has spurred the current resurgence of interest in the Austrian tradition.

The emergence of neoclassical economics

During the last three decades of the 19th century, mainstream economics underwent a series of drastic alterations. In 1870 a frayed and battered classical orthodoxy, represented typically by John Stuart Mill's *Principles of Political Economy* (1848), still struggled—in the face of widespread undercurrents of skepticism and incipient rebellion—to maintain its position of dominance. By 1900 fresh winds had conclusively swept out the old orthodoxy and had firmly installed its successor—a body of thought by no means homogeneous or monolithic, but one nonetheless often referred to generically as "neoclassical economics," in the broadest possible interpretation of that term. Mainstream historians of economic thought tend to see the various separate schools which made up the neoclassical revolution as having made their separate contributions within a broadly shared consensus. Before World War I, the various schools pursued their work with relatively little international crossfertilization. Marshall in Cambridge, England; Walras, and later Pareto, in Lausanne, Switzerland; Menger and Böhm-Bawerk in Vienna, Austria; J. B. Clark in the United States, carried on their work, each in his own way, within the broadly-shared neoclassical world view. It has come to be held that between the two World Wars the various strands of neoclassicism merged naturally, as a result of more vigorous international flows of ideas, into the body of thought which has, since World War II, dominated Anglo-American thought. Thus, in this view, the current orthodoxy has beneficially absorbed the special strengths of all these various schools. The "subjectivism" of the early Austrians, the "general equilibrium" system of Lausanne, joined the mainline of Marshallian and Clarkian economics to produce what is today taught on both sides of the Atlantic. From this historical perspective the Keynesian attack on neoclassical orthodoxy appears now, in retrospect, to have had relatively little permanent *revolutionary* impact. Although Keynesian macroeconomics successfully dominated the stage during the immediate postwar decades, it has since then come to be significantly assimilated to neoclassical orthodoxy, first through Samuelson's "neoclassical synthesis," and more recently as a result of sustained growth of interest in the "micro-foundations" of macro theory.

The Austrian perspective on the same historical period in the development of modern economics sees the picture somewhat differently. Careful study of the various schools at work before World War I reveals that the differences which separated them probably exceed in significance the elements generally held to justify grouping these schools together under the neoclassical umbrella. It is true that all the great post-1870 economists were attempting to recast economics along lines which (in contrast to classical economics) recognized the role of the consumer, of marginal utility, and of the demand side of markets. But, except for the Austrians in Vienna, this emphasis came to be subordinated to other, more dominant, themes. For both the Walrasians and the Marshallians, economic theory came more and more to point primarily towards the derivation of the conditions for market equilibrium. In these treatments the role of the entrepreneur came to be lost sight of, the dynamics of the market process came to be overlooked or misunderstood, and the role of competition came to be recast until its meaning for technical economics was almost the exact opposite of what it had meant to Adam Smith (and still means to the layman).

From this Austrian historical perspective, the absorption into Anglo-American orthodoxy of the ideas developed by the various separate pre-World War I schools assumes a different aspect. It was not that the various schools made their contributions to the development of an already commonly-shared body of understanding. Rather it was a case of the dominant Marshallian neoclassical strand assimilating important features of Walrasian economics, as well as, in some degree, certain insights from other traditions. The confluence of Walrasian and Marshallian traditions had the consequence, it is now clear in retrospect, of decisively turning modern economics away from an appreciation of capitalism as a market *process*. It is in a number of respects ironic that the very injection of certain fundamental Austrian ideas into the Anglo-American orthodoxy (as occurred, for example, in 1932 with the appearance of Lord Robbins' justly celebrated *Nature and Significance of Economic Science*) seems to have helped crystallize the new direction taken by neoclassical thought.

As a result of the dominance achieved by this new direction, the older Austrian tradition came to be almost completely submerged. By the mid-1940's the dynamic view of the competitive market process shared (despite their differences!) by Austrians, such as Schumpeter, Mises, and Hayek, had become a view completely alien to the mainstream perspective. The success achieved during this period by Keynesianism contributed still further to the eclipse of the Austrian tradition. To an observer of the profession in the mid-1950's, the Misesian view appeared as one thoroughly discredited—or at least ignominiously ignored—by the mainstream of economic thought. That mainstream, by constrast, was enormously busy in developing sophisticated mathematical models, elaborate econometric techniques, and massive programs of empirical studies.

It is only in recent years that the younger members of the economics profession, in the United States, in Great Britain, and elsewhere, are finding it no longer possible to ignore the major flaws in the dominant view. A small but growing group of scholars has rediscovered the Austrian tradition and are engaged in a broad effort toward the restatement of economics along lines embodying the brilliant, neglected insights developed by the modern exponents of that tradition, Mises and Hayek. In what follows, I examine briefly the nature of the principal flaws in modern economics as seen from the Austrian perspective. This perspective is that which particularly emphasizes: the purposefulness of individual action; the role of knowledge in economic choice; the subjectivity of the phenomena that interest economists; the competitive-entrepreneurial character of the market process; and the *ex ante* role in which time affects economic activity.

Some flaws in neoclassical economics

Although Austrian critics of the modern neoclassical tradition often refer critically to the excessive technical sophistication affected by the present-day exponents of that tradition, such criticism should not be misunderstood. It is not so much that Austrians are driven to question the relevance, even in principle, of the mathematics and the econometric techniques which today fill the pages of the professional economic journals, nor is it even the conviction (often shared by non-Austrians) that the sheer bulk of the technical baggage is too massive and too abstract to be fruitfully applied in explaining the real world with which we wish to deal. Rather, Austrian skepticism of the technical sophistication that pervades modern economics stems from painful awareness that the attention paid to the formal apparatus has been responsible for failure to appreciate a number of insights crucially important for economic understanding. As a result, modern mainstream economics displays a number of related features which, for Austrians, appear as serious flaws. These features include especially: a) an excessive preoccupation with the state of *equilibrium*; b) an unfortunate perspective on the nature and role of *competition* in markets; c) grossly insufficient attention to the role (and subjective character) of *knowledge, expectations,* and *learning* in market processes; and, d) a normative approach heavily dependent on questionable *aggregation* concepts and thus insensitive to the idea of *plan coordination* among market participants. Together these flaws represent very serious distortions, at best, in the understanding of the market process in capitalist economies which modern neoclassical economics is able to provide.

Equilibrium. Probably the central notion in modern neoclassical economics is that of market equilibrium. A very large part of economics is concerned with working out the mathematical conditions which must be satisfied in order for particular markets to have achieved equilibrium—i.e., the state of affairs in which all plans are successfully carried out without disappointment and without reason for subsequent regret. A very large part of applied economic theory proceeds by assuming that market data can be treated as consistent with the hypothesis of markets being *already* in equilibrium. To a large extent the mathematicization of economics, as well as the disappearance of the entrepreneur from the theory of markets, can be attributed to the central role of equilibrium theory. For Austrians this preoccupation with equilibrium represents a serious shortcoming. Without in any way denying the usefulness of the equilibrium concept as a tool of analysis, Austrians see the neoclassical emphasis on equilibrium as a failure to recognize the really important aspects of a market economy—namely, those which relate to the nature of market *processes*. Equilibrium economics has tended simply to take these processes for granted, treating them in effect as working so rapidly, and as being so definitely equilibrating in their character, as to permit the analyst to assume instantaneous attainment of equilibrium. This is not only unrealistic; it leads to a totally false perception of the social usefulness of the market.

The inadequacies of equilibrium theory have not escaped the attention of contemporary theorists. I will a little later comment on the attempts being made, within the neoclassical framework, to address these inadequacies. For our present purpose it is sufficient to point out that, despite these well-meaning attempts, the corpus of mainstream economics is still heavily dependent on the equilibrium assumption. It is precisely the widespread awareness of this crippling handicap which contributes to the crisis-like atmosphere surrounding contemporary discussion of economic theory.

Competition. Economists have always emphasized the beneficial role of competition in market processes. Sad to say, neoclassical economics long ago developed a technical notion of *static* competition which is not only antithetical to that used in everyday layman's speech, but which, more seriously, fails entirely to appreciate the nature and enormous importance of dynamic competition. Not only did neoclassical economics introduce a meaning to the term "competition" which is almost the opposite of its ordinary meaning, but, in so doing, it diverted attention from market *processes*.

For neoclassical economics a "perfectly" competitive market means a market already in full equilibrium, in which individual buyers and sellers have no discretion with respect to price whatsoever—price having been already somehow set at the level such that utility-maximizing buyers and profit-maximizing sellers make the set of decisions which will clear the market. Competition is thus a state of affairs in which there is no need and no opportunity to "compete," in the everyday sense of striving to outdo one's competitors.

This notion of competition is so obviously bizarre, unrealistic, and unhelpful in understanding markets, that it long ago led to attempts within the neoclassical paradigm to replace it with more realistic models, notably that of "monopolistic competition." In the 1930's and 1940's Joseph A. Schumpeter (who in this respect, at least, was thoroughly Austrian) ridiculed the standard competitive models. Unfortunately, the attempts to replace the unrealistic economists' notion of competition by and large failed. On the one hand, the substitutes that were offered suffered from serious limitations of their own. On the other, the mainstream of economics still proceeded to use—almost without compunction—the standard, unrealistic, static concept of competition.

For Austrians, an economics built around this unfortunate notion of perfect competition is seriously inadequate. Not only does it reinforce the regrettable preoccupation with equilibrium, it has also been responsible for a disastrous failure to understand the requirements for, and benefits of, the dynamic kind of competition (in which the conditions of the economists' static view of perfect competition are in fact *necessarily violated*). The results of this failure include, among other matters, a misunderstanding of the role of advertising in modern economics, as well as an approach to the economics of anti-trust which has seriously threatened the efficiency and vitality of American industry. Instead of recognizing the critical importance for dynamic competition of *freedom of entry* (and of the harmfulness of all the well-meaning governmental regulatory actions which have eroded this freedom in modern times), mainstream economics has supported the view that sheer size is *per se* anti-competitive, and that the presence of any discretion to a firm, with respect to price, is essentially sinister.

The work of industrial-organization theorists has also come to recognize the harm wrought by the dominance of the perfectly competitive model in mainstream economics. A good portion of the widespread dissatisfaction with contemporary theory must indeed be laid at the door of this model.

Knowledge, Expectations, and Learning. The shortcomings associated with neoclassical preoccupation with equilibrium and "perfect" competition, can be traced to a deeper flaw—a failure to recognize the role of knowledge in the face of radical uncertainty, and of learning processes in dynamically competitive markets. For mainstream economics, objective data are viewed as somehow able instantly to determine the decisions of market participants. Until quite recently the main body of neoclassical theory was entirely comfortable with the assumption of perfect knowledge. No attention was paid to the extent to which buying and selling decisions must express the expectations being held with respect to *other* people's buying and selling decisions. No attention was paid to Hayek's demonstration that market equilibrium means the possession by market participants of sets of mutually-sustaining expectations with respect to one another's actions.

This neoclassical lack of appreciation for the role of knowledge and expectations has gone hand in hand with failure to recognize the nature and significance of *entrepreneurial discovery* in an uncertain world. In particular it has been responsible for misunderstanding the nature of competitive market processes, and for failure to ask the relevant questions with respect to whether or not the *learning* sequences, of which such processes consist, are likely to be equilibrating. For Austrians, sensitized to awareness of these matters, all this adds up to a powerful indictment of mainstream economics.

Allocation, Aggregation, and Social Welfare. Economic theory has always been pursued not only for the light of understanding which it promises, but also for the fruit of improvement in the well-being of society for which such understanding might be deployed. The neoclassical framework within which mainstream economics has pursued these latter ("normative") interests, contains certain key features which, in the opinion of Austrians, compound the faulty perception of market capitalism which that tradition represents.

First, normative economics is conducted in terms of a notion of *social allocational efficiency* which begs the very essence of the normative problem. Second, the economic well-being of society has (partly under the impact of macroeconomic thinking popularized by Lord Keynes) come to be identified with such deeply flawed *aggregate* notions as gross national product and the like.

For Austrians, to see the economic problem of society as one of efficiently allocating scarce social resources for the attainment of social goals, is not only to extend misleadingly the notion of choice from the level of the individual (where it properly belongs) to that of society as a whole (where it can only apply as a metaphor). Far worse, it is in effect to assume away essential elements of the question. For the notion of social allocation of resources must assume that *somehow it can already be known* (how? to whom?) exactly what the available resources of society are, and exactly what is to be the relevant priority ranking of social goals. As Hayek has shown, it is the essence of the social-economic problem to grapple with the obvious circumstance that these matters are in fact *not* known to any single mind at all. Indeed, from the Austrian perspective the social relevance of the market process lies precisely in the extent to which it facilitates the way in which scattered (and even as yet entirely undiscovered) information is mobilized and brought to bear upon decision making.

Austrian criticisms of *aggregate* notions of social economic welfare derive both from the methodological individualism and from the subjectivism embedded in the Austrian tradition. Aggregate notions of welfare imply that there is some objective entity such as "output" which can be aggregated across individuals for purposes of welfare comparisons. For Austrians this raises well-nigh insuperable conceptual problems. The circumstance that such aggregates rely on market prices to achieve value homogenization of physically heterogeneous products only compounds Austrian unhappiness.

The truth, as seen by Austrians, is that economic welfare—consisting as it does of nothing but the subjective sense of well-being of separate *individuals*—displays an interpersonal incommensurability which simply defies aggregation. Moreover, market prices at any given time are sure to be *dis*equilibrium prices, and thus wholly inappropriate for purposes of aggregation (even if aggregation were unconcerned with welfare aspects of output). More fundamentally, perhaps, the Austrian emphasis on the individuality of choice and on the crucial significance of mutual expectations, on the basis of which choices are made in society, focuses attention on normative issues that have been wholly neglected by mainstream economics. For Austrians such questions as the coordination of plans, the extent to which decisions of different individuals can be systematically modified by market experience to more correctly anticipate each other's preferences, and the degree to which disequilibrium prices contribute to such improved anticipation through generating opportunities for entrepreneurial discovery, are all at the heart of normative discussion. But they are nowhere to be found in mainstream normative economics.

The monetary framework: further flaws

For market capitalism to work smoothly and effectively in the coordination of the plans of market participants, a reasonably stable monetary framework is an important requirement. For Austrians one of the gravest consequences of mainstream economics during the present century has been persistent mismanagement by governmental monetary authorities—mismanagement that has again and again brought in its train inflationary booms followed by bouts of depression. Mainstream Keynesian economics, it is now fairly widely felt (by non-Austrians as well as by Austrians), has failed miserably to live up to its presumptuous claims of having rendered economic instability obsolete. Contemporary disillusionment with the Keynesian mainstream has in large measure arisen from a shrewd suspicion that Keynesian policies are not only inadequate to ensure stability, but have in fact been to blame for its disappearance. For today's intelligent layman to put the mainstream economist in his place, it is only necessary for him to ask the now well-known and troublesome questions about inflation and stagnation.

To Austrians these mainstream failures appear as natural consequences of neoclassical misunderstanding of market processes and of its blindness towards the critical importance of plan coordination. The decades of Keynesian ascendancy emerge as a period during which it was somehow blithely believed possible to analyze the interaction of various "macro" variables without any examination of the micro-underpinnings of these aggregate entities. It was held possible, for example, to examine the impact of changes in the money supply without considering their structural consequences, as manifested through the market interplay of individual transactions. To put it somewhat differently, it was held possible to talk, say, of "price level" changes consequent upon increases in the supply of money, in a manner assuming that possible changes in *relative* prices (and the consequences of such changes) may be safely ignored. It was held possible to talk, say, of changes in aggregate "investment" without regard to the delicate web of plans governing the social structure of capital utilization, and the role of relative prices in achieving and modifying this structure of production. The insight that market forces—with all the scope they provide for action based on erroneous information, and for the incentives they offer for the entrepreneurial discovery of such errors—govern monetary phenomena as well as "real" phenomena, was missed. The tragic result of all this has been that mainstream economics has, to its shame, come to appear to endorse the popular and dangerous folklore that in order to stimulate economic activity and to avoid depression, it is necessary merely to inflate the money supply. That such inflation may induce serious distortions in the economy, that it may systematically foster failures of coordination among the decisions of individual market participants, are concerns that have tended not to disturb mainstream economists.

Rescue and reconstruction

Contemporary mainstream theorists have not remained entirely unaware of all the shortcomings that have been briefly noted here. A good deal of work appearing in current journals is in fact directed at extending mainstream economics to deal with such matters as market processes during disequilibrium, the role of uncertainty, and the search for information. The need to provide "micro foundations" for macroeconomics is by now almost universally conceded, and considerable work in this direction has been achieved, much of it involving careful attention to the role of individual expectations in market responses to macro policy. These efforts are most encouraging, as far as they go. Nevertheless, to Austrians these efforts seem unlikely to effect the radical repairs so sorely needed by the leaky structure of contemporary neoclassical theory.

The fact is that these efforts at improvement are directed at specific perceived limitations of existing theory. Unfortunately, they appear generally not to recognize the extent to which the entire theoretical structure needs reconstruction. Instead of dismantling the elaborate equilibrium models of which neoclassical economics consists—and appreciating the subtle processes of spontaneous learning made possible by market interaction under imperfect knowledge—the new work seeks to address the problems by constructing even more complicated equilibrium models. Instead of recognizing the high price (in fundamental economic understanding) paid in order to deploy sophisticated technical tools of dubious practical value, the new work has largely taken the form of pouring still more intellectual investment into the technical tool kit. Instead of seeking to escape the mechanical quality which neoclassical theory has imparted to economic analysis, much of the new work (notably that centered around the "economics of search") has tended to extend that mechanical quality to areas (such as those of knowledge and discovery) which had, until recently, mercifully escaped it. The Austrian economist is compelled to conclude that the new work is being conducted along lines that, unfortunately, simply do not point in the required direction.

For Austrians the present state of economics is seen to stem naturally from its historical development. Consideration of this background appears to identify very clearly the direction of required reconstruction. Neoclassical mainstream economics possesses great virtues. With all its faults, it does perceive the market economy as an interlocking array of individual decisions. It perceives the pattern in which decisions at the level of production are inextricably linked with expected decisions of resource suppliers and of prospective consumers. What is required is to retain these fundamental insights, and to begin to explore, with a humility which sophisticated model building is somehow unsuited to generate, the way in which individual decisions are likely to be modified by the discovery of error, by the awareness of radical uncertainty, and by the awareness of the *futurity* of the perceived time dimension within which decisions must be made. Economic theory needs to be reconstructed so as to recognize at each stage the manner in which changes in external phenomena modify economic activity strictly *through the filter of the human mind.* Economic consequences, that is, dare not be linked functionally and mechanically to external changes, as if the consequences emerge independently of the way in which the external changes are *perceived,* of the way in which these changes affect expectations, and of the way in which these changes are discovered at all.

Of course, these are very "Austrian" prescriptions. Contemporary Austrian economists indeed believe that the tradition which they have rediscovered offers the strongest hope for economics in its present time of crisis.

8

General Equilibrium Theory

FRANK HAHN

In decentralized economies a large number of individuals make economic decisions which, in the light of market and other information, they consider most advantageous. They are not guided by the social good, nor is there an overall plan in the unfolding of which they have preassigned roles. It was Adam Smith who first realized the need to explain why this kind of social arrangement does not lead to chaos. Millions of greedy, self-seeking individuals, in pursuit of their own ends and mainly uncontrolled in these pursuits by the State, seem to "common sense" a sure recipe for anarchy. Smith not only posed an obviously important question, but also started us off on the road to answering it. General Equilibrium Theory as classically stated by Arrow and Debreu (1954 and 1959) is near the end of that road. Now that we have got there we find it less enlightening than we had expected. The reason is partly that the world has moved on and is no longer as decentralized as it used to be, and partly that the road we pursued was excessively straight and narrow and made—we now feel—with too little allowance for the wild and varied terrain it had to traverse. We have certainly arrived at an orderly destination, but it looks increasingly likely that we cannot rest there.

Here is a simple account of General Equilibrium Theory. The basic building block is the individual agent. Agents are divided into two types: households and firms. Start with the latter. A firm is an agent that transforms inputs into outputs. There may be many ways of doing this (there may be many *activities*), and the firm is assumed to know a book of blue prints or *production set* which gives the menu of activities from which it must choose. Given the prices of all inputs and outputs which the firm regards as beyond its own control, the firm will choose from the menu the activity which is most profitable, that is, which gives the maximum difference between the value of outputs and the value of inputs. The activity choice of each firm thus depends in principle on the prices of all goods.

At this stage, a crucial convention and a crucial assumption is introduced. The convention is this: Goods are distinguished by their physical attributes, their location, the date of their delivery, and by the state of nature. (A state of nature is a complete description of the environment which is independent of the actions of agents.) The crucial assumption is that all goods thus defined have markets, that is, each of them has a price. Thus, for instance, there is a price quoted today for umbrellas to be delivered in Cambridge on Christmas Day 1980 if it rains. This is not a very realistic assumption and I return to it. Here we may note that at least some of the disorders of a capitalist society which Keynes considered can be traced to the absence of some of these Arrow-Debreu markets. With this crucial assumption, profit maximization entails the choice of an activity which specifies inputs and outputs at each date and location and in each contingency. Since all goods as defined have current markets, the firm undertakes no uncertainty.

The household, when the story starts, is endowed with a basket of goods (which includes its stock of leisure of a certain type which it can supply as labor to firms), and with certain entitlements to shares in the profits of firms.[1]

The household takes prices as given. Its choice menu consists

[1] The taking of these initial endowments as exogenous has been criticized and much misunderstood, in particular by Marxist critics. For instance, it is often argued that this makes the distributions of income and of wealth exogenous. But to go from the distribution of physical endowments to the distribution of wealth, we need to know the value of the endowment and that depends on prices and these are fully endogenous. In any case, even Marxists have to start the clock sometime after Neanderthal man, and when they do they will find people equipped with axes, seed, and the like, and they will not attempt to explain these possessions further.

of all those bundles which it could physically consume and which it can also "afford." A bundle can be afforded if the cost of purchases does not exceed the receipts from sales. With our definition of goods and our assumption on markets, borrowing and lending and indeed all intertemporal transactions are included in this notion of affording. For instance, selling (or buying) a dollar for delivery next year is equivalent to borrowing (lending) a certain sum now. The household is now supposed to choose a bundle such that there is no other bundle in its choice menu which it prefers. The household choice will thus in general depend on all prices and on the household's endowment.[2]

An equilibrium of the economy is a state in which the independently taken decisions of households and firms are compatible. Thus it is a set of prices such that if they ruled there is a profit maximizing choice of firms and a preference maximizing choice of households *such that the total demand for any good is equal to the amount of it initially available, plus the amount of it produced.* The equilibrium prices impose order on potential chaos. To show that these equilibrium prices can indeed be found, one needs a number of further assumptions. The most important of these is the absence of significant economies of scale in production.

But the theory goes further than showing that order is a possibility in a decentralized economy. It shows that an equilibrium has this property: that there exists *no* reallocation of goods such that *every* household attains a position preferred by it to its equilibrium position—*at least one household must be made worse off by every such reallocation.* The equilibrium allocation is thus shown to be *Pareto-efficient.* It is important to understand that this does not mean that the allocation is just. Indeed, there are many Pareto-efficient allocations (in general a continuum). Under certain assumptions, in particular the absence of increasing returns to scale and non-convex preferences,[3] one can show that each of these allocations could be a competitive equilibrium for some distribution of endowments. That is, by varying the distribution of endowments we change the equilibrium allocation (and prices), but every equilibrium is Pareto-efficient. Or put differently: Every Pareto-efficient allocation can be decentralized into a competitive

---

[2] We do not have to include its entitlement to profit here separately, since we already know these themselves are, uniquely, given once prices are.

[3] Suppose a household is indifferent between a and b, two points in commodity space (one axis each good). Preferences are non-convex if some point c, with $c = \alpha a + (1-\alpha)b$, $0 < \alpha < 1$, is inferior to both a and b.

equilibrium. Hence the moral questions concern the distribution of endowments, and equilibrium as such is only of limited moral relevance. A bad nomenclature (Pareto-optimum) in the literature, together with much carelessness in textbooks, often misleads people into thinking that there is some theorem which claims that a competitive equilibrium is socially optimal. There is no such claim.

It is convenient to break off the account here and to take stock. It is clear from what has already been said that in part at least General Equilibrium Theory is an abstract answer to an abstract and important question: Can a decentralized economy relying only on price signals for market information be orderly? The answer of General Equilibrium Theory is clear and definitive: One can describe such an economy with these properties. But this of course does not mean that any actual economy has been described. An important and interesting theoretical question has been answered and in the first instance that is all that has been done. This is a considerable intellectual achievement, but it is clear that for praxis a great deal more argument is required.

Friends and critics

The theory itself has often suffered a good deal from its friends. Some friends—in what might be called roughly, and a bit unfairly, "Chicago" economics—have taken the theory in practical applications a good deal more seriously than at present there is any justification for doing. Paradoxically they are rather hostile to its abstract foundations, yet are happy to put a great deal of weight on them. For instance, Milton Friedman's definition of the natural level of unemployment is a good example of application outrunning applicability. I return to these friends again briefly below. Other dangerous friends are certain textbook writers. Enemies find their books an endless mine of careless language and slipshod claims. Whole books have been written to refute some textbook scribblers, whose besetting sin is that they use the theory mechanically and apparently without understanding. For instance, there are many accounts to be found of the proposition that a free-trade equilibrium is Pareto-efficient for the world as a whole. Very rarely do these textbooks spell out completely and precisely what is required to reach this result, in particular, absence of increasing returns and a complete set of Arrow-Debreu markets. If these assumptions were stated and discussed, they might be less inclined to declare free trade "optimal." As it is, their concentration on the case of two goods, for "expository reasons," leads them to forget that this device stops them from discussing intertemporal problems, that is, at least half the story. I often wonder whether other subjects suffer as much from textbook writers.

The enemies, on the other hand, have proved curiously ineffective and they have very often aimed their arrows at the wrong targets. Indeed if it is the case that today General Equilibrium Theory is in some disarray, this is largely due to the work of General Equilibrium theorists, and not to any successful assault from outside. Before I discuss this disarray, I shall very briefly consider some recent critics.

One view frequently expressed is that the neoclassical theory is preeminently concerned with the allocation of given resources among alternative uses and that it is thus best considered as relevant to a theory of exchange, rather than to a theory of production and growth. For example, it is said that the theory begins "not with production but with exchange" and then "adds on" production "to make possible the indirect exchange of factor services for final commodities" (Walsh and Gram, 1979). This is then contrasted with classical theory which apparently "starts" with production. It is very hard to make anything of this argument. I do not see in what sense General Equilibrium Theory, except perhaps historically, "starts" with exchange or, for that matter, with production. Both take place and are incorporated in the theory. Nor is it easy to see why so much fuss has been made about exogenously given endowments. No sensible theory would, as I have already noted, start with Neanderthal man. At whatever date we start, we had better take the available resources at that date, and their distribution, as exogenously given by history. Starting with these endowments, an economy has a large number of possible futures which, among other things, depend on technological "knowhow" and the rate at which durable inputs are augmented. General Equilibrium Theory considers a very narrow subset of these futures, i.e., those which are Arrow-Debreu competitive equilibria. This is indeed restrictive, but that is not the issue here. These futures are characterized by accumulation, and the distribution of wealth is an outcome and not a given. Among other things which the theory accomplishes is an end to the nonsensical view that intertemporarily, or because there is production, the notion of opportunity cost loses its relevance either for explanation or planning.

It is possible that the outputs produced in an Arrow-Debreu

economy in the far distant future are independent of its initial endowments. That would mean that in such an economy the relative scarcities prevailing now would have no influence on the relative prices and rentals in the distant future. This should be enough to persuade the critics that the theory is not committed to a relative scarcity theory of distribution, though they seem to believe it is and that often motivates them in their attacks. General Equilibrium theorists are aware that some inputs are reproductive and production is an integral part of the theory they study.

It is of course the question of distribution which is the most urgent for many of the critics. Many of them are after a theory which will explain the distribution of income between classes, specifically between workers and capitalists, and they wish to formulate the theory in such a way that class conflict and power become central explanatory variables. It is perfectly true that General Equilibrium Theory is not suitable for this project; the question is whether it is in direct conflict with it, or more modestly, whether it can be of use in the ambitious projects of the critics.

Suppose that it was claimed that a particular class-conflict theory can explain the prevailing level of wages. In looking at this claim, one might ask whether at those wages any one capitalist could increase his profits by hiring more labor than he does. If the answer is yes, and more labor is not hired, then there is something to explain. Or it may be a way of explaining something, such as a more or less explicit convention not to compete for labor. If, on the other hand, no capitalist is tempted to change his hiring, then each worker is worthy of his hire and the marginal productivity relations hold. *The point of the argument is this: The fundamental element of neoclassical theory, that agents will, if it is open to them, take actions they consider advantageous, cannot be ignored by any grand theory of power and conflict*. Indeed, if such theories ever mature, this feature of the situation may also be central for them. There may of course be more sociologically based definitions of "advantageous" and a much broader class of actions than the neoclassical ones may have to be considered. But it is very hard to see how anything can be achieved without at some stage coming to grips with the agent and his interests. It is therefore not at all clear that from the vantage point of such an achieved theory, General Equilibrium analysis will not be seen as a stepping stone rather than as a *cul de sac*.

There are two further points to make. The first one is this: There exists at present no alternative theory which explains what General Equilibrium Theory seeks to explain, and in particular none which does this by means of consideration of power and class conflict. Ask the Marxist economist why the composition of output is what it is and at best you will get a Leontief answer which is a linear General Equilibrium answer. Ask him to explain relative prices and you get the "transformation problem" which you surely do not want. Ask him to predict the "subsistence" wage of Western industrial workers on the basis of power and conflict; ask him to study the impact of OPEC on techniques of production; indeed, ask him to explain recent trends in the distribution of income, and you will find that he has either nothing to say or that he gives answers which in no way conflict with an analysis starting from neoclassical premises. He may have deep things to say about the "innate laws of history" but he is likely to offer stones in those areas where General Equilibrium Theory provides the basis for some answers. These answers, of course, may be wrong. But the point remains: There are no credible rivals in answering the particular questions which General Equilibrium analysis has posed. (On the other hand, as I argue below, these questions may be too narrowly and academically based.)

Does not the classical revival led by Sraffa (1960) present a valid challenge and a well formulated alternative to General Equilibrium Theory? My second point is that the answer to this question is no. I have documented this answer at length elsewhere[4] and it would be inappropriate to repeat it here. I accordingly simply assert that there are no logically coherent propositions of Sraffian analysis which are not also true propositions of General Equilibrium analysis, and although the classical revivalists often speak of the importance of power and of conflict, these find no formal place in their theory. They do sometimes argue that the rate of profit is determined by these forces, but they leave the manner of it impenetrable.

Buttressing the defenses

The ease with which so much current critique of General Equilibrium analysis can be countered is potentially dangerous. For as I said at the outset, the citadel is not at all secure and the fact that it is safe from a bombardment of soap bubbles does not mean that it is safe. Fortunately, those "inside" have begun to build new walls and to lay new foundations.

[4] In a forthcoming book, *Neo-classical Economics and its Critics.*

The first important need is to develop the theory so that it can deal with a larger range of questions than it now does. For instance, it is not possible to pose any monetary questions in the context of an Arrow-Debreu model since, according to that construction, money would have no role and hence would not be viable. Similarly, the theory cannot explain a market in shares, and it cannot take account of certain forms of uncertainty and certain forms of market expectations which are important in Keynesian theory and important for policy. Oligopoly and imperfect competition have also been abstracted from and the theory does not allow one to answer interesting questions which turn on the asymmetry of information among agents. For all of these purposes, the strict assumptions of the theory will have to be restyled—with possibly fateful consequences.

There is also a canker at the heart of the theory. This arises from the logical necessity that a theory based on rational self-seeking actions ensures that its equilibrium notion is indeed that of a state in which no agent can improve himself by any action. But all General Equilibrium Theory has done is ensure this *provided market prices are independent of these actions.* Moreover, we have not considered the possible actions of agents which consist in forming a coalition. When these matters are seriously considered, the set of economies for which General Equilibrium could be the appropriate theory shrinks. In particular, it is generally true that the theory can apply only to "large economies," i.e., economies with many (indeed perhaps a continuum) of agents.

Recent work by Ostroy (1976) and Makowski (1979) allow one to clarify part of this problem. Consider an equilibrium allocation for an economy with "n" agents. Suppose now that one agent withdraws from the economy. If in the equilibrium with "n-1" agents all of these do as well as before when there were "n," if indeed their allocations remain unchanged, then the withdrawing individual has no power in the economy—he cannot harm or indeed aid anyone. This is called by Ostroy the "no surplus" condition. Each agent contributes exactly as much to the economy as he takes out. It can be shown that "no surplus" is a condition which must be satisfied if rational agents are to treat prices parametrically as General Equilibrium Theory supposes to be the case. For if the no-surplus condition does *not* hold, an agent can by his actions affect the equilibrium prices of the economy. In general, this condition will only be satisfied in large economies, although there are some special small-economy examples.

This line of analysis has close but not yet completely understood connections with the theory of the core. Consider any arbitrary allocation of goods in an economy without production. Ask whether any group of agents (which includes the group of all agents) could each feasibly improve themselves by re-allocating the goods which they have among themselves. If such a group exists we say that it blocks the given allocation. An allocation is in the core if it cannot be blocked by any group (coalition). Notice that prices and markets do not enter into this definition and that the core could be considered a sort of social equilibrium.

Now it can be shown that for large economies the only allocations in the core are in fact the equilibrium allocations of General Equilibrium analysis. On the other hand, for "small" economies there are core allocations which are not equilibria of this kind. But such allocations have considerable claim to be called equilibrium allocations. Production causes further problems.

The outcome of all of this is that one must agree that the Arrow-Debreu theory will run into logical difficulties in small economies; that is, those in which the actions of a single agent can affect equilibrium outcomes. Yet as formulated, the theory stipulates a finite number of agents and takes these as given. Strictly speaking, then, the received theory is inconsistent. It is also incomplete. For though one can argue that it is reasonable to take the number of households as exogenous, this is not so when it comes to the number of firms. In fact we have here another difficulty with the theory which does not turn on its realism and relevance.

For the firm is a shadowy figure in General Equilibrium Analysis. It is simply an agent which converts inputs into outputs. But why is not every household its own firm when increasing returns have been ruled out? Why does not every firm produce all the goods there are? Why is the number of firms finite? It would seem that to make sense of firms at all we must at least stipulate the existence of set-up costs and so allow for some increasing returns. Once again, by excluding these the existing theory is dangerously close to being inconsistent. It certainly has not answered the question why the number of firms is what it is. Recent work by Novshek and Sonnenschein (1978) and by Hart (1979) has gone some way to rectifying this difficulty regarding economies which are large relative to the set-up costs of firms. But for economies which are not large in this sense, we have no theory at present. (It should be added that the work referred to relies on a Cournot-Nash approach which itself is not free from objections.)

Thus, there are purely theoretical problems which General Equilibrium Theory has left unresolved, and it is only quite recently that logical holes have been plugged by an appeal to large economies. The latter in a loose sense are economies in which agents are without economic power. Therefore, as I have already argued, those who regard power as central to economic understanding must look beyond classical General Equilibrium Theory. I rather count myself among those, and my earlier strictures were directed at the unfortunate fact that no serious work in new directions is available.

If Arrow-Debreu economies take no heed of power, they are also cavalier in their treatment of time. *The assumption that all intertemporal and all contingent markets exist has the effect of collapsing the future into the present.* A man who wants to exchange labor today for orange juice tomorrow *if he has a cold,* can do so today by selling current labor and buying the contingent contract: orange juice tomorrow if I have a cold and nothing if I do not. Such a man must form expectations on the probability of getting a cold but not of any market variables. This scenario can be attacked on the grounds of realism and relevance. We know that many of the stipulated markets do not exist.

But it can also be questioned on more fundamental grounds. These are of two kinds. First, in the example it may not be possible for a second person to observe whether I have a cold or not, and so the seller of the contingent orange juice would be in trouble. In general, when agents have different information, some of the required markets cannot exist (Radner, 1971). Second, if exchange is costly (because agents must find one another and/or shops and advertising are required), then certain markets will not open because it does not pay to do so. Both these considerations suggest that the conditions for all Arrow-Debreu markets to exist are very restrictive indeed.

Once these markets are incomplete, rather terrible things happen to the theory. The economy will now have trading at every date—we are dealing with a sequence economy. Agents' actions at any date will now depend on their beliefs concerning *future* events (e.g., rain or shine, war or peace, cold or no cold) and on the prices which will rule *given these events.* But we have no theory of expectations comparable to our theory of household or firm choice; that is to say, we certainly have no axiomatic foundations for such a theory and scarcely have we a psychologically plausible account.

Two steps

There are two steps one can take. One is to take expectation formation as exogenous and to restrict attention to short period equilibria. That is, consider only those current prices which, given the expectation formation and given that agents have done their best for themselves with the expectations, will clear current markets. (See Grandmont, 1977, for a survey.) In the next period, of course, expectations may be falsified and a new equilibrium in then current prices may be established. Taking this route means that the price mechanism will no longer ensure Pareto-efficiency in the usual sense. On this account, then, the economy staggers from one short period equilibrium to another, and a good deal of this rests on unexplained expectations formation.

The other route is to invoke Rational Expectations. Price expectations are rational if each agent correctly predicts the equilibrium prices which are associated with every possible state of nature.[5] A Rational Expectation Equilibrium obtains if the optimizing actions of agents in the light of their rational expectations lead to the clearing of markets at all dates. Once again, such an equilibrium (if it exists) is not Pareto-efficient in the usual sense, since the absence of some markets still prevent mutually advantageous exchanges between agents. Rational Expectations themselves are justified by the argument that rational agents will learn what is the case. The argument at present is ill-founded in theory for it must be shown that agents *could* learn. That, except for examples, has not been demonstrated. Just as classical General Equilibrium Theory has never been able to provide a definitive account of how equilibrium prices come to be established, so Rational Expectation Theory has not shown how, starting from relative ignorance, everything that can be learned comes to be learned. The obvious route here is via Bayes' Theorem but there are formidable difficulties in General Equilibrium application.

Put at its mildest, the sequence economy has presented problems of market expectations which are not yet resolved. Unfortunately, this is not all. In a sequence economy, it is not at all clear what it is that the firm should maximize; or, to put it differently, it is not clear what we mean by the best interest of shareholders. Once again, the villain is the absence of some markets. Suppose shareholder "a" wants the production plan of his firm to change by substituting some output of rainwear for summer frocks. He at-

[5] There are other more econometrically based definitions which are more or less equivalent to the above.

taches a high probability to a rainy summer. Shareholder "b" wants the reverse change because his climatic beliefs are the reverse of those of "a." In an Arrow-Debreu economy, this situation would lead to mutually beneficient exchange in contingent contrasts between "a" and "b." As it is, the two just disagree. A very large literature has grown up on this subject (most recently Grossman and Hart, 1979). But while there are many suggestions, the issues are fundamentally unresolved. This is extremely serious for neoclassical theory since simple profit maximization has been a cornerstone of the analysis. It may well be that the theoretical difficulties which we face when we have decided to take missing markets seriously will only be resolvable by a managerial theory of production.

As I have already noted, the lack of some Arrow-Debreu markets can be partly explained by the difference in information available to different agents. But the problems with information do not stop there. Classical General Equilibrium Theory assumes that every agent knows all prices and that every agent has all the information that is needed about every good. Think of a second-hand motor car or the hiring of a new Assistant Professor to see that it would be interesting to relax the last assumption. Once again, it turns out that the received theory is less robust than one might wish.

All sorts of new problems arise, but also all sorts of new insights have been gained. One of these is this: Sellers must find a way of signalling the quality of what they have to sell. In the labor market, this may be done by means of educational qualifications. These are costly to acquire but one may reasonably postulate that the better worker has a lower cost of doing so. One then studies a "signalling equilibrium" which is a schedule of wages such that no worker has an incentive to change the qualifications he acquires and employers have no incentive to change the schedule relating wage to qualification. In a splendid early work, Spence (1974) showed that there are many such equilibria, so that there is no presumption that the resources used in acquiring qualifications are used efficiently. Recently certain weaknesses in this analysis have been corrected. But this is only one example and many other cases have been studied. In particular, much attention has recently been given to cases where information is market dependent. For instance, in accident insurance the choice of contract by the agent may reveal to the insurer his accident probability. In a most fruitful paper, Rothschild and Stiglitz (1976) have shown that in these cases no equilibrium may exist. The reasons for this have been further investigated by Hahn (1977).

None of this has yet been properly integrated into General Equilibrium analysis. At the first attempts, some unexpected problems were encountered. If agents have asymmetrical information before the market opens, it may be the case that when it does open the market price will reveal all the information there is to everyone. (Think of someone with special knowledge trying to cash in on the stock exchange.) But then special information is worthless to its possessor. On the other hand, if no one had the special information, then the equilibrium would be different and it would be worthwhile to acquire it. This paradox—crudely summarized here—has been much studied recently and with some success. It appears that the situation will arise rarely or not at all if the information mart is noisy (Radner, 1979).

Lack of information concerning prices leads to search for the best bargain. This has been much studied in the context of the labor market. One can, on certain hypotheses, calculate the optimum search strategy. There is interest now in the idea of a search equilibrium—that is, a state where there are always some agents engaged in search but there is no tendency for their number or the relative prices to change. This is at the bottom of Friedman's "natural rate hypothesis," the proposition that there is an equilibrium account of unemployment of those engaged in search. This literature has led to the view that most of the unemployment which we observe is voluntary, and it leads me to the last topic which space permits.

No meaning can be given in classical General Equilibrium Theory to the notion of an equilibrium with involuntary unemployment. The neoclassical axiom, that wages will fall as long as not all those wishing to work can find a job, sees to that. In this world, there is no occasion for Keynesian policies. Indeed no very good sense can be made of the Keynesian opus, a circumstance reinforced by the fact that Keynes and most of his followers never attempted to ground their theory rigorously. But certainly Keynesian theory and policy cannot be reconciled with classical General Equilibrium Theory.

But General Equilibrium Theory has never justified its pricing axiom and certainly has not given any account of how wages are set when the economy is out of equilibrium. When, however, one looks for such a theory taking account of hiring costs, the divergence of interest between the employed and unemployed, the risk aspects of the labor contract and the possible formation of coalitions of workers, it becomes clear that there may be no inducement to change wages even when there is involuntary unemployment. There is as yet no definitive theory, but there are strong indications that the rational interests of the agents involved may result in some wage inflexibility. This line of research also reveals quite generally that if price changes are themselves the outcome of rational assessment of their consequence for the agent making the change, then we can no longer take the neoclassical axiom for granted. This in turn means that we must consider new equilibrium notions. At least this is so for economies which are not large in the appropriate sense.

In this new equilibrium we think of agents observing not only the prices at which they can trade, but also any limits there may be on the amount they can trade. Thus an unemployed worker notices that the likelihood of selling his labor at the going wage is less than certain and he adjusts his other actions, such as his consumption, accordingly. Agents must now consider whether they can affect the limitations on their trading by offering to trade at different prices. The farmer who cannot sell all his apples must consider the consequences of lowering his price. An employer who sees workers have been constrained in their sale of labor must consider whether to lower the wage. If there are monopolistic elements in the economy and, more generally, if the economy is not large enough, there may now be states in which agents are constrained in their transactions and yet prices do not change. Such a state would have strong claims to be regarded as an equilibrium. It is clear that this could be consistent with involuntary unemployment.

The correct path

These new, non-Walrasian equilibrium concepts are in their infancy. No complete or fully convincing theory is available. But I consider them to be on the right lines for the following reason. There is overwhelming evidence to suggest that production and investment decisions are taken on the basis of calculations of expected demand. If you gave General Motors all the prices which will rule in 1981 and nothing else, they would not be able to formulate plans for 1981 simply because they know that they cannot sell (and buy) all they want at these prices. If you like, nonperfect competition must be invoked to account for this. General

Equilibrium Theory as we now have it cannot deal with this situation. But it is a situation for which we should like to have a theory. When we have it, the present theoretical disillusionment with Keynes will, I conjecture, be reversed.

If we think of an economy in non-Walrasian equilibrium with involuntary unemployment, it would seem that Keynesian policies would once again come into their own. To this it has been objected that fully foreseen policies—as all systematic ones in principle can be—will be ineffective. For example, if, when there is X percent unemployment, government spends Y percent more, and this is anticipated, then it will be known that prices will be higher and agents will demand less and offset the government injection. These arguments seem false and are certainly unproven. Those which I have seen are based on unexplained linear macro equations, and essentially rely on the neoclassical axiom that prices must change as long as there is a constraint on transactions. I cannot here develop the full argument,[6] but only dogmatically assert that there are good grounds for believing that we shall soon have satisfactory theories of non-Walrasian equilibria and that these are highly likely to leave scope for government macro-policy to be effective.

There is, of course, much more to say that is outside the confines of this article. As I see it the situation can be summed up as follows. Classical General Equilibrium Theory is a major intellectual achievement. It describes a situation where private self-interest, governed only by market prices, can be consistent with a coherent and orderly economy. We now know that, generally speaking, the original postulates must be augmented by appealing to "large" economies. This leaves an obvious lacuna—the "small" economy. Similarly, we know now that the theory is very sensitive to the postulate that all goods have markets and that it has assumed away many interesting informational problems. The journals are full of papers addressed to these matters and while we are still in the tunnel there are also chinks of light. If we successfully reach the end, I believe it will be found that the route has been straighter and cleaner than it would have been had we not started from General Equilibrium Theory. The theory itself, however, is likely to recede and be superseded. There seems absolutely no reason to believe that the new theory will have been anticipated by some defunct 19th century economist or that it will be in the form of linear identities. Nor, on the other hand, does it seem likely

[6] But see McCallum, "Professor Hahn on Unemployment," and my reply in *Economica* (forthcoming).

that it will give much support to those who are now teaching politicians from vulgarizing neoclassical textbooks.

BIBLIOGRAPHICAL NOTES

K. J. Arrow and G. Debreu: "Existence of an Equilibrium for a Competitive Economy," *Econometrica,* 1954.
G. Debreu: *Theory of Value,* John Wiley and Sons, 1959.
M. Friedman: *The Optimum Quantity of Money,* Macmillan and Co., 1969.
J. M. Grandmont: "Temporary Equilibrium," *Econometrica,* 1977.
S. J. Grossman and O. Hart: "A Theory of Competitive Equilibrium in Stock Market Economies," *Econometrica,* 1979.
F. H. Hahn: "On Equilibrium with Market-Dependent Information," in *Quantitative Wirtschaftsforschung Studien,* J. C. Mohr, Tubingen, 1977.
O. Hart: "Monopolistic Competition in Large Economies with Differential Commodities," *Review of Economic Studies,* 1979.
Hollis and Nell: *Rational Economic Man,* Cambridge University Press.
L. Makowski: "A Characterisation of Perfectly Competitive Economics with Production," Economic Theory Discussion Paper No. 25. Cambridge.
W. Novshek and H. Sonnenschein: "Cournot and Walras Equilibrium," *Econometrica,* 1978.
J. Ostroy: "The No-Surplus Condition as a Characterisation of Perfectly Competitive Equilibrium," mimeo, 1976.
R. Radner: "General Equilibrium with Uncertainty," *Econometrica,* 1971; "Rational Expectations Equilibrium: General Existence and The Information Revealed by Prices," *Econometrica,* 1979.
M. Rothschild and J. Stiglitz: "Equilibrium in Competitive Insurance Markets," *Quarterly Journal of Economics,* 1976.
A. M. Spence: *Market Signalling,* Harvard University Press, 1974.
P. Sraffa: *The Production of Commodities by Commodities,* Cambridge University Press, 1960.
V. Walsh and H. Gram: *Classical and Neo-Classical Theories of General Equilibrium,* Oxford University Press, 1979.

9

Real and nominal magnitudes in economics

KENNETH J. ARROW

THERE has been a long-standing doctrine that high levels of employment tend to be accompanied by inflation. Closely related is the view that unemployment or slack economic conditions in general can be relieved by increases in the supply of money. These views have been held by economists of widely varying persuasions and particularly with widely varying views on appropriate economic policy. During the postwar period, the concept of a trade-off between inflation and unemployment was studied empirically and also used as an extension of the basic Keynesian framework of analysis (a needed supplement since the *General Theory* had little to say about price movements in the absence of full employment).

These doctrines imply that "money matters," at least to some extent. They are contrary to the main thrust of general economic theory; rational individuals are interested in the commodities they can exchange and produce. Their motives are measured in "real" terms (in terms of goods), not in "nominal" terms (values expressed in money). If all prices doubled, for example, the real magnitudes are unaltered, and therefore, according to the so-called neoclassical doctrines, all economic behavior should be unchanged. Anything to the contrary is derided as "money illusion."

Thus the theory and practice of economic stabilization have been at variance with the main lines of economic theory. In the last 10 years or so, there has been a tendency to argue that movements in output and employment are governed primarily by real measures. It is held that there is no systematic relation between employment and inflation and that monetary policy can have no predictable effect.

In this article, I argue that the choice between these viewpoints is deeply related to the existence of involuntary unemployment. The view that only real magnitudes matter can be defended only if it is assumed that the labor market (and all other markets) always clear—that is, that all unemployment is essentially voluntary. In this theory, individuals may be unemployed because of errors of judgment—they believe that higher wages can be found by search or waiting. But, it is held, at each moment there is a going wage, and any worker who wishes to work at that wage can do so. The view that only real magnitudes matter, even over the short periods of the business cycle, can only be defended on this extreme view of smoothly working labor markets. If the contrary view is held, that actual unemployment is to a considerable extent involuntary, then monetary magnitudes retain some of their traditional importance for the analysis of and policy toward short-term economic fluctuations.

The choice of numeraire

The neoclassical theory of general equilibrium, expounded elsewhere in this issue by Frank Hahn, argues that *relative* prices guide the allocation of resources. Under competitive conditions, any individual with a supply of one commodity perceives that it can be exchanged for another at some fixed ratio. These exchange ratios must further be consistent with each other: Given three commodities—for example, wheat, washing machines, and medical services—the exchange ratio of wheat for medical services must equal the exchange ratio of wheat for washing machines multiplied by the exchange ratio of washing machines for medical services. If this were not so, any individual could secure any amount of goods of any kind without giving up any by repeated arbitrage. Hence, all exchange ratios between pairs of goods can be determined by singling out a specific good and by knowing the exchange ratios of all other goods for it. These exchange ratios can be thought of as the *prices* of the goods. The good singled out was named the *numeraire* by the French economist Léon Walras (1874), and the term has passed into the English-language literature; the numeraire's price is taken to be 1.

The numeraire in this simple theory has no special significance. Shifting from one numeraire to another should not affect the direction in which resources are allocated. Indeed, instead of choosing a particular commodity as numeraire, one could choose prices so as to stabilize a price index, the cost of a fixed bundle of goods. All such a rule does is to fix the absolute level of prices, which has no significance.

From the beginnings of the equilibrium formulation of economic theory, the question has been raised of how equilibrium prices are to be achieved. General equilibrium theory is supposed to describe a highly decentralized world in which information is widely dispersed. No one can know the prices which will clear all markets or have information to determine them.

General equilibrium theorists have tended to model an adjustment process in which prices are altered according to the discrepancy between supply and demand until the two are equated on all markets. That is, the price of any one commodity increases when the demand for that commodity exceeds the supply and decreases in the opposite case—the familiar "law of supply and demand." Walras, Marshall, Hicks, and Samuelson have all told variations of this story. Notice that, since the supply and demand for any one commodity depends in general on the prices of all commodities, the model implies that the rate of change of any one price depends on the current values of all prices.

This story recognizes the possibility of disequilibrium, of differences between supply and demand on any one market. Unemployment of labor, for example, is certainly not excluded. However, it is postulated that disequilibrium alters a price in such a way as to reduce a market imbalance, at least as far as the effect on that market is concerned. (Since a change in one price affects supply and demand on all other markets, it can be that a movement toward equilibrium on one market will destabilize some other markets. There is no general theorem that price adjustment according to supply and demand leads to the wiping-out of market imbalances on all markets. But this is another issue, best not treated here.) For example, the model implies that wages fall when there is unemployment of labor (supply of labor exceeds demand for labor).

The model is inadequate in not supplying any mechanism by which prices are changed. Who or what changes them? But it would seem to be superior from this point of view to models which postulate a permanent equality between supply and demand, for which the mechanisms are even more mysterious.

What I want to emphasize here and repeat later in varying contexts is that this price adjustment mechanism is *not* independent of the choice of numeraire.

More specifically, the movements of relative prices can be different with different numeraires. Suppose, for example, that at some point of time there is disequilibrium. In particular, suppose that both gold and silver have excess demand—that is, demands exceed supplies for both. If gold is the numeraire, then its price is fixed. If the price of silver responds only to the difference between supply and demand on the silver market, then its price will rise. Hence the price of gold relative to that of silver falls. But, if silver were the numeraire, then exactly the same reasoning shows that the price of silver falls relative to that of gold. Equivalently, the price of gold is now *rising* relative to that of silver.

To be sure, if the prices in fact do move toward equilibrium levels then eventually the choice of numeraire will be immaterial. But in the process of adjustment, which may, after all, be lengthy, the choice even of the unit in which accounts are reckoned may not be irrelevant.

Disequilibrium and the future

A major part of economic activities have a future orientation. An investment is an input now with a view toward future outputs. In a complex market economy, the investor is usually interested in future output not for his or her own consumption but for exchange with others. Saving is refraining from consumption today in order to have consumption in the future, for oneself or one's heirs; or, more precisely, to have the power to consume in the future. Overall, savings must equal investment, for current output set aside as an input to future production must necessarily be unavailable for current consumption. (For simplicity, I ignore here foreign trade.)

If it were possible to have current markets for future as well as present delivery of commodities, then the general equilibrium theory can be extended into the future. Would-be savers can sell their claims today and purchase commodities for delivery in the future. Investors can purchase inputs and finance the purchases by selling today the outputs for future delivery. But very few such forward markets exist in fact. There are some, for a few years in advance, for agricultural commodities and minerals; there are long-term leases of real estate; there are some, not many, insurance contracts which extend into the future; and above all there are credit instruments.

There are good reasons why these markets do not exist, even though they would serve a social purpose. It would be a distraction here to discuss these reasons in detail. Suffice it to say that 1) uncertainty about the future, particularly about the specification and technological production conditions of future commodities in a changing world, 2) differences in information about these uncertainties among the agents in the economy, and 3) the costs of operating markets in narrowly-defined commodities relative to their benefits, together explain the almost complete absence of forward markets.

Under these conditions, how does a system based on current markets allocate resources between the present and the future? In particular, consider for the moment how this allocation would operate in the absence of money.

Consider first the problem of saving. The saver is willing to give up some of his present commodities in return for commodities in the future. Since we do not have markets today for specific future commodities at specific times, repayments must be in the form of some unit of account, which can then be translated into commodities at the prices prevailing at the time of repayment. These contracts are credit instruments, bonds and the like. They may, for example, be denominated in terms of numeraire.

However, there are qualities needed in these credit instruments if they are to be serviceable for saving. The saver does not want to specify too closely the timing of future consumption. There are many accidents and uncertainties in life; in particular, if the saving is destined for bequests, the timing is intrinsically uncertain. In the absence of forward markets, the prices at which future consumption will take place are uncertain, and this uncertainty will affect not only the goods consumed but also the timing of the consumption.

The saver must thus have flexibility in the timing of future spending. This can be achieved in two ways: 1) markets in the credit instrument themselves, so that an individual holding, say, a five-year bond, can sell it if desired after three years; and 2) very short-term bonds, whose repayments can be reinvested if the saver is not ready to consume.

It should now be observed how implicit in this mechanism is the assumption by the saver that future markets always clear. If the bond is denominated in terms of a numeraire, the repayment can be transformed into desired commodities for consumption by selling the rights to the numeraire and buying the desired goods. But the ability to do this depends on the assumption that markets clear. If there is an excess supply of the numeraire, then the saver might not be able to realize the proceeds; if there is excess demand for the goods, he or she might not be able to obtain them. Similarly, if there is an excess supply of bonds, a saver holding bonds may be unable to convert them to consumption when he or she wishes to. The last point creates a premium on short-term securities which achieve the desired flexibility without concern about equilibrium on the securities markets in the future.

To sum up, if it is anticipated that markets may be in disequilibrium in the future, the motives will be altered.

Future disequilibrium is an even more serious problem for investment. If markets are sure to clear in the future, then the amount invested is completely determined by the anticipation of future relative prices (which may well be uncertain). However, suppose that there may be excess supply in the market for the product of the investment process. Then the investment will be geared to the anticipated volume of sales and be much less affected by prices; for if there is excess supply, the amount sold is no longer determined by the firm alone but is also affected by the level of demand.

We touch here on the Keynesian doctrine of effective demand. If markets do not necessarily clear, then on those markets where there is excess supply, the general conditions of demand determine sales. Therefore, if excess supply is anticipated, investment will be restricted accordingly as compared with a situation in which markets are anticipated to clear at all times. In the latter case, investment will be determined solely by prices, since the firm anticipates selling whatever it chooses to produce.

Certainly, businessmen in their calculations consider their future sales as limited by demand; and most empirical work on investment has taken the anticipated output as one of the main determining variables. Neither of these observations is decisive, but they both give support to the idea that investment decisions do not depend solely on anticipations of relative prices and that firms do not anticipate automatic market clearing.

The money supply in disequilibrium

This lengthy exercise has been designed to bring out the importance of disequilibrium to the workings of the economy, in the absence of money. The first part argues the adjustment process precipitated by disequilibrium is likely not to be describable solely in terms of relative prices. This is true even though the equilibrium toward which the system tends does depend only on relative prices. The second part argues that the anticipation of future disequilibria will have important effects on the decision to invest and to save.

How are these observations altered by the presence of money? Money is something more than a numeraire. It is useful to have one commodity which enters as one side of all transactions. It is not merely that exchanges of goods are denominated in terms of a numeraire; the only exchanges that occur directly are between a commodity and money, even though they are primarily intended as intermediate links in the exchange of commodities for commodities.

Since transactions do not occur instantaneously or simultaneously, individuals who sell will be holding money for some short period of time before they buy. Holding money becomes valuable because it makes easier the transitions. Therefore money becomes valuable as such. It may also be a commodity with a use-value of its own, as gold was, but it acquires an additional value because it is the only way of achieving command over goods (I ignore the small role of barter in our economy, though it may be increasing because it eases tax evasion). Modern paper money shows this tendency in an extreme—it has no intrinsic use-value but is valued because of its ability to purchase other goods.

There is an oddly circular characteristic in the value of fiat money —sellers are willing to accept it because other sellers are willing to accept it. However that may be, and several hundred years of speculation and empirical study have not removed the perplexity, we can take the acceptability of money for granted.

We assume then that money is used in all transactions. In particular, prices are denominated in money terms. Further, individuals are willing to hold money to bridge the gaps between buying and selling. This gives rise to demand for money balances. It is reasonable to assume that the desired money holding is proportional to the *money* value of the individual's transactions. It is this observation that gives rise to the well-known quantity theory of money. If the supply of money is given—for example, set by the government issue of notes—then equilibrium requires that supply of and demand for money are equal. Imagine two economies, one of which has twice the money stock of the other, but otherwise identical. Suppose we have determined the equilibrium prices for the second economy. If we guess that the equilibrium prices for the first economy are just twice as large, we find that the money value of transactions is twice as great. In the second economy (with the smaller money supply) the demand for money equalled the supply, since the economy is in equilibrium. Since the first economy has twice the money volume of transactions, the demand for money to be held will be twice as great and will therefore equal the supply for that economy.

Hence, it can be concluded that, in economies which differ only in their supply of money, *relative* prices will be unchanged, and the price levels will be proportional to the money supplies. Thus, money is a "veil" for the real factors which remain dominant. More exactly, monetary policy is "neutral" in the sense that alterations in the stock of money affect no real variables. (The term "real" is used, as usual in economic discussions, to refer to physical quantities as opposed to values denoted in money terms, which are referred as "nominal" magnitudes.) Not only are the flows of commodities unaltered but also the real value of the stock of money—that is, the amount of money deflated by some suitable index of prices. Since, in the pure theory, all prices move together, any index will do.

No one really supposes that a sudden alteration in the quantity of money would have no real effects. On the contrary, there is a long analytic tradition, of which Milton Friedman is the outstanding representative today, which regards fluctuations in the stock of money as the main cause of the disturbances to which the capitalist economic system has been subjected. The abrupt change will produce a disequilibrium which is corrected only over time. Nor does Keynesian theory differ on the implications of monetary disturbances, though it does tend to emphasize the empirical importance of other causes of economic fluctuations.

We have already seen that the process of adjustment in a nonmonetary economy cannot be stated completely in terms of relative prices. In a monetary economy, there are several observations to be made. In the first place, money is always acceptable. Hence, there really cannot be any excess demand or excess supply of money. People hold what they wish to hold. However, there can be disequilibria in other markets, such as unemployment in the labor market or excess supply of goods.

If the money "market" clears, then the quantity theory can still be valid, if properly interpreted. It simply states that the money held is proportional to the money value of transactions (i.e., national income in nominal terms) and equal to the supply. National income in nominal terms can be regarded as equal to the product of real national income by an index of the price level. In equilibrium, real national income is uniquely defined by the conditions that supply and demand are equal on all markets. But in disequilibrium, by definition, the real national income may deviate from the equilibrium value. When labor or other resources are idle, the real national income will in general be below the equilibrium level. There is therefore room for it to increase. The quantity theory of money predicts that an increase in the supply of money will lead to an increase in nominal national income. But it cannot say whether this increase will take the form of an increase in price or in real national income.

There is no really settled theory about the process of adjustment on markets other than that for money. The simplest view would be that the existence of money permits a decentralization among commodities. The movement of any one money price, such as money wages, will depend in the first instance only on the excess demand or supply on the corresponding market. It may still be that the process can come to rest only at an equilibrium in which money is neutral. The relative prices still govern supply and demand themselves, so that the process can come to rest only at an equilibrium in which money is neutral. But the process itself would not be neutral. Suppose there were excess supplies on most markets. An increase in the money supply would have the immediate effect of increasing the real stock of money, so long as prices were responding slowly. This would increase demands and thereby reduce the excess of supply over demand. Hence, real national income would rise. The reduction in excess supply would mean in turn that prices fell more slowly or even rose. Hence, monetary policy could be effective, at least in the short run. The closer the system moved to full employment and market clearing in general, the less the increase in the money stock could translate itself into an increase in outputs and the more it would affect prices.

The simple dynamics suggested above would, in the case of the labor market, relate the rate of change of money wages to unemployment. In a modified form, this relation is known as the Phillips curve, after the Australian economist, A.W. Phillips, who studied it empirically, and was much used in policy analysis during the later 1950's and early 1960's. However, as the era of general price stability gave way to rising prices, the inadequacies of the formulation became empirically evident. It appears that rising prices themselves cause an increase in wages. Even before the empirical evidence was strong, both Friedman and Edmund Phelps were arguing that general principles of economic rationality suggested that the dynamics of wage adjustment should imply movement in real wages. That is, whatever caused workers to seek high wages should cause them to seek high real wages rather than higher money wages.

The present state of knowledge is confused. On the one hand, there is possible evidence that the dynamics of the labor market runs in terms of real wages. None of this evidence can be conclusive because of the difficulties of drawing inferences from such highly interdependent data. On the other hand, there seems no consistent way of setting up a disequilibrium dynamics which can operate exclusively in terms of relative prices.

One way out of this dilemma is suggested by the "rational expectations" school (Robert Lucas, Thomas Sargent, and Robert Barro are leading exponents). They assert that all markets always clear. This indeed means, as we have seen, that money is neutral and that only relative magnitudes matter. But it leaves out several important features. One is the evidence of everyday observation that some people are unemployed and that some businesses would like to sell more at the current prices and cannot find customers. Another is the statistical observation that the economy is volatile in real as well as nominal terms. To meet this, it is necessary to suggest mechanisms whereby the equilibrium magnitudes may change rapidly from one period to the next. This is related to their emphasis on the importance of anticipation in economic life, which will be touched on in the next section.

Anticipating disequilibrium

Let me turn, if briefly, to the influence of money in an economy spread out in time. Again, the possible role of disequilibrium will be emphasized.

Some of the difficulties pointed out earlier in allocating resources over time in an economy without money are alleviated with the introduction of money. Credit instruments are now denominated in money terms; hence, when paid, the lender has a universally valid commodity. Money is itself a means of saving for short periods of time, so that flexibility in future consumption behavior can be achieved. It is, to be sure, a means of saving for long periods also, but an inferior one when interest rates are significantly above zero.

As already clear, the intertemporal nature of the economy implies the importance of anticipations of the future in determining the present. The critical question is whether the anticipation of future disequilibria is an important factor or not. If it is, then it is difficult to maintain the view that nominal magnitudes are unimportant or that money is neutral.

If markets always clear and are always expected to clear, then only current prices and anticipations of future prices affect savings, investment, and other economic decisions. The only way that the economy can change from period to period is for unexpected changes to occur and thereby alter price expectations. Thus it is recognized that an unanticipated increase in the money supply can have a real effect, but an anticipated increase cannot. However, the explanation is a little odd. After all, according to the quantity theory even an unanticipated increase in the money supply should simply manifest itself in a corresponding increase in prices with no real consequences. The rational-expectations school has tended to argue that the willingness to work and produce is influenced by a difference between actual and previously anticipated prices. If the money supply goes up and prices begin to rise, suppliers find that prices are higher than anticipated and therefore produce more. This effect is, of course, not permanent, because the price anticipations are now revised to take account of the new information about the money supply. However, there are temporary real effects. That the productive sector is really that responsive to unexpected fluctuations in prices is not easy to understand. However, the rational-expectations school needs some version of this story to explain why the economy varies as much as it does.

Disequilibrium theorists, such as Robert Clower, Axel Leijonhufvud, and Edmond Malinvaud, stemming from Keynes, argue that the anticipation of future disequilibria can explain why random fluctuations such as occur all the time are amplified (the so-called "multiplier" effect). Consider the demand for consumption goods by workers. If they anticipate unemployment, their demand is reduced from its normal relation with the amount of labor they wish to supply. Suppose at the same time firms anticipate, for whatever reason, that there will be excess supply on their product markets, so they cannot sell as much as they wish at current wages and prices. Then their demand for labor will be reduced below the level of the amount corresponding to what they wish to sell. Clearly, the two anticipations can be consistent with each other, producing the situation observable in most recessions where idle men and idle capacity coincide.

In this situation, an increase in the money supply leads to increased demand, which in turn changes anticipations and that in turn leads to further increased demands.

To be sure, if money prices are decreasing in response to the excess supplies of both labor and goods, the real stock of money is rising, and demand will eventually rise without policy, as noted in the 1930's by Gottfried Haberler, A.C. Pigou, and Tibor Scitovsky. But whatever the magnitude of this effect, it certainly can be enhanced by suitable monetary (or fiscal) policy if the disequilibria are sufficiently persistent.

To repeat myself still once more: The key question, in determining whether changes in monetary magnitudes can have planned effects on real quantities, is whether the fluctuations in our economic system are best described by a model in which prices clear markets at every instant or by one in which market disequilibria persist over months or even years.

10

Post Keynesian economics: solving the crisis in economic theory

PAUL DAVIDSON

THERE appears to be a crisis in economic theory. The tide of events in the last decade has diminished the stature of economists of both neoclassical-Keynesian and monetarist persuasion in the eyes of the public, and the corpus of orthodox neoclassical theory is a shambles. Meanwhile, and even more importantly, there appears to be an economic crisis in the real world which is not unrelated to the crisis in economic theory. For this economic crisis—the second great economic crisis of the 20th century—is being precipitated by policy advice derived from irrelevant schools of neoclassical economic thought.

The Keynesians of the so-called "neoclassical synthesis," who reigned supreme in the American economics profession during the 1950's and early 1960's, must bear some responsibility for this state of affairs; for, despite its name, the neoclassical synthesis was not really a synthesis of neoclassical with Keynesian ideas (as it purported to be) but merely the reassertion of the neoclassical framework with the addition of some Keynesian "macro" terminology. The flavor of some of Keynes' specific policy recommendations was retained, but the essential *logic* of Keynes' economic theory was discarded. Thus the neoclassical synthesis had the result that the fundamental Keynesian revolution was aborted before it could establish roots in the economics profession.

The bearing of this on the present crisis is that the logic of the neoclassical synthesis is essentially pre-Keynesian. Since the pre-Keynesian systems were inadequate for analyzing the real-world economic problems of the 1930's, it is not surprising they are incapable of dealing with the more complex problems of the 1980's.

Keynes was preeminently a monetary theorist. The words "money," "monetary," or "currency" appear in the titles of all his important economic books. Keynes was a firm believer in the importance of money and a passionate advocate of monetary and banking reform, both domestically and internationally. Keynes' writings provide a monetary framework for the analysis of 20th-century production economies involving markets, contracts, money-wages, expectations, time, employment, and output. Although Keynes emphasized the problems of mass unemployment, he also provided a basic framework for dealing with the stagflation problems of modern economies. Economists who have worked to foster the further development of this logical approach are Post Keynesians.

In recent years, there has developed a "Post Keynesian" literature and even a *Journal of Post Keynesian Economics*. As the brace at the bottom of the table on pages 154 and 155 indicates, Post Keynesian economists[1] are primarily an amalgam of those from the Keynes and Neo-Keynesian schools, but are also joined by some right-leaning members of the socialist-radical group, such as Galbraith. Moreover, certain left-leaning members of the neoclassical Keynesian school have exhibited much sympathy for Post Keynesian analysis in recent years (e.g., John Hick's writings of the late 1960's and 1970's). Thus Post Keynesians do not represent a monolithic or puristic approach to the study of either micro or macroeconomics. The analytical framework utilized by Post Keynesians does, however, share certain common propositions (which tend to be downgraded by the other schools, if they are noticed at all).

Post Keynesians also share the view that Keynes provided a revolutionary new *logical* way of analyzing a *real world* economy; and, like Keynes, Post Keynesians believe that only models which are relevant to the contemporary world are worthy of economists' attention. Thus, in a chronological sense, the economists who share these features and views are the only Post Keynesians among the

[1] There is no hyphen between the words "Post" and "Keynesian." In the past there has been a lack of uniformity in labeling schools of thought; hence perceptive readers will note that others have used the term Post-Keynesian (with the hyphen) to designate the school that I have labeled Neo-Keynesian. In order to provide a nonambiguous terminology I have eliminated the hyphenated term from this text and request others to do the same.

various schools of economics listed in the table. The other schools rely primarily on analytical foundations which were developed before Keynes and hence represent regress and not progress in economic science, despite a veneer of mathematical and econometric sophistication.

Economic models and the real world

Economics is a science of thinking in terms of models joined to the art of choosing models which are relevant to the contemporary world. . . . Good economists are scarce because the gift for using "vigilant observation" to choose good models, although it does not require a highly specialized intellectual technique, appears to be a very rare one.
J. M. Keynes, *Collected Works,* Volume IV.

Models used in economics are of two basic types: (a) general equilibrium models, which are characteristic of all neoclassical economics; and (b) historical humanistic models, which were used by Alfred Marshall and by Keynes and are the models favored by Post Keynesians.

Equilibrium is a concept that has not always been well understood, even by economists (see Hahn, 1973). Economists have often used the term with different meanings in different contexts. In the broadest, most generic, sense of it, a market is said to be in equilibrum when, given an initial set of conditions, the market price is such that neither buyers nor sellers wish to alter their market offers. General equilibrium theory, however, uses a restricted definition of equilibrium which asserts that a market is in equilibrium if, at the equilibrium price, the market *clears*—meaning that the quantity demanded equals the quantity supplied. It can be shown, however, that market clearing is a sufficient but not a necessary condition for market equilibrium in the generic sense (see Davidson, 1967). In other words, although it is true that any market which clears will be in a state of equilibrium (in the sense given above), there are conditions under which a market may be in a state of equilibrium—meaning that there are no market forces inducing buyers and sellers to change their offers at the going price—*even if the markets do not clear.* When Keynes and Post Keynesians use the term equilibrium (for example, when they speak of less-than-full employment equilibrium) they are using the concept in its generic sense. Neoclassical economists, on the other hand, use the term equilibrium to mean market clearing.

The notion of a general equilibrium is formed by taking this re-

A Table of Political Economy

	Socialist-Radical	Neo-Keynesian	Keynes	Neoclassical synthesis Keynesian	Monetarist-Neoclassical
Politics	Extreme left	Left of center	Center	Right of center	Extreme right
Money	Real forces emphasized—money merely a tool for existing power structure.	Real forces emphasized, money assumed to accommodate.	Money and real forces intimately related.	Money matters along with everything else.	Only money matters.
Wage rate and income distribution	Wage rate basis of value. Income distribution the most important economic question.	Money wage is the linchpin of the price level. Income distribution very important.	Money wage rate fundamental; income distribution question of less importance.	Wage rate one of many prices. Income distribution is the resultant of all the demand and supply equations in a general equilibrium system. Income distribution a matter of equity, not of 'scientific' inquiry.	
Capital Theory	Surplus generated by reserve army.	Surplus needed over wages.	Scarcity theory (quasi-rents).	Marginal productivity theory and well-behaved production functions.	

Employment Theory	Any level of employment possible. Assumes growth in employment over time. Full employment creates crisis for capitalism.	Growth with any level of employment possible, although growth at full employment emphasized.	Any level of employment possible; full employment desirable.	Full employment assumed; unemployment is a disequilibrium situation.	Full employment assumed in long run; no explicit short-run theory of employment.
Inflation	Primarily due to money wage changes, but can also be due to profit margin changes.	Due to money wage or profit margin changes.	Due to changes in money wages, productivity and/or profit margins.	In long run primarily a monetary phenomenon being related to money supply via portfolio decisions. In short run may be related to Phillips curve.	Primarily a monetary phenomenon in the sense of being related to the supply of money via portfolio decisions.
Well-known representatives:	Galbraith, Bowles, D. Gordon, All Marxists	Mrs. Robinson, Kaldor, Sraffa, Pasinetti, Eichner, Kregel, Harcourt	Harrod, Shackle, Weintraub, Davidson, Minsky, Wells, Vickers	Solow, Samuelson, Tobin, Clower, Leijonhufvud, J.R. Hicks	Friedman, Brunner, Meltzer, Parkin, Laidler
	Post Keynesians				

This is entitled "A Table of Political Economy" because it attempts to associate the various schools of modern economic thought with different positions on the political spectrum, from extreme right to extreme left. Obviously the divisions are not watertight, but the views of individuals within any one school tend to be very close, and where there is overlap among the schools, the overlap tends to be greatest between individuals in schools that are adjacent in the table.

stricted definition of equilibrium, which originally applied only to a single-commodity market, and applying this concept to the whole economic system, which consists of a large number of interacting markets. Thus general equilibrium theory addresses the interaction among markets. This mode of analysis proposes to understand an economic system by positing, instead of a single market-equilibrium price, a set of relative prices at which, if they were simultaneously achieved, all markets would be in a state of equilibrium, both internally and with respect to one another.

Simply stated, a general equilibrium economic system is one in which there exists a set of relative prices for all goods and services (including labor and capital) which will bring about the simultaneous *clearing* of *all* markets. In such a system it is impossible (by definition) to have a situation of (less than full) employment (i.e., an uncleared labor market in which labor market exceeds labor demand).

In the 1950's neoclassical economists (e.g., Patinkin), using this limited equilibrium concept, were able to "prove" (by definition) that Keynes' theory was "*disequilibrium*" analysis, where unemployment occurred only because money-wages were "too high" and were "rigid," so they would not decline in a recession. Of course, neoclassical economists before Keynes were well aware that unemployment was "caused" by wage rigidities, and if Keynes was merely emphasizing these aspects he contributed nothing new to economic theory.

In a famous letter to George Bernard Shaw, Keynes claimed to be "revolutionizing" the way the world thinks about economic problems. As a trained logician, Keynes knew that in order to transform the way the world thinks about economic problems, he had to displace the existing approach by a new set of axioms and logical analysis. He specifically denied that, in his logical framework, reducing money-wages would automatically assure full employment equilibrium (Keynes, 1936, pp. 260-2). Thus Keynes' analytical framework is logically incompatible with all general equilibrium systems for a number of reasons, not the least being that it is based on a wider definition of equilibrium than merely market clearing. Accordingly, Keynes' wider definition must provide a more *General* Theory.

The most crucial limitation of general equilibrium models, however, is their inability to deal with the passage of calendar time. All general equilibrium systems are essentially static or timeless, despite claims by some economists that they can be made to handle time. General equilibrium is timeless in the sense that the equilibrium position is thought to be uniquely determined by an initial set of conditions, preferences, and decisions, all taken at an arbitrary initial instant. Logically there can be no activities which occur after the initial event which were unanticipated (at least in an actuarial sense). Thus there can be no activities which happen after the initial instant that have any effect on the predestined final outcome. Accordingly, the logic of general equilibrium analysis implies that such systems *cannot* provide practical answers for policy makers facing hard decisions when unforseen complications arise and involve activities which will have important ramifications in the uncertain, unpredictable future.

In effect the general equilibrium model depicts a world in which all contracts are signed (*and paid for*) in the Garden of Eden, without any erroneous (false) trades, and in which the "initial instant" decision process completely determines the future history of mankind for every conceivable trick of Mother Nature. In the future course of events, economic actors merely read their agreed-upon lines, and the economic play is performed, though all know—or expect with actuarial certainty—that Hamlet and the others will die in a certain sequence in the last act.

There are certain purely imaginary intellectual problems for which general equilibrium models are well designed to provide precise answers (if anything really could). But this is much the same as saying that if one insists on analyzing a problem which has no real-world equivalent or solution, it may be appropriate to use a model which has no real-world application. By the same token, if a model is designed specifically to deal with real-world situations it may not be able to handle purely imaginary problems.

Post Keynesian models are designed specifically to deal with real-world problems. Hence they may not be very useful in resolving imaginary problems that are often raised by general equilibrium theorists. Post Keynesians cannot specify *in advance* the optimal allocation of resources over time into the uncertain, unpredictable future; nor are they able to determine how many angels can dance on the head of a pin. On the other hand, models designed to provide answers to questions of the angel-pinhead variety, or imaginary problems involving specifying in advance the optimal-allocation path over time, will be unsuitable for resolving practical, real-world economic problems. Moreover, even with regard to this question of optimal allocation, it has been shown by F. H. Hahn that by means of general equilibrium models one can only demonstrate that leaving allocation to market forces will *not* guarantee an optimal solution.[2] In fact, general equilibrium systems were not (and logically cannot be) designed to provide positive guides to resolving the macro-political-economic problems of inflation, unemployment, economic growth, or even the energy crisis. These horrendous economic problems are, however, the perfect grist for the Post Keynesian mill, because it is precisely this sort of problem that the historical and humanistic models employed by Post Keynesian economists are best suited to deal with.

Three propositions

Post Keynesians recognize, of course, that all theories are abstractions and, hence, simplifications of reality. But the purpose of the theory is to make the real world intelligible, not to substitute an ideal world in place of it. The general equilibrium model, however, abstracts from precisely those features that make the real world real —namely, the irreversibility of time and the uncertainty of the future. The characteristics of the historical and humanistic models employed by Post Keynesians may be summarized in the following three propositions: 1) The economy is a historical process; 2) in a world where uncertainty is unavoidable, expectations have an unavoidable and significant effect on economic outcomes; and, 3) economic and political institutions play a significant role in shaping economic events.

1. *The economy is a process in historical time.* Time is a real-world device which prevents everything from happening at once! The production of commodities takes time; and the consumption of capital goods and consumer durables takes time. These processes of production and consumption are essentially irreversible. Thus real time

[2] Intelligent advocates of general equilibrium systems have come to realize that the one and only useful function of general equilibrium analysis is to demonstrate why optimal allocations can *never* be achieved in the real world. In this view, neoclassical systems are only:

> very useful when for instance one comes to argue with someone who maintains that we need not worry about exhaustible resources because they will always have prices which ensure their 'proper' use. Of course there are many things wrong with this contention but a quick way of disposing of the claim is to note that an Arrow-Debreu equilibrium must be an assumption he is making for the economy and then to show why the economy cannot be in this state. The argument will here turn on the absence of futures markets and contingent futures markets and on the inadequate treatment of time and uncertainty by the construction. This negative role of Arrow-Debreu equilibrium I consider almost to be sufficient justification for it, since practical men and ill-trained theorists everywhere in the world do not understand what they are claiming to be the case when they claim a beneficent and coherent role for the invisible hand. But for descriptive purposes of course this negative role is hardly a recommendation. (Hahn, 1973, pp. 14-15.)

is an asymmetric variable, which means, among other things, that we know the past but cannot know the future. Yet economic decisions taken in the present require actions which cannot be completed until some future date. Hence, as Marshall stated in the preface to the first edition of his *Principles*: "(The) element of time is the center of the chief difficulty of almost every economic problem." Keynes' revolution is in the Marshall tradition of emphasizing the presence of time at the center of economic problems. The neoclassical synthesis, on the other hand, by attempting to reformulate the Keynesian revolution in general equilibrium terms, emasculates it by removing from the Keynesian terms their original reference to the historical process.

2. *In a world where uncertainty and surprises are unavoidable, expectations have an unavoidable and significant effect on economic outcomes.* In an uncertain world, economic decisions are continually affected by the decision makers' expectations, and these expectations are shaped by the "inherited stocks" possessed by economic actors—the accumulated results of past guesses, both correct and incorrect. In other words, economic decisions are rarely made on anything like a clean slate. As different individuals or groups approach the same economic circumstances with different "slates," so their expectations and hence their decisions may also differ. Post Keynesians, therefore, emphasize the role played by this heterogeneity of expectations, as well as the importance of the fact that future events *cannot be fully anticipated.* As J. R. Hicks recently noted, "One must assume that people in one's models do not know what is going to happen, and know that they do not know what is going to happen. As in history!" (Hicks, 1977, p. vii.) And Keynes himself clearly recognized that money matters only when we wish to analyze the "problems of the real world in which our previous expectations are liable to disappointment and expectations concerning the future affect what we do today." (Keynes, 1936, pp. 293-4.)

In a neoclassical world, on the other hand, all decisions involving present and all future actions are taken at a single initial instant in time; errors are (at least in the long run) *by assumption* impossible. Thus neoclassical economics implicitly denies human fallibility, for to admit the possibility of error is to admit that a general equilibrium solution via market prices (which are suppose to coordinate people's plans and expectations without altering the initial parameters) need not exist. In a neoclassical system, the existence of competition *guarantees* that no one undertakes erroneous (wasteful) activities, as resources must always be "optimally" allocated.

Neoclassical theorists assume that the uncertainty of the future can be adequately represented by means of probability statements about an economic world which, without being absolutely determinate, is at least statistically predictable. The monetarists Laidler and Parkin, for example, have noted that in neoclassical theory:

> [E]xpectations—even if erroneous—are usually treated as if held with certainty, or it is assumed that any variance in expectations does not influence behaviour. There exists a well-developed analysis, based on probability theory, of individual behaviour in the face of risk elsewhere in our subject and there surely are gains to be had from applying this analysis to aspects of the problems of inflation. This at least would be our view, but there are many economists, notably Davidson (1972) and Shackle (1955), who would presumably regard the application of such analysis as misconceived (though possibly better than assuming all expectations to be held with certainty). They would stress that *uncertainty* in the Knightian sense as opposed to risk lay at the root of the problem. Certainly an analysis of behaviour of this kind would provide an interesting alternative to the approach based on probability. There can be no guarantee *ex ante* as to which line of work will prove more fruitful, as a means of replacing the widespread assumption (often unstated) that people's actions are the same as if their expectations were held with certainty. (Laidler and Parker, 1975, p. 795.)

Replacing the concept of certainty by the concept of a known probability distribution merely replaces the assumption of perfect foreknowledge by the assumption that economic agents possess actuarial knowledge. In such a situation actuarial costs and benefits can be calculated, and the economic agent can act "as if" he possessed absolute foreknowledge (or, in modern monetarist parlance, expectations are "rational" and "fully anticipate").[3] This semantic legerdemain permits neoclassical economists to develop sophisticated theories which replicate the solutions of pre-Keynesian perfect-certainty models while giving the specious appearance of dealing with time and decision making by economic agents facing an uncertain (but fully anticipated!) future. Such literary deceptions are, in fact, required by the neoclassical economists to enable them to reach their invariable conclusion that government intervention to improve employment (by means of fiscal policy) or to fight inflation (by means of incomes policy) is always bound to be ineffective. In the "rational expectations" models, for example, the conclusion that government intervention is futile is connected with the concept

[3] Moreover, in a general equilibrium world, *all* expectations must be realized by events; surprises and disappointments are logically incompatible with general equilibrium.

of a "natural rate of unemployment" (which is the equivalent of full employment in a world of perfect certainty). As Laidler has argued,

> . . . any rate of inflation is consistent with a state of zero excess demand in the economy provided it is *fully expected*. If to this we add the proposition that there is a unique level of unemployment in the economy associated with a situation of zero overall excess demand then we have it by implication that this *so-called "natural" employment rate is consistent with any fully anticipated rate of inflation.* (Laidler, 1976, p. 59, emphasis added.)

Is there really a difference between "fully anticipated" events and perfect certainty?

Modern neoclassical economists have developed models of expectation formation in an attempt to shore up their collapsing analytic structure.[4] These models are, as even their advocates have admitted, "naive," "arbitrary," or "inconsistent." (Laidler, 1976, p. 62f.) "The simplest lesson to be learned from consideration of the rational expectations hypothesis," Laidler concedes, "is that there is likely to be far more to the formation of expectations than the blind application of some mechanical formula to a body of data. . . . [Moreover] we must face the implication that heterogeneity of expectations at any moment is more likely to be the rule than homogeneity." (1976, p. 69.)

Yet the fundamental monetarist concept of a "natural rate of unemployment" *requires,* as the monetarists admit, a "fully anticipated future"—which means a future which "can only be perfectly anticipated in any actual economy if *all* people hold the same expectations since otherwise some expectations are bound to be wrong." (Laidler and Parkin, 1975, p. 743.) Elaborate monetarist models which show that controlling the rate of growth of the money supply is an effective method of fighting inflation (in the long run!) are based, however, on a "natural rate of unemployment" and hence on a fully anticipated future with everyone holding the same expectations.

---

[4] The monetarists have attempted to shore up their collapsing system by adding various expectational-formation hypotheses to their system. "Expectations" permits any outcome in the short run, while expectations either "adapt" or are "rational," and therefore monetarists assume that economic actors either know *at the initial instant* what are the true parameters of the economic system or learn (adapt to) these unchanging parameters. Consequently "in the long run," though we are all dead, the monetarist expectational analysis will be verified! (Elsewhere I have demonstrated that even with such expectational formationmodels added to general equilibrium systems, one cannot rescue the neoclassical system [Davidson, 1978, pp. 370-72].)

Heterogeneity of expectations, which Laidler admits to be the more likely real-world situation, however, precisely means that people have differing expectations about the future. This guarantees that most of those holding expectations today will find, as events unfold, that their expectations were in some degree incorrect.[5] Certainly mistakes, false trades, and, above all, changing economic parameters are unavoidable in the real world. Consequently, the monetarist proposal to fight inflation simply by controlling the money supply has no sound basis. It appears merely to be an article of faith!

In contrast to this neoclassical approach that handles uncertainty as if it were the same as predictable risk, Post Keynesians build upon the fact that the future is uncertain, and as Hicks observed, people know that they do not know the future when they undertake economic actions. By recognizing this obvious fact of life, the Post Keynesians aim, when discussing future events, to be approximately right; whereas the neoclassical economists, in aiming to be precise, end up being precisely wrong. The economic future, Post Keynesians note, is *created* by man, not simply discovered.

3. *Economic and political institutions are not negligible and, in fact, play an extremely important role in determining real-world economic outcomes.* The logical world of general equilibrium theory contains no significant real-world institutions—not even organized commodity or financial markets. That is to say, general equilibrium theorists treat institutions as theoretically negligible, for the same reason that they are committed to the view that the particular configuration of institutions *cannot* have any effect on the final outcome (i.e., the general equilibrium position). In the Post Keynesian world, on the other hand, the real world in which the future is uncertain and events take place in time—in that world economic and political institutions are both influential and prominent in determining economic outcomes, and policy makers neglect them at their peril.

The distribution of income and power is a basic concern of Post Keynesians, particularly in regard of the problems of inflation. With the growth of an industrial society and democracy, people have learned that they can and *should* attempt to control their own destinies. If one gains control of one's income, then one's fate is largely in one's own hands. In modern societies, there are three ways to affect and control one's own income: 1) possess a unique, market-

[5] The rational expectations hypothesis, on the other hand, assumes that the public has complete knowledge of the parameters of the real economic system and hence cannot be "fooled" by government intervention.

able qualification and exercise the monopoly power it provides; 2) organize with others who have similar market capacities in order to exercise some joint monopoly control; and 3) organize and employ political activities to tilt government policy towards improving one's income.

Post Keynesians recognize that in a world whose future is not predetermined by the initial conditions, continuing inflation involves a redistribution of real income *from* the weaker groups to the more powerful. This induces powerful economic *and* political forces, as competing groups attempt to catch up with one another. Thus inflation is symptomatic of a struggle between organized groups, each trying to obtain a larger share of the available national or world income for themselves. Post Keynesians emphasize the importance of bearing in mind that every price is ultimately somebody's income. For example, OPEC's price increase is the way the oil cartel extorts real income from consumers who, if they have any market or political power, demand "cost-of-living" adjustments to their pay so that they will not lose income to the Arabs. If the United States cannot or will not break the OPEC cartel, then we must give up some of our GNP to OPEC. The remaining income must be distributed some way. In an unfettered market system with large business, labor, and governmental units, where all are reluctant to accept a reduction in real income or profits, the struggle over the remainder of the pie will induce a continuing wage-price inflation. If one ignores this phenomenon, one cannot properly compare the effectiveness of incomes policies designed to restrain the income demands of competing groups with that of "planned recessions" achieved by means of tight monetary or fiscal policy.

The goal of restrictive monetary and fiscal policy as anti-inflation devices is to so weaken the various domestic and foreign groups (the euphemism is "squeezing out inflationary expectations") by creating business losses and unemployment that they will not have the strength to continue the struggle. Unfortunately, those that are most likely to be weakened are those with the least power to begin with, while any success with such a severe policy requires, as even its advocates would admit, several years of impoverishing the entire society (by means of recession or slow economic growth). Incomes policies, on the other hand, are designed to obtain a social agreement among the domestic competing groups to limit their demands for real income in a manner which is socially responsible for distributing the remaining GNP and hence limiting current inflation to the size of the OPEC tax on our resources.

In the general equilibrium world, the problem of how to deal with income redistributions over time due to *unanticipated* inflation cannot even arise, because, as we have seen, the system assumes the future is predictable and "fully anticipated." Thus the logic of neoclassical analysis does not even permit the analysis of the problem of distribution over time due to unanticipated inflation, despite pontifical neoclassical statements about the desirability of "indexing" to avoid unanticipated inflation.

The importance of money

Post Keynesians, following Keynes' lead, give particular attention to the human institution of money and other institutions with which it is organically connected. These include the banking and monetary systems; time-oriented markets for goods, factors of production, and financial assets; money contracts for spot and forward transactions; and especially, the money-wage contract as a necessary condition of liquidity over time in any market-oriented production economy organized on a forward money-contracting basis. (A production economy is one in which goods are produced as well as marketed. A pure exchange economy is an abstraction, used by many neoclassical economists, in which production is disregarded and only trade in pre-existing goods is studied. Liquidity involves the ability to discharge one's money-contractual obligations as they come due; this ability depends on either holding sufficient money balances to meet these obligations or holding readily marketable assets which can be quickly sold for money when needed.)

Keynes and the Post Keynesians base their logical analysis on the following inductive propositions: 1) modern monetary economies do not possess any automatic mechanism that assures a tendency towards full employment of resources over time; 2) underemployment equilibrium is a recurring phenomenon in money-using production economies; and therefore, 3) the existence of underemployment equilibrium must be associated with the characteristics of money and related institutions, and with how production is organized.

Money is first and foremost a human institution, organically connected to other economic institutions including the banking system; time-oriented markets for goods, factors of production, and financial assets; and money contracts for spot and forward transactions—especially the money-wage contract. The existence of these interrelated economic institutions produce the need for liquidity over time in any market-oriented, production economy organized on a basis of forward contracts in money terms.

In all modern market-oriented production economies, production is organized on a forward money-contracting basis. A forward contract is simply one that specifies a future date (or dates) for both delivery *and* payment. Since production takes time, the hiring of factor inputs and the purchase of materials to be used in any productive activity must precede the date when the finished product will be at hand. These hiring and material-purchase transactions will therefore require forward contracting if the production process is to be efficiently planned.

The financing of such forward production-cost commitments (the taking of a "position" in working capital) requires entrepreneurs to have money available to discharge these contractual liabilities at one or more future dates before the product is sold and delivered, payment received, and the "position" liquidated. This is the ubiquitous liquidity problem of entrepreneurs in capitalist economies, a problem which, however, is left unattended by mainstream neoclassical economists.

The logic of general equilibrium theory requires that *all* payments be made at the initial instant, and therefore neoclassical theory cannot logically deal with the question of meeting contractual payment obligations at any point of time after the initial instant. Consequently neoclassical economists, by remaining faithful to their theory, truly earn the businessman's traditional gibe: "They have never had to meet a payroll!"

In a general equilibrium world, it is *assumed* that all goods are traded simultaneously in spot markets and all payments are also made simultaneously on the spot, while each person's expenditures are assumed to equal the value of his simultaneous sales. There is never a liquidity problem, for neoclassical models are actually barter systems where, in essence, goods pay for goods at equilibrium prices on the spot. In such a world there is no logical niche for the institution of money, a money price level, or future events that are not already "fully anticipated" and dealt with on the spot. If the real world were similar to, and could therefore be represented by, a logical world of barter economies, then indeed money would *not* matter! Money only matters in an economic world where numerous interconnected sequences of forward contracts in money terms are used to organize productive activities. *But that is our world!*

In a decentralized market economy, then, moving irresistibly through historical time into the uncertain future, forward contracting for production inputs is essential to efficient production planning. And the most ubiquitous forward contract of all in such an economy, as long as slavery and peonage are illegal, is the money-wage contract. Since labor hiring and payment precede in time the delivery of newly produced goods, the price level of new goods depends in large measure on the relationship between the money wage and the productivity of labor. As Arrow and Hahn have written:

> The terms in which contracts are made matter. In particular, if money is the good in terms of which contracts are made, then the prices of goods in terms of money are of special significance. This is not the case if we consider an economy without a past and without a future. Keynes wrote that "the importance of money essentially flows from it being a link between the present and the future" to which we add that it is important also because it is a link between the past and the present. If a *serious monetary theory* comes to be written, the fact that contracts are indeed made in terms of money will be of considerable importance. (Arrow and Hahn, 1971, p. 356f. Emphasis added.)

If Arrow and Hahn are correct, a "serious monetary theory" must give serious attention to the economic role of the *money-wage contract*. It is the "stickiness" of money wages and prices (i.e., the absence of rapid movements), as guaranteed by the law of contracts, that permits capitalist economies to engage in time-consuming production processes and provides a basis for a "sticky" price level of producible goods. Accordingly, forward contracting can be considered as the way entrepreneurs in a "free market" environment attempt to maintain wage and price controls! Indeed, such controls are fundamental to the financing of production processes.

The existence of fixed money contracts for forward delivery *and* payment is fundamental to the concepts of liquidity and money. In such a setting, changes in money-wage rates—Keynes' wage unit—determines changes in the costs of production and the price level associated with the production of goods that profit-oriented entrepreneurs are willing to undertake. The view that inflation (i.e., a rising money-price level of newly produced goods) is a monetary phenomenon makes logical sense only in an economy where time-oriented money contracts (especially labor hire) are basic to the organization of production activities. For clearly, as long as the time duration of fixed-money wage contracts exceeds the gestation period of production, entrepreneurs can limit their liabilities when undertaking any production process. If, however, the institution of long-duration fixed-money contracts begins to break down, the entrepreneur's liabilities may become prohibitively uncertain. Then a "social contract" to limit wage and price movements over long periods of calendar time must be developed to buttress the private institution of lengthy forward contracts, if production processes which require lengthy periods of time are to be maintained.[6]

Post Keynesians contend, therefore, that the existence of some human institution which will guarantee income (i.e., production-cost) restraint over time is a necessary adjunct to developed capitalist economies. Devices that have been proposed for achieving this objective are frequently referred to as "incomes policies."

Liquidity

Liquidity involves the ability to discharge one's contractual obligations when they come due. The capacity to remain liquid requires holding sufficient money balances to meet known upcoming obligations and, in an uncertain world, to meet unknown but potential obligations. (Instead of holding cash one can hold readily marketable [liquid] assets which can be quickly sold for cash when needed and which do not incur significant carrying costs while they are being held.)

According to Keynes (1936, Chapter 17) money and all other liquid assets possess two "essential properties," and it is these two properties which cause unemployment when people reduce their purchases of goods and increase their demand for liquid assets instead. Thus, in the real world, where the future is uncertain, any unexpected event which creates fears for the future may induce a rush toward liquidity which can thereby cause additional unemployment. The two essential properties of liquid assets are: 1) their elasticity of production must be zero (or negligible); and 2) their elasticity of substitution must be zero (or negligible).[7]

When a good is said to possess a positive elasticity of production, this simply means that any increase in the demand for this com-

[6] It would be foolish for entrepreneurs in a free enterprise, market-oriented system to enter into a production process whose gestation period greatly exceeded the duration of forward contracts with his workers (or even his material suppliers). To do so would be to undertake a potentially unbounded liability with no controls on the costs of production and hence no assurance that the entrepreneur had sufficient finance to meet his future payrolls and complete the production process.

[7] For a complete discussion of these technical requirements see Keynes (1936, Ch. 17), Davidson (1978, Chs. 6-9), Davidson (1980). The latter item is followed by a discussion by Bronfenbrenner (1980) and a reply which discusses these matters and their relation to gold.

modity will induce private suppliers to produce more of it by hiring additional workers. To say that money has an elasticity of production of zero is merely to state in the language of the economist the old adage that "money does not grow on trees." Hence money cannot be harvested (produced) by the use of labor. (Most laymen would be appalled to know that the weighty pronouncements and econometric projections given by neoclassical economists are based on a logical structure which assumes that money [or the "numeraire" as it is called in general equilibrium models] can be any commodity and that it is often associated in such analysis with *peanuts*—which, if it does not grow on trees, does grow on bushes. If the logical foundations of neoclassical economists had any relevance to the real world, President Carter might have done better to name brother Billy rather than Mr. Volker to the chairmanship of the Federal Reserve Board.)

Money's zero elasticity of production does not mean that its supply is unalterable. Obviously the money supply can be expanded exogenously by means of deliberate actions of the central bank, or endogenously when the banking system responds to an increased demand for finance. But money's zero production elasticity does have the consequence that an increase in the demand for money does not induce a commensurate increase in the demand for workers to produce it.

If a good possesses a positive elasticity of substitution, this means that, if the *price* of this good *rises*, some of the demand for this commodity will be diverted to some other good (or goods) which is then said to be a substitute for the first. Thus if the price of coffee rises, some people will switch to tea; others may attend the movies more often. The greater the relative diversion of demand away from coffee for any given percentage *increase in its price*, the greater the elasticity of substitution between coffee and other producible commodities. (One of the fundamental axioms of neoclassical theory is "gross substitution," which assumes that ultimately anything is a substitute for anything else, so that if the price of anything rises, people will spend less on it and more on other producible things.)

The importance of these elasticity properties, and their implications for the Post Keynesian, as against the neoclassical, theory of employment, is easily illustrated. Suppose we start from a period of close-to-full employment and then hypothesize that some event causes people to become more worried and cautious about the uncertain future. Many people will wish to postpone or even permanently reduce their current purchases of goods and services, and use more of their current income to buy liquid assets (or just store it in the form of money). This reduction in the public's demand for goods will immediately reduce the sales of industry and cause lay-offs. The increased demand for liquid assets will cause *their* price to increase. But if liquid assets have a zero elasticity of production the laid-off workers cannot be re-employed to produce (or harvest) money or any other liquid asset. (In a neoclassical world where peanuts can be money [the numeraire], laid-off workers would be reallocated and re-employed—by the invisible hand of the rising price of liquid assets—in the peanut fields to harvest more numeraire in response to the increase in demand.)

Moreover, since the elasticity of substitution between liquid (non-producible via the use of labor) assets and producible goods is zero, the hypothetical increased demand for liquidity will *not* be diverted by the rising price of liquid assets back to things which are readily produced by labor (whose prices have not changed). Thus in a Post Keynesian world, the rush to liquidity not only causes workers to be laid-off in industry, but also they cannot be re-employed in producing more of the (liquid) objects that the public now desires.

In my recent published debate with Professor Friedman, he specifically indicates that, in contradistinction to the Post Keynesian analysis, his theoretical framework assumes easily reproducible commodities are good substitutes for money. Accordingly, any change in the demand for liquidity will, on Friedman's model, be diverted into a change in the demand for producible goods such as furniture, household appliances, clothes, and the like. Thus Friedman's logical framework requires the full employment of labor, *in the long run*, since he assumes that everything demanded by people as they spend their income leads, either directly or through a substitution effect, to an equivalent demand for workers. Hence, there can never be a shortage of effective demand.

Keynes thought differently, however, as he made clear in his *General Theory*:

> Unemployment develops, that is to say, because people want the moon; —men cannot be employed when the object of desire (i.e., money) is something which cannot be produced and the demand for which cannot be readily choked off (p. 235).

The acceptance of the "essential properties" approach to liquidity, then, represents a fundamental logical difference between Post Keynesians (who reject the universality of the gross substitution axiom) and *all* neoclassical theorists. These essential properties entail that underemployment equilibrium *can* occur whenever there are what Hahn calls "resting places for savings other than reproducible assets" (1977, p. 31). Neoclassical doctrine holds that equilibrium can occur only in a state of full employment; hence unemployment is regarded merely as a blemish due to some friction in an otherwise perfectly functioning market system. For this reason neoclassicists argue that unfettered markets will, in the long run, work out these blemishes and that government interference merely accentuates them.[8]

Post Keynesians, however, see unemployment as a fundamental problem of any money economy where liquidity considerations are important. Post Keynesians believe that unemployment tendencies are an inherent weakness in any money economy and that only public policy can prevent this weakness from manifesting itself and perhaps destroying an otherwise desirable system of organizing economic activities.

Some closing remarks

The purpose of this essay was to illustrate that there are fundamental logical differences between Post Keynesian theory and neoclassical general equilibrium analysis of either the Keynesian or monetarist persuasions.[9] If the neoclassical view is adopted as the starting point of any economic theory, observed real-world unem-

[8] Logically consistent general equilibrium analysts would argue, for example, that unemployment can be cured by lowering the money wage so that businessmen *substitute* workers for other productive inputs without lowering the level of GNP (income). Keynes and Post Keynesians, on the other hand, argue that reducing wages will not directly increase employment, for such wage cuts will *parri passu* reduce consumers' incomes and hence lower the demand for the output of industry. Instead, if government increases income, employment will rise both directly and indirectly via the multiplier.

[9] Solow, on the other hand, believes that "thus far so-called Post Keynesianism seems to be more a state of mind than a theory" (Solow, 1979, p. 344). Of course, Solow (as he readily admits) is far from an impartial judge of the merits of Post Keynesian analysis *vis-a-vis* neoclassical Keynesianism. Although Solow concedes that he now finds "bits of unorthodoxy incomparably more credible than the things that impeccably orthodox equilibrium theory asks me to believe about the world" (1979, p. 348), he still concludes: "It is much too early to tear up the . . . [neoclassical synthesis] chapters in the textbooks" (1979, p. 354). Perhaps it is "too early" for professors who have made fame and fortune out of such models to be ready to abandon them, despite their common sense which suggests the incredible nature of neoclassical theory; for others who have an earnest desire to resolve the economic problems which are threatening the Second Great Crisis of Capitalism in the 20th century, and who have no vested interest in neoclassical theory, time is running out.

ployment and stagflation phenomena can only be "explained" as *temporary* phenomena due to frictions, short-run price and wage rigidities, or (adaptive? rational?) expectational reactions. In the long run it is believed that a state of economic bliss will be attained by means of unfettered market processes. (This latter is, of course, not a conclusion of the analysis but merely a reiteration of the initial supposition of neoclassical systems.) The object of neoclassical modelling is an "idealized state," i.e., the long-run equilibrium solution, and *all* neoclassical theorists begin with the assumption that full employment is the necessary long-run position of modern production economies.

Arrow and Hahn have shown that in "a world with a past as well as a future and in which contracts are made in terms of money, no [general] equilibrium may exist" (1971, p. 361). In other words, even the *existence* of a full-employment equilibrium position cannot be logically demonstrated for a world of time and money contracts. Thus, economies such as ours—organized on a money-contracting basis over time—may settle down to equilibrium at any level of employment; that is, they may exhibit an unemployment equilibrium *in the long run*, as well as in the short run.

Keynes believed that from the outset economists should model the actual state of the real world, rather than idealized long-run solutions. He wrote in a famous passage:

> But this long run is a misleading guide to current affairs. *In the long run* we are all dead. Economists set themselves too easy, too useless a task if in tempestuous seasons they can only tell us that when the storm is long past the ocean is flat again. (Keynes, 1971, p. 65.)

For members of the Post Keynesian schools the notions discussed above—historical time, uncertainty, expectations, political and economic institutions (especially money and forward contracts)—represent fundamental characteristics of the world we inhabit—*the real world.* We have seen that the idealized state of the neoclassical model cannot exist, even as an ideal, in the temporal setting of the real world. Accordingly, Post Keynesian economists oppose neoclassical analysis as irrelevant to the macroeconomic problems of the 20th century. They believe that their own approach, even if incomplete, is the only one that is able to look with unclouded vision at the problems which most earnestly require attention.

BIBLIOGRAPHICAL NOTES

K. S. Arrow and F. H. Hahn, *General Competitive Analysis* (Holden, San Francisco, 1971).

M. Bronfenbrenner, "Davidson on Keynes and Money," *Journal of Post Keynesian Economics, 2,* Spring 1980.

P. Davidson, "The Dual Faceted Nature of the Keynesian Revolution: The Role of Money and Money Wages in Determining Unemployment and Production Flow Prices," *Journal of Post Keynesian Economics, 2,* Spring 1980.

P. Davidson, *Money and the Real World,* 2nd edition (Macmillian, London, 1978).

P. Davidson, "A Keynesian View of Patinkin's Theory of Employment," *Economic Journal, 77,* 1967.

P. Davidson, "Why Money Matters: Lessons from a Half Century of Monetary Theory," *Journal of Post Keynesian Economics, 1* (1978).

P. Davidson and E. Smolensky, *Aggregate Supply and Demand Analysis* (Harper & Row, New York, 1964).

A. S. Eichner, *The Megacorp and Oligopoly* (Cambridge University Press, 1976).

J. K. Galbraith, "On Post Keynesian Economics," *Journal of Post Keynesian Economics,* (1978).

F. H. Hahn, *On the Notion of Equilibrium in Economics* (Cambridge University Press, 1973).

F. H. Hahn, "Keynesian Economics and General Equilibrium Theory," in G. C. Harcourt, ed., *Microeconomic Foundations of Macroeconomics* (Macmillan, London, 1977).

R. F. Harrod, *Money* (Macmillan, London, 1969).

J. R. Hicks, *Critical Essays in Monetary Theory* (Oxford University Press, 1967).

J. R. Hicks, "Some Questions of Time in Economics," in *Evolution, Welfare and Time,* ed. by A. M. Tang, F. M. Westfield, and J. J. Worley (Heath, Lexington, 1976).

J. R. Hicks, *Economic Perspectives* (Oxford University Press, 1977).

J. R. Hicks, *Causality in Economics* (Basic Books, New York, 1979).

N. Kaldor, *Essays on Value and Distribution* (Free Press, Illinois, 1960).

N. Kaldor, *Essays on Economic Stability and Growth* (Duckworth, London, 1960).

J. M. Keynes, *The General Theory and After: Part II; The Collected Writings of John Maynard Keynes,* Vol. XIV (Macmillan, London, 1973).

J. M. Keynes, *The General Theory of Employment, Interest and Money* (Harcourt, New York, 1936).

J. M. Keynes, *A Tract on Monetary Reform,* reprinted as Vol. IV of *The Collected Writings of John Maynard Keynes* (Macmillan, London, 1971).

J. A. Kregel, *Rate of Profit, Distribution and Growth: Two Views* (Aldine, Chicago, 1971).

J. A. Kregel, *The Reconstruction of Political Economy* (Halsted, New York, 1973).

D. Laidler, "Expectations and the Phillips Trade Off: A Commentary," *Scottish Journal of Political Economy, 23,* 1976.

D. Laidler and M. Parkin, "Inflation—A Survey," *Economic Journal, 85,* 1975.

A. Marshall, *Principle of Economics,* 1st ed. (Macmillan, London, 1980).

H. P. Minsky, *John Maynard Keynes* (Columbia University Press, New York, 1975).

L. L. Pasinetti, *Growth and Income Distribution* (Cambridge University Press, New York, 1974).

J. Robinson, *The Accumulation of Capital* (Macmillan, London, 1956). *Essays in The Theory of Economic Growth* (Macmillan, London, 1962).

A. Roncaglia, *Sraffa and the Theory of Prices* (Wiley, New York, 1978).

P. Sraffa, *Production of Commodities By Means of Commodities* (Cambridge University Press, 1960).

R. M. Solow, "Alternative Approaches to Macroeconomic Theory: A Partial View," *Canadian Journal of Economics, 12,* 1979.
S. Weintraub, *An Approach to The Theory of Income Distribution* (Chilton, Philadelphia, 1958). *Capitalism's Inflation and Unemployment Crisis* (Addison-Wesley, Reading, 1978).

10

Value and capital in Marxian economics

EDWARD J. NELL

NEOCLASSICAL theory roots value in the act of exchange, which is undertaken by the parties in order to gain. The theory shows that under the postulated conditions all parties will gain from exchange in terms of their subjective preferences. This then generalizes into the theory of optimal allocation of scarce rewards by means of the price mechanism, which makes it possible to incorporate production into the theory as a special case of indirect exchange. Value arises from the interactions of isolated, rootless "individuals" acting in terms of their abstract "preferences," expressed as a consistent ranking of the bundles of commodities assumed to be "available" on the one hand and "scarce" on the other. Where these individuals come from, how they are supported, what their preferences are based on, how and by whom the commodities have been produced, and by whose authority the "initial endowments" were conferred—all are assumed to be irrelevant to the foundation of value-in-exchange. Whatever the answers to such questions, value arises because the parties to exchange stand to gain in terms of their preferences, so long as these are consistent and "convex," and goods are scarce. Value arises from convex preferences coupled with scarcity.

One feature of this approach is worth mentioning. Value, which appears to be a relationship between commodities—the value of this chair in apples or in gold or paper money—is shown to be a relationship between, on the one hand, economic agents (their preferences), and between these agents and nature (scarcity) on the other. At this very general level, the neoclassical approach meets Marx's definition of the task of the theory of value, explaining how "exchange of commodities [which] is a definite social relation between men . . . has assumed in their eyes the fantastic form of a relation between things." Beneath this appearance lie the real relationships which hold between people. On this, neoclassicals and Marxists can agree. But then the paths diverge. Neoclassicals ground value in the act of exchange, which in turn is governed by preference and scarcity. For Marx, value arises from the relationships governing the process of production and reproduction—the process which maintains the social order. The key to the working of that process lies in the relation of wages to labor, which is therefore the foundation upon which the theory of value must be built.

Mainstream or mud puddle?

Swimmers in the mainstream of economics have noted how cloudy the waters have become, even at the source. The neoclassical theory of value is no fountain of inspiration, bubbling and sparkling with new ideas. To an increasing number of economists it is a source of intellectual pollution. It doesn't explain demand; its concept of production is naive. Thus it doesn't help with the theory of prices. It is difficult, arcane, and finally rests on assumptions that are not only "unrealistic," but quite simply false. Four sets of complaints are commonly articulated.

First, it bases value on exchange, treating production (in rather an afterthought) as a special kind of exchange. But reproduction-commodities used to produce commodities used to produce commodities . . . (counting support of labor as an input)—makes exchange a moment in the circuit of production and reproduction. Such an input-output account is arguably essential to any analysis of a social system's continued ability to support itself or expand. It therefore seems more fundamental than any account which takes the agents and the supplies of goods to be traded as *given*. But in that case the mainstream theory has its starting point wrong.

Secondly, the agents involved in exchange are typically described with extreme abstraction, although the environment in which they operate is one in which quite definite and historically-specific rules of property apply. Surely it would be more appropriate to develop the theory based not on abstract agents but on the institutional forms, abstracting only from inessential details. This, however, would require a close study of the history and sociology of labor, of the different social classes of households, of the business corporation, and so on, to determine at different periods what were and were not inessential details. It would mean trading generality for content.

Thirdly, the central notion of preference itself is so abstract as to be virtually inexplicable. Interpersonal comparisons of "utility" generally are forbidden; preference scales are usually considered "ordinal," although in certain game theory situations cardinal utility is held to be permissible. But what are these preferences based on? This we are told is a question the economist cannot ask. The grounds of choice are a matter of the agents' ultimate decisions, and the descriptive sciences can do no more than record what their subjects choose. This is a position, central to positivism, which modern moral philosophy has largely thrown over, and economics would do well to follow suit. The observing economist can—and must—question the choices he observes being made, not in terms of his own values and social philosophy, but in terms of the agents'. An agent has not revealed a preference if he has made a mistake, or miscalculated, or forgotten. The point of (theoretically) constructing preference scales from "market data" is to show that the law of demand (that the sign of the substitution effect is negative) can be derived. But this is a "lawlike proposition"; it supports counterfactual conditionals—statements, that is, of the form "what would happen, if. . . ." So the *actual* behavior must reveal the agents' *typical* disposition or commitment to behave in a certain way. And how can we tell whether the behavior we are observing is typical?

The course we normally take in everyday life is to discover whether the agent has *good reason* to behave that way typically. If so, then we can count the behavior as "projectible"; in similar circumstances, he will normally choose such a course of action; it will be a means to an end, or will fulfill his obligations, or is expected and socially approved behavior. In the case of the theory of the firm, this can be done. Selling for a certain price, or buying a quantity of input at a certain price, will contribute to maximizing profit (or growth, or sales, or the value of invested capital—although there is little agreement about which of these is the appropriate target and when). But in the case of consumers, or in the pure theory of exchange, there is nothing to go on. There are no reasons for preferences; they are simply postulated to be there. More of any good is always better, but increasing abundance provides diminishing improvement. No other explanation is given—and within the framework none is possible—of why a consumer prefers one bundle of commodities to another, or is indifferent to the choice. But this is obviously wildly at variance with everyday life and with the informal logic of the process of making comparisons and choices. When we choose a bundle of goods we can always explain why, and we frequently have to, to our wives, children, employers, and tax collectors. More is not always better, not even somewhat better. Goods are chosen because they have characteristics that serve needs or functions. These needs, in turn, depend on what kind of household it is; that is to say, on status, family, and employment. The characteristics of a commodity and the fact that these will serve or help serve certain clearly defined functions provide the reasons for choosing the good. Choices must be made subject to a budget, and this sets up a very typical economic problem. But the details of this problem are not abstract at all. They depend on what kind of household it is, the social as well as economic constraints it faces, the ordering of priorities among the needs that have to be met, and so on. Since the kind of household depends, in part at least, on the job of the breadwinner, household demand will be influenced by the structure of production. Causality runs from the supply side to the demand side, just the reverse of "consumer sovereignty."

Finally, there is the notion of scarcity itself. Scarcity in neoclassical theory is, as is choice, essentially *timeless*. Moreover, it is a relationship between output or "endowments" and wants, which is assumed to be insatiable. But an economy exists through time only by continually replacing the material basis for production. What is left over after such replacement—the *net* output—is what is available for purposes other than the support of continued existence. And an obviously central question is, who will control that surplus and decide how it is to be used? Scarcity for some may be the result of plenty for others. Moreover, over time the relationships may change, or *be* changed, by conscious political action.

The traditional alternative to the mainstream theory of value is the Labor Theory of Value (LTV). Both can be said to agree that the problem is to show how what appear to be relations among things are really social relations among persons. But neoclassical theory treats these as timeless relations between the abstract preferences of socially unspecific individuals, in conjunction with given endowments and postulated scarcity, whereas the Marxian tradition grounds value in the class positions of agents in a specifically capitalist system engaged in a continual process of reproducing itself over time.

But, notoriously, the Marxian theory of value is a mare's nest of tangled issues and unresolved problems. Even among serious scholars there are disputes over exactly what is being claimed, and whether certain propositions are or are not true; that is, provable within the accepted framework of the theory. One could agree, as argued above, that the Marxian approach is superior, yet still shy away from the intense and sometimes rancorous dispute. How can concepts that will reveal the interconnections of the system we live under come out of such often graceless polemics? Yet the fierceness of the debates stands in reasonable ratio to the magnitude of the issues involved. *For what is at stake is our understanding of the central concepts of the system: value and capital.*

The General Labor Theory of Value

Broadly speaking, all recent work on the LTV written in the Marxian tradition agrees that the starting point must be a conception of the economic system as capitalist; that is, as characterized by ownership of capital, institutionalized in business firms, employing workers who live on their wages, and engaging in production which uses up commodities in producing them. But from the common starting point very different roads are taken. One group led by Ian Steedman strenuously rejects all consideration of labor values, arguing that the representation of the system in terms of the physical inputs used up or consumed and produced is completely adequate for all serious analysis, and that further consideration of "labor value" is a metaphysical exercise and a waste of time. Worse, the labor theory stinks of dogmatism and is haunted by the ghost of Stalin. A second group argues that the so-called "detour through labor values" is necessary or useful in revealing the underlying relations of exploitation. A large set of authors, however, reject much of this discussion as "economistic," and regard the LTV as a set of philosophical propositions about the nature of capitalist commodity exchange with no particular implications for the specific values of variables in economic models, though defining the meaning of such variables. A related group also holds that the LTV is basically philosophical, but argues that its world-historical meaning implies that at bottom relative prices are "governed by values" in some ill-defined sense. Some of these writings are distinctly fundamentalist; Marx is the Word, and the Word, like butter, is there to be spread, not analyzed. "Obscurantist" is Steedman's Word, and it fits.

First, what exactly does the Labor Theory of Value say? This, of course, is part of what the argument is about. But certain points can be made. At a general level it says that the fact that commodities "have value" is to be explained by the fact and only by the fact that they are products of wage labor, which is to say exploited labor. To "have value" is to be exchangeable in a regular way for a universal equivalent. For a universal equivalent to exist, exchange ratios between any two commodities must be consistent with the exchange ratios of either with any third. The ultimate insight of the LTV in its most general form is that value as a society-wide phenomenon, expressed in universal equivalence with money ("everything has its price"), can only arise in social circumstances of class conflict. If commodities exist, if things have exchange-value, then there must be exploited labor, and so at least potential class conflict. No "harmony" is possible through the market, since value and commodity exchange, and so class conflict, are preconditions for markets.

Let's call this general doctrine the GLTV and take a closer look at the claim that value is the reflection of class conflict in the mirror of economics. All activities which can be privately organized are commodities, and so have value—and the key condition for this arrangement is that labor be exploited. This is a large claim, and it is not the way everyone has read Marx. For instance, it has become commonplace to remark, and to lament, that Marx simply took over Ricardo's position on the LTV, in the process, of course, both developing it and placing it in a social and historical perspective. But on this view, Marx's theory is still substantially that of Ricardo; embodied labor is what explains exchange-value and so prices, whereas the level of wages in relation to total output is what explains profits. As Ricardo recognized, however, these two propositions cannot coexist under free competitive conditions, except in the special case, assumed by Marx in *Capital,* Volume I, of all industries or departments having equal organic compositions of capital. For capital will flow to where rates of return are highest, thus establishing a uniform rate of profits, and the resulting prices will not reflect embodied labor.

But in fact the first nine chapters of *Capital,* Volume I are devoted to a completely different set of issues in which prices and the rate of profits figure neither as the targets of the inquiry, nor among the explanatory concepts. When Marx finally does set about to determine a quantitative concept, it is not the rate of profit but the rate of surplus-value (rate of exploitation), and this comes only in Chapter IX. Are the first eight chapters just a prelude, presenting the social and historical background? *That certainly is not what Marx thought!*

Capital begins with a discussion of commodities and money, moves on to the transformation of money into capital, and then shows that the production of surplus-value in the labor process is the foundation of the earning power of capital. The entire discussion, although illuminated by examples drawn from history, moves on the plane of theory. It is *not* a presentation of socio-historical background; it is the central core of Marx's theory, leading up to the determination of the rate of surplus-value.

Commodities, the form in which the wealth of capitalist societies presents itself, have two aspects, use-value and exchange-value. These in turn correspond to two aspects of the labor which produces them: concrete, specific labor which produces use-value, and abstract labor which generates exchange-value. Concrete labor is easy to understand, but exactly what abstract labor is and how it produces value is not yet explained, partly no doubt because the Ricardian LTV was the most common currency of political economy at the time he wrote and could be taken for granted. Instead, Marx enters on a long and detailed examination of the forms of exchange-value, culminating in the General Form of Value which "results from the joint action of the whole world of commodities. . . . A commodity can acquire a general expression of its value only by all other commodities, simultaneously with it, expressing their values in the same equivalent. . . ." The general form of value requires some commodity to act as universal equivalent. But insofar as a commodity does so, it cannot be used as a means of production or of subsistence or of luxury consumption. It no longer is the use-value it once was; it is money. "The difficulty lies, not in comprehending that money is a commodity, but in discovering how, why, and by what means a commodity becomes money."

The commodity which becomes money already has value. "When it steps into circulation as money, its value is already given. . . . This value is determined by the labor-time required for its production. . . ." Exchange requires not only a universal equivalent, but a fit and proper one. "The truth of the proposition that, 'although gold and silver are not by nature money, money is by nature gold and silver,' is shown by the fitness of the physical properties of these metals for the functions of money." For there to be general commodity production, there must be fully developed exchange, and for Marx that *requires* that exchange-values be expressed (and compared) in universal equivalent form, and carried out by means of circulating money.

But if money is the universal medium by which commodities are exchanged, then capital will have to circulate in money form. The capitalist advances money for commodities, then sells commodities for money.

But this makes no real sense. Selling commodities for money and then buying commodities again is practical enough. The exchange-value of the two sets of commodities may be the same; but the use-value of the second set to the owner will be higher.[1] By contrast, buying commodities for a sum of money and selling them again for that same sum is a complete waste of time. (Marx is assuming all commodities sell for their cost of production, and that all exchanges are fair and equal; no agents in the market have any special privileges.) To assume that on resale commodities can fetch more than they cost, *in general,* is contradictory. "Suppose, then, that by some inexplicable privilege" a seller is able to sell at some percentage above what he previously paid. He seems to pocket a gain. Then he goes to buy, and finds all other sellers now offering only at the higher price. Or suppose one capitalist is clever enough to take advantage of another; what the one gains the other loses. The total amount of value in circulation is unaltered. "If equivalents are exchanged, no surplus-value results, and if non-equivalents are exchanged, still no surplus-value. Circulation, or the exchange of commodities, begets no value."

At this point Marx states exactly what he is up to: "The conversion of money into capital has to be explained on the basis of the laws that regulate the exchange of commodities, in such a way that the starting-point is the exchange of equivalents. Our friend, Moneybags, who as yet is only an embryo capitalist, must buy his commodities at their value, must sell them at their value, and yet at the end of the process must withdraw more value from circulation than he threw into it at starting. His development into a full-grown capitalist must take place, both within the sphere of circulation

[1] "So far as regards use-value, it is clear that both parties may gain some advantage. Both part with goods that, as use-values, are of no service to them, and receive others that they can make use of. . . . With reference, then, to use-value, there is good ground for saying that exchange is a transaction by which both sides gain. It is otherwise with exchange-value." Marx, *Capital*, Volume I, Chapter 1.

and without it. These are the conditions of the problem. *Hic Rhodus, hic salta!*"[2]

We began from universal commodity production; all activities are commodities, so human work will be also. And the solution lies in the buying and selling of labor power. The buyer pays its cost of production, the (socially determined) subsistence wage, but obtains its use-value, namely the worker's capacity to work for a period of time. What the worker does in this time depends on what the buying of labor power can get out of him. Workers work; work means changing the form of materials—cutting, shaping, processing, and so on. The faster, harder, or longer a worker works for subsistence pay, the more material input he converts to output.

Marx analyzes the labor process with great care, and his chapter on "The Working Day" has never been surpassed for controlled outrage in exposing injustice. Material input, wear and tear of machinery, and so on, summed up, form the "constant" capital that must be advanced. Such capital is simply converted into output, adding its own value, but no more. The wage bill, however, is "variable" capital; it is spent on the purchase of labor power which, if coerced or cajoled suitably, can produce in a day more than the value needed to pay its subsistence. The ratio between the time worked "for the capitalist" and the time worked "for himself" (producing what it would take to buy his subsistence) is the rate of exploitation.[3] Thus by buying materials, equipment, and labor-power at cost or true value, and selling goods produced by labor for cost or true value, a capitalist is still able to turn a profit.

In short, the first nine chapters of *Capital* are devoted to relating commodities, values, and free exchange to capital and the exploitation of labor. And the latter explains the earning power of capital,

---

[2] Marx attached an important footnote to this passage which explains why he insisted on assuming the SLTV throughout Volume I: "[T]he formation of capital must be possible even though the price and value of a commodity be the same; for its formation cannot be attributed to any deviation of the one from the other." He knew perfectly well that, in general, prices deviate from value—Volume III was drafted before Volume I was written—but he wanted to forestall the notion that the existence of profit could be explained by a systematic discrepancy between price and value. Hence "to explain profit at all, it must first be explained on the assumption that prices equal values." Dobb made this point in 1939.

[3] It should be evident that this argument does not depend on whether the true values of goods are measured by ratios of embodied labor times or by prices. The subsistence goods support labor for a given time; whatever their prices are, the real wage is thus the equivalent of a certain amount of labor time. Hence the rate of exploitation can be expressed in terms of the division of the working day. Steedman is surely right on this point.

which in turn explains the driving force of its circulation—the motivation which runs the whole system.

The Special Labor Theory of Value

A more specific level of theory holds that the value of a unit amount of a commodity is the sum of the abstract, socially necessary labor directly and indirectly embodied in it. Let us call this SLTV. This is not a simple claim and is widely misunderstood. For one thing, the terms are complex. "Abstract labor" means labor conceived simply in terms of its status as wage-labor, and measured in time, regardless of the specifics of job or skill.[4] "Socially necessary labor time" means the time needed according to the best methods known and in use at the historical moment in question. Labor indirectly required, of course, is the labor required by the non-worker inputs. So the formula for value gives the amount of time —put in by those with the status of wage earners—that *would be required,* directly and indirectly, to produce the commodity. What results is a set of simultaneous linear equations, easily handled by matrix methods. Value in exchange, then, is the ratio of the labor value of any good with any other good taken as a standard.

Now a very important implication of this definition of value is that the exchange ratios implied are such that the excess of the value of every department's output, over the value required to replace its means of production and subsistence, will stand in the same ratio to the cost of supporting direct labor. That is, the ratio of "value of output minus value of means of production and subsistence" to "direct labor time employed" is the same in every department or industry. This has important implications.

First, since the surplus is measured in labor time, we have a pure ratio expressing the productivity of the direct labor employed. If

[4] The distinction between abstract and concrete labor must not be confused with the distinction between simple and skilled labor, both of which are concrete. The reduction of skilled labor to simple is, for Marx, largely a matter of history and custom, including the ability (or lack of it) of groups to entrench themselves and enhance their status. It "rests in part on pure illusion, or to say the least, on distinctions that have long since ceased to be real, and that survive only by virtue of a traditional convention, in part on the helpless condition of some groups of the working class" (Marx, Volume I, p. 192, No. 1). Concrete labor is the practical work of producing use-values; abstract labor is the condition of being exploited, measured as the amount of time in simple labor equivalents spent working in that status. A good deal of academic labor has been expended on the question of determining the reduction of skilled to simple labor. It is not clear that such labor is socially necessary; Marx regarded the reduction as exogenous to value theory. (For a related view, cf. Bowles and Gintis, 1978.)

the surplus is appropriated by the owners of the means of production, then the ratio can be interpreted as showing the time workers worked to produce what they needed to replace their own means of subsistence in relation to the time they worked to produce surplus-value for their employer—the rate of exploitation. Moreover, the existence of the mathematical dual to the set of equations implies that means of production and labor could be reallocated among the departments so that the physical net output consisted only of means of subsistence.[5] Thus the rate of exploitation can be expressed as a ratio of quantities of surplus consumer goods to required consumer goods.[6] If these consumer goods were used to support servants, entertainers, police, and the like, this would then be interpreted as the ratio of unproductive or surplus labor to necessary or productive labor. Note also that since the rate is expressed in labor-time, its reciprocal is the proportional "slowdown" or work-to-rule which, if carried out in every department, would totally eliminate the surplus. That is, a proportional slowdown in every department, equal to the reciprocal of the rate of surplus-value, would result in an output the value of which would just cover replacement of means of production and subsistence.

This leads directly to a fundamental point. For Marx, in *Capital,* the labor process is one in which workers *work,* that is, convert material inputs into output by means of their labor power. So there are two different kinds of "technical coefficients," those which tell us the material inputs required per unit output (regardless of how long production takes), and those which tell us the labor *time* needed for unit production (regardless of the amount of input required). Of course, there may be interactions, but the first depends on engineering, while the second depends on incentives and morale, the willingness of workers to work, or the ability of capital to

[5] It is now widely recognized that Marx had unusually acute insight into the mathematical structure of economic problems (Morishima, 1974). His attempts to formulate his system were often cumbersome and inept, but he was developing arguments for which there were as yet no adequate mathematical tools. Matrix algebra was 40 years in the future. The Perron-Frobenius theorem was first proved in 1907.

[6] "In the 'transparent' modes of exploitation, the rate of exploitation is immediately obvious: the serf works for three days on his or her own land and for three days on the master's. Neither the serf nor the lord is blind to this fact. But the capitalist mode of exploitation is opaque. On the one hand, the proletarian sells labor power, but seems to be selling labor, and is paid for the eight hours of work put in, not just for the four that would be necessary for maintenance; on the other hand, the bourgeois realizes a profit which is calculated in relation to the capital owned, not to the labour exploited, so that this capital seems to the capitalist to be productive." From Amin, 1977, p. 13.

coerce them. Marx runs the first kind of coefficients under the heading "constant capital," and the second under "variable capital." It is variable capital, then, which produces surplus-value; labor works faster or harder, so converting more input into output. A general slowdown can eliminate surplus-value (and, in the dual, the surplus product). Only as much would be produced in a given length of time as is needed, directly and indirectly, to replace the means of subsistence needed to support labor for that time. A faster rate of production, more intensive work or longer hours per day, applied across the board, would increase surplus-value.[7]

But suppose workers performed no work. Suppose machines, carefully programmed robots, carried out actual production, drawing energy from sunlight, the tides, geothermal sources, etc. Computers might devise most of the programs. The human being would then relate to the production process "more as watchman and regulator," stepping "to the side . . . instead of being its chief actor" (Grundrisse, p. 705). Of course, there will be paperwork concerned with the bureaucracy, or with the struggle for markets and against taxes.[8] But no matter how fast or slow, well or badly, such work is done, within wide limits the output produced would be unaffected. How, in such a situation, could we speak of "variable capital" or define a rate of exploitation?

Marx himself seems to conclude that the SLTV must be set aside: "As soon as labor in the direct form has ceased to be the great well-spring of wealth labor time ceases and must cease to be its measure, and exchange-value [must cease to be the measure] of use-value. The *surplus labor of the mass* has ceased to be the condition for the development of general wealth, just as the *non-labor of the few,* for the development of the general powers of the human head." If labor's direct work is not the source of the surplus, labor time is not the measure of value.

---

[7] But wouldn't industries or departments all produce at different speeds, depending on the particular working conditions in each? Industries, however, are interdependent. One which produced faster than the rest will find, on the one hand, its supplies used up before its suppliers have completed production, and on the other, its product finished before its customers are ready to buy. Inventory policy smooths this out, of course, but *given* an inventory policy, a speed-up out of line with its customers and suppliers will lead an industry to where it has to lay off workers and wait. The basic industry, therefore, with the slowest rate of production regulates all the rest, a familiar result from critical path analysis.

[8] It is important to realize that faster or better work in circulation (sales, finance, etc.) does produce a faster turnover, and therefore *does* contribute to surplus-value in Marx's sense. The robot economy suggested is very far removed from any advanced capitalist economy today.

But does this mean throwing over the GLTV as well? Quite the contrary. Whereas manual labor can only be appropriated once, while it is being expended, some kinds of mental labor can be appropriated, as it were, once and for all. For the result of such mental labor is "the business of invention," "when . . . all the sciences have been pressed into the service of capital." This dramatically heightens the contradiction between the essentially social nature of production and the private mode of organizing it and appropriating its fruits. The processes of scientific discovery and engineering development depend on the accumulated knowledge of the human race. But they are tied down to the making of profit for the benefit of particular capitalists. What is exploited here is not the power to perform material work, but humanity's potential to think creatively. The difference, and it is a crucial one, is that the return to capital is not immediate, but is spread out over an indefinite and unpredictably long period of time. But the scientist is paid his wages, and the use-value of his product—of his ideas—is appropriated by capital.

Scrapping the SLTV

It is time for a closer and more critical look at the Special Labor Theory of Value. If, in fact, commodities exchanged at ratios of labor-values, employers would then obtain surplus-value in relation to the labor they employed, not in relation to the total value of the means of production advanced. That total value is the value of their capital, and under capitalist production capital will be moved about until all capital tends to earn the same return on its value. The implication of this is that exchange-ratios must be such that the "exchange-value of output" minus "exchange-value of means of production and subsistence" stands in the same ratio for every department to the "exchange-value of means of production and subsistence," not to the "direct labor time employed." So in capitalism relative prices will not be equal to ratios of labor-values, except in the case where the ratio of the value of means of production to the value of subsistence is the same in all departments.

But Marx defines the rate of profit as $S/(C+V)$, where "S" is surplus-value, "C" is constant capital, and "V" variable capital, all expressed in labor-values. So if prices are governed by the rate of profit, his definition of the rate of profit will not, except by a fluke, be correct. Nor, in fact, will his definition of the overall organic composition of capital. What should we conclude?

The most controversial position (Steedman, 1977; Hodgson, 1976) may be the easiest to start with. If exchange-values are governed by the rate of profit, and will therefore not usually equal labor-values, why bother with the Labor Theory of Value at all? It was an interesting insight, and of importance in the history of the subject, but as a proposition about relative prices, it is wrong. So forget it. Moreover, the Sraffa system is perfectly capable of dealing with cases like the robot economy above, where even Marx acknowledges that labor-values are inapplicable. This does not necessarily mean throwing over the general insight—the GLTV.[9] (Still less does it offer any consolation to partisans of supply and demand or choice theory.) All it means is scrapping the specific labor-value formulae. But it has sometimes been taken to mean that, given the quantities of inputs and outputs, exchange-values can be calculated on various assumptions about the disposition of the surplus, quite regardless of class positions or class conflict. Some have argued that the same equations could be used to describe systems in which supposedly there was "no class conflict," leading critics to charge that "neo-Ricardians" think of socialism simply as "capitalism without capitalists."

On the face of it, such a use of the equations is inconsistent with the GLTV, which holds that the existence of commodity exchange, a precondition for generalized value-in-exchange, implies that there is exploited labor. If it is argued that the prices are calculated simply for "accounting purposes," the question becomes, why are the accounts kept? What costs are being minimized, at whose expense and for whose benefit? If labor is a cost, what does cost minimization imply for workers? These "accounting calculations" are not neutral in their implications. Not to see this is to miss—or reject—the point of the GLTV.

Abandoning the SLTV while retaining the GLTV, however, leads to some striking positions, which may prove of considerable importance to the future development of Marxism. First, labor-values have nothing and the rate of profit has everything to do with prices. So traditional supply and demand are out the window, and we have a new general equilibrium theory in which prices are a function of the rate of profit, and so of distribution. Secondly, distribution in its turn reflects the balance of class forces; distribution is not determined by purely economic relationships, contrary to neoclassical

[9] Abandoning values and relying on physical quantities has sometimes been taken as equivalent to rejecting Marx's insights into exploitation (Roosevelt, 1974). Steedman specifically denies this.

thinking. The model shows precisely how and when class struggle affects economic variables, so it helps to locate "economic laws" in the wider field of historical materialism generally. Thirdly, the approach is capable of great mathematical sophistication—in effect, Sraffa and von Neumann are conjoined to Marx, producing a Marxian dynamic general equilibrium-disequilibrium approach (Morishima, 1974; Abraham-Fois and Berebi, 1976). Many normal topics of mainstream concern can be dealt with (e.g., the effects of taxes, subsidies, welfare) while many traditional Marxian subjects, such as the reserve army, mechanization, and the falling rate of profit, can be dealt with in a far more elaborate and sophisticated way.

Apparently, then, there are great advantages to developing Marxian economics by dropping the SLTV while retaining the GLTV. Yet this trend has met strong resistance. One line of argument holds, in effect, that the distinction between the GLTV and SLTV is artificial. They are inseparable: They stand or fall together. Marxism is an organic unity, the parts of which are mutually supportive and cannot be questioned. Like an oyster, but less digestible, it must be swallowed whole.

A better argument, but still defective (Amin, 1978), is that the use of physical quantities permits no comparison of changes in the economic base. When new products or processes are introduced the physical system changes, and the new exchange-values cannot, in general, be compared with the old. But labor-values can be compared. Hence it is argued the SLTV is superior to an approach based on physical quantities and exchange ratios. However, both rates of profit and rates of exploitation, being pure ratios, can be compared. This is the point of the "switching" arguments. And under capitalism it will be the rate of profit that will govern the movement of capital. All that is necessary is to calculate which processes or products, if introduced, will generate the highest rate of profit. These will be the ones eventually adopted unless, of course, there are institutional or political barriers. There is no need to detour through labor-values.

The fundamentalist arguments are wrong, though the last point can be restated in a more acceptable form, as we shall see. So long as the GLTV is taken as the basis for the interpretation of the variables of the model, the case for dropping the SLTV as (part of) the account of exchange-values looks sound enough, so far. But the matter cannot be left there. There is the not altogether irrelevant question of what is, in fact, the case.

It has been customary for decades among economists of all stripes to dismiss the SLTV as "unrealistic." Yet this dismissal has been based on theoretical grounds, not on empirical investigation. The argument has already been presented. Capital-to-labor ratios differ in different industries, and capitalism tends to establish a uniform rate of profit. Therefore prices cannot equal ratios of embodied labor. Good, but what do the *facts* say?

Unfortunately, the facts are a little shy of speaking right up, but with a bit of coaxing they can be heard to murmur something like, "perhaps Ricardo was right after all." To study the problem one has to make use of input-output tables, and the data collected there are not presented in "physical" terms. So the coefficients have to be adjusted, and this (along with many other things) may introduce bias. Nevertheless, allowing for such problems, labor-values can be calculated from input-output data, and so can the theoretically correct (uniform rate of profit) prices. Then the labor-values and the "correct" prices of production can be compared to the "actual" prices (which of course are highly aggregated). Preliminary calculations, surprisingly enough, suggest that labor-values are much closer to actual prices than the theoretically superior prices of production (Shaikh, forthcoming). Moreover, it appears, and is well known from other studies, that changes in labor productivity account for by far the greatest part of price changes. If this is so, then it would seem that labor-values and changes in labor-values provide a simple and reasonably accurate working hypothesis for predicting both the prices ruling at a given time, and changes in prices over time. This ought to be of interest to practical economists. Indeed, it is something of a comment on the ideological state of mind in the profession that this suggestion provoked such vicious attacks that the effects can only be described as chilling; some of those working on the idea came to feel they might be endangering their careers. The idea that the SLTV might be a reasonable empirical approximation, though theoretically inadequate—for Marxist reasons—was too much. Economists don't appreciate irony.

The SLTV reinterpreted: the fundamental theorem

Nevertheless, this is a sideshow. So far the partisans of Marx after Sraffa seem to have a good case theoretically. The second group of writings, however, whittles this down. Understandably, in view of ambiguities in the tradition, Steedman, et al., have misconceived the role of the SLTV by treating it, in Ricardian fashion, as a theory of price. But it is not; like the GLTV it is a theory of the origin (or grounds) of the surplus—that is, of the basis of profits and other forms of net income (and also, in the dual, of net output).[10] GLTV shows that commodities having value is the consequence of the exploitation of labor, where labor is itself a commodity. SLTV, then, determines the rate of exploitation and the associated commodity values. What is needed to complete this is the demonstration that to any given rate of exploitation there corresponds a definite and unique positive rate of profit. And that is given by the solution to the transformation problem.

In other words, the relation between labor-values and prices of production is a red herring. The correct transformation is not of values into prices, it is the proof that to every rate of exploitation there corresponds a unique rate of profit—that is, exploitation and the rate of profit are functionally connected. This Morishima terms the Fundamental Theorem of Marxian economics.

But Steedman still has a point. Values and the rate of exploitation are determined *along with* prices and the rate of profit, by the same fundamental data. So why are they any more or any less important? They are simply the solutions to the same system of equations when the rate of profit is zero, and the entire surplus is appropriated in proportion to direct labor. However, this argument misses the point that when labor works, the speed, intensity, and the like, of that work is what determines the rate of exploitation.

So there is no "detour" through labor-values. The issue is not to explain prices; it is to explain *profits*. The point of the SLTV is to determine the rate of exploitation, to uncover the underlying grounds for the existence of profits, and to demonstrate a formal connection between these grounds and the rate of profit.

Changes of technique

Now we come to an apparently devastating objection, which is, perhaps, the centerpiece of Steedman's position. Suppose there are several "techniques" of production for some or all of the commodities. The choice of technique which maximizes the rate of exploita-

[10] This is brought out very clearly in a note circulated by Steedman concerning a long-standing problem in the interpretation of "socially necessary labor-time." Steedman holds that this *must* mean the labor time required in the best-practice technique; otherwise the exchange ratios will not be the correct equilibrium ones. Marx, however, several times asserts that required labor is that with "the *average* degree of skill and intensity prevalent at a given time" (*Capital* I, p. 39, my italics). Steedman is correct for his purposes, but his method would *overestimate* both the actual surplus-value produced and the rate of exploitation. Marx is right, if his purpose is the theory of exploitation.

tion (notoriously) need not be the same as that which maximizes the rate of profits. So the rate of exploitation is not only irrelevant; it would also be misleading. Or, put another way, a given rate of exploitation implies different profit rates in different techniques. But the techniques will be adopted on the grounds that they maximize the rate of profit. So we have to know the rate of profit to know the technique in order to calculate the corresponding rate of exploitation. The Fundamental Theorem has it just the wrong way around. Again the rate of exploitation *et hic omnia genus* seem to have led us to red but indigestible herrings.

This conclusion is strongly bolstered by two further arguments which are not easy to explain intuitively. One concerns joint production. The other, fixed capital, in the Sraffa-von Neumann tradition is a *special* case of joint production. [Each year the industry both ("jointly") produces its product(s) and depreciates its machinery.] In both cases some labor-values can turn out to be negative, even though prices and the rate of profit are positive. So a paradox can be constructed: positive profits and negative surplus value. "Marxists should therefore concentrate on developing the materialist account of why production conditions and real wages are what they are, leaving the discussion of 'value magnitudes' to those concerned only with the development of a new Gnosticism."

Admirers of the caves of Nag Hammadi may wish to rephrase this, but the message is clear and strong. The mechanics of these arguments are mathematically formidable. But the framework in which they move has drawn fire. Critics, especially Morishima, have charged that the joint-production arguments depended on an arbitrary and unjustified assumption that the number of products just equalled the number of processes. Instead, all the possible processes should be considered, and the choice of the best made in accordance with cost-minimization. In other words, the "choice of technique" problematic should be extended to cover joint production. Steedman accepts this, and agrees with Morishima's revised analysis of the joint-production case. So there is no need to go over the paradoxes of "negative value"; we can concentrate on choice of technique, taking single-product industries as the illustrative case.

There are serious problems here. First, (unlike the "method of physical quantities" generally) the choice of techniques problematic, borrowed from neoclassical production-function theory, is genuinely asocial and ahistorical, as Joan Robinson never tires of stressing. Secondly, the choice of techniques argument moves on a different level of abstraction than the claim that the rate of exploitation explains the rate of profit. And, thirdly, the argument, once it is set in historical time, *does* require a specification of the rate of exploitation. These three points are closely related.

A set of techniques—one for each commodity—makes up a technology according to modern theory. At any moment there will normally be known a number of different ways of producing at least some commodities. So the different techniques can be grouped together in different technologies. In a technology, then, a given level of the real wage will imply a set of prices and the rate of profit. But the technology *chosen* will be that one which maximizes the rate of profit. For simplicity, assume *either* with Marx, that all the techniques in each technology have the same organic composition of capital, *or* with Sraffa, that all technologies are in standard proportions. Then the real wage, rate of profit trade-off is a downward sloping straight line. The vertical axis represents output of consumer goods, so the real wage can be marked out on it. The horizontal axis represents the rate of profits. The slope of each line, then, is the capital-labor ratio for that technology.

At any given time there will be an actual technology in place. Social systems do not rise full-blown, like Venus from the waves. For this actual system the rate of exploitation will be determinate. In each sector an actual labor force is employed under established working conditions, and between them and their employers there will be a *modus vivendi*. Both sides will be constantly pushing to change this, employers to increase productivity and reduce costs, employees to raise wages and improve working conditions, but Steedman is surely right that for many purposes it is legitimate to "freeze" the balance of forces in the workplace and analyze the working of the system for a given level of productivity and real wages.

Now let us say that we are examining a prospective change in a currently existing technology. We know the present rate of exploitation (output per worker divided by the wage); we know its output over capital, profits over capital, and its capital-labor ratio (output per worker divided by the output over capital).

The new technology does not yet exist. (Of course, this new technology may include many of the same industries now in place, but at least some must be new.) The present real wage may carry over in the new situation. That presumably depends on the labor market. But new technology creates a new workplace situation; new jobs will have to be defined, and new factories built. Relations in these new work situations cannot be "frozen"—no one knows what they will be. Of course, assumptions about work intensity can—and must—be made, but until they are it will be impossible to determine how much the new technology's capital-labor ratio varies from that of the currently existing technology. (For simplicity, I am basing the discussion on the non-Marxian assumption that profit is not figured on advanced wages.) Productivity will vary considerably depending on how long, how hard, and with what care and attention workers will work; and if workers do not like the new set-up and are careless and wasteful, unit costs will rise and profits decline. But leaving this aside, suppose that engineers can predict with reasonable accuracy what the material inputs per unit output should be, and that the number of workers needed to operate the technology, and the wage required to sustain a worker for a given period of time are also known. This is enough to tell us the horizontal intercept of the wage-profit frontier. For whatever the speed with which workers work, the input per unit of output remains the same. But it does not give us the frontier's vertical intercept, nor consequently its slope—which is to say, we cannot yet know whether the new technology is superior to the existing one at all levels of the existing wage, or at only some levels, or not at all. For that we have to know also how much work—processing input into output—workers will do in a given amount of time. *And that is simply asking, in Marx's sense, what is the rate of exploitation?*

If we turn back to the paradoxes of "negative value," we find the same thing. Steedman does not distinguish coefficients falling under constant capital from those under variable capital. The effects of changes in the speed or intensity of work are therefore not examined. So he has not really confronted Marx's problem, though his examples do call attention to the importance of the patterns of technological interdependence. Where these are complex, conclusions from simpler cases may not carry over. However, not much work has been done analyzing what kinds of industries engage in what kinds of joint production; indeed, not much has been done defining categories of joint production. (Definitions have been developed for "by-products" in which most of the conclusions from the single-product case carry over. See Nell, 1964; Schefold, 1971.) But the question is too technical to go into further. As for fixed capital, there are two serious problems with the Sraffa-von Neumann approach that have not yet received the attention they deserve. First, if fixed capital is to be treated as a joint product, how much should appear as output when capacity is under or over-utilized, that is, when we adapt the analysis to the consideration of questions of effective demand?

(Nell, in Lowe, 1976, p. 292.) Presumably if the normal output is down when capacity is under-utilized, the equipment appearing as joint product will be *up*, since it has been depreciated less. But it may all have been used at less than normal intensity, or some of it left idle, while the rest ran as usual. Are these equivalent? Do managers have a choice? Secondly, for Marx capital must be continually turned over from commodities into money form. Thus, when the part of constant capital corresponding to the depreciation of fixed equipment is realized in the sale of the product for money, it will then be invested in a sinking fund, which will earn interest. Hence the total capital will be unchanged in amount, and in earning power, if the rate of interest equals the rate of profit. Only the form will be changed, progressively, with more of it in funds and less in the value of equipment, until the time for replacement comes when the sinking fund matures (Nell, 1964). These questions, capacity utilization and turnover, need answers before the Sraffa-von Neumann approach can claim to be an adequate concept of fixed capital for Marxian analysis.

So the "choice of technique" and related arguments fail. The analysis moved at too abstract a plane; it was developed without regard to the fact that any change of technology involves moving from one concrete, actual situation, in which the balance of forces in the workplace can (often) reasonably be taken as known and "frozen," to a new, as yet untried, situation in which it can only be estimated. More importantly, the "balance of class forces"—and therefore the position of the wage-profit frontier—depends on different kinds of factors from those determining material input into output. Social and political questions predominate in the former, engineering in the latter. Marx sought precisely to separate, and then relate, these two categories of influences on the rate of profits.

How do we get there from here?

So what does it all amount to? The Sraffa-based critique of Marx is surely correct that, theoretically, labor-values are of no relevance in explaining prices (though, ironically, they may yet prove a useful empirical approximation). Marx's account of the rate of profit as $S/(C+V)$ is wrong, and his attempts to solve the transformation problem failed. Attempts to defend Marx on these specific points are a waste of time and effort. But the LTV played a larger and a different role for Marx. In its general form it relates capitalist commodity production and the existence of exchange-value to the exploitation of wage-labor, and more specifically, it determines the rate of exploitation in a sense which shows it to be a causal determinant of the rate of profit. So Steedman's claim that socio-technical conditions and the real wage are all that count is misleading, and his claim that "the rate of profit is . . . *logically prior* to any determination of value magnitudes" must be rejected. On the contrary, it seems the rate of exploitation must be known in order to determine the rate of profit.

Where does this get us, though? We undoubtedly understand Marx much better, and a powerful array of mathematical techniques has been developed for Marxist and other non-standard economics. A coherent and sophisticated alternative to conventional value theory seems to be taking shape, though no doubt still containing many unresolved issues. *But how is a better understanding of Marx, or for that matter of value and capital, going to help us understand the economic crisis of our times?* What does all this argumentation, ingenious and abstruse as it is, promise in the way of insight into the malignant follies of our age? Marx, after all, wrote about a very much earlier stage of capitalism.

Consider some of the economic issues of today: inflation and unemployment, formerly thought to be opposites, moving together; stagnant productivity in the West; runaway energy pricing by cartels and powerful multinationals; massive dependency on armaments spending; ubiquitous waste and social misallocation; ill-designed and unmanageable cities; dwindling supplies of essential resources and a world population explosion; widespread destruction of ecological balance; the pillage of the Third World and the resulting reactions; and on and on. All this in the context of a period of historically unparalleled scientific and technological creativity. What have value and capital, or Marx's theories, to do with this?

It is surely impossible to answer this here. The best I can do is sketch the outline of an answer. To begin with, the Marxian approach is rooted in the actual situation of the system, at a moment of historical time. It has become what it is as the result of a particular path of historical development. The pure logic of the system can and must be considered, *but it is the logic of a system on a path of historical development.* Moreover, that development is powered by internal tensions and conflicts—"contradictions"—which are tending to undermine the very processes by which it works. Conflict, latent or open, is absolutely endemic to the system—buyer vs. seller, employer vs. employee, borrower vs. lender, as well as firm vs. firm and worker vs. worker. Some conflicts are more fundamental than others, and the GLTV holds that the most fundamental of all is capital versus labor, taken in all its dimensions.

Secondly, no clear line can be drawn between economic and social or political conflicts, or even between economic and political processes. Politics, very often, is simply economics pursued by other means. This applies to capital as well as to labor. Not surprisingly the scope of state activities, and the cost of them, expands to encompass these demands, and to try to keep the conflicts within bounds. (Of course, there are political and social issues that are not, at least in any immediate way, related to economic concerns. In this connection there is an extensive Marxist literature about the influence of material factors "in the last instance.") Neoclassical theory, however, defines a sharp boundary between what can be analyzed by its methods, and what falls outside its purview. Since it is a theory of choice under constraints, it can be applied widely, if unsuccessfully, in explaining many political choices, marriage and divorce, job discrimination, and other issues. "Widely," because being abstract, it is quite general; "unsuccessfully," because it starts from the individual with given preferences operating in a given environment, where both "preferences" and environment are conceived in limited and misleading ways. Neither the development of the individual's consciousness, nor the development of the institutions in and through which individuals function are possible subjects of inquiry. "What are the effects of mechanization upon worker alienation" is not a question that can be raised in orthodox labor market analysis; it is inescapable in the Marxian framework.

Thirdly, capital is not a "factor of production" earning a return in virtue of its "productive contribution" at the margin. It is a social relationship; it is the way production is organized and the product appropriated. The existence of capital as self-expanding value depends upon the exploitation of wage-labor. This again is the point of the GLTV. So when multinational capital moves into new areas, formerly organized non-capitalistically, new institutional arrangements must be created. A proper "climate for investment" must be established. This means a labor force, labor discipline, protection for property in the means of production, suitable finance, and so on. These can involve major social upheavals and political changes, all too evident throughout the Third World, from South Korea through South America to South Africa.

Some of these changes are the results of conscious political decisions. (One should never underestimate the conspiracy theory of history. Even paranoids have *real* enemies.) But many, and perhaps the largest, are not. They are the outcomes of the process of capital accumulation. This is not steady-state growth. It is the creation and management of a force of wage-laborers by capital in pursuit of its only legitimate goal, high and steady profit. The massive shift of people to the cities in search of work, for example, is an indirect and largely unintended result of technical progress and reorganization resulting from the invasion of agriculture by corporate capital.

Fourthly, the Marxian approach forces us to recognize that productivity and technical change have social and political dimensions. We have already seen that productivity depends on the clash of interests—and wills—in the workplace. It also depends on common interests; the more successful the business, the higher the wage it can afford. Productivity is the outcome of a complex symbiotic process, an important aspect of which is the development of technology. For technology is not merely control over Nature, it also provides control over Man. The division of labor and the factory system provided ways of *controlling* the pace and quality of work, as do modern assembly-line methods. Technology provides for social control and discipline in the workplace. So the development of technology is not socially neutral; it will reflect class interests and sociopolitical pressures. "Economies of scale," for example, may refer to lower unit material costs, or to greater effectiveness in controlling markets or disciplining labor. The appropriation of science and engineering for private interests, setting up walls of secrecy, distorts and even comes to block scientific development.

Fifthly, we get a very different perspective on markets. For one thing the "labor market" and the "capital market" are quite different in nature and working from the markets for goods. To understand a market requires having a clear picture of the respective positions of the parties on either side of it. The GLTV provides this for the labor market, and moreover, in doing so, explains the origin of the net returns which are the subject of the bargaining among the different types of capitalists in the capital markets. The SLTV explains the size of such returns and the "transformation" relates exploitation and productivity to profits. But besides the relationship of the labor market to capital, the LTV also provides insight into employment and effective demand. Returns must be realized in money form; if sales are not made, exploitation merely means piling up inventory. The rate of exploitation will not be reduced, however; instead, workers will be laid off. Lay-offs, in turn, reduce consumer spending, so lead to lower sales revenue and hence lay-offs. The SLTV, in fact, can be developed as an employment multiplier, showing the repercussions of a change in sales of final goods on employment throughout the system. This offers a practical alternative to marginal productivity theory, and has been extensively developed, first by Kalecki, and now by the contemporary "post Keynesians."

Prices, in turn, must be explained in terms of the mark-up required to obtain a target rate of return. Here Steedman's themes are paramount. Long-term prices are determined by the rate of profits, which depends on real wages, productivity, and technical coefficients. Exploitation depends on real wages as well as intensity of work, and real wages depend on money wages in relation to prices. Effective short-run pricing policies can, therefore, contribute to a favorable rate of exploitation. Such policies are the results of collusion, power plays, politics and governmental regulation, marketing, mergers and takeovers, and many other strategies designed to bring about stable and profitable markets. Price competition is one route to this end, but only one. Competition is a short-lived state of affairs; it is the race to get the monopoly—but it ends like the race between whales and minnows, with the winners swallowing the losers. The neoclassical picture of "the price mechanism efficiently allocating scarce resources" should be hung next to the round square in the Gallery of the Theatre of the Absurd. The Invisible Hand, if it is to be found anywhere, is likely to be found picking the pockets of the poor.

I could go on. The Marxian theory of value and capital provides a framework for re-thinking population questions, for re-examining the historical growth of capitalism in the Age of European Expansion, for re-thinking the role of the State and the causes of its growth. It provides the basis for a new approach to the development of technology. But most of all, it provides the conceptual linkages showing how all these different aspects of human society are bound together in a central unity: the organization of production by capital. The problems outlined earlier are all, in some part, attributable to the consequences, and normal working, of this form of organization. "[T]hey belong to a state of society, in which the process of production has the mastery over man, instead of being controlled by him. . . ."

BIBLIOGRAPHICAL NOTES

An excellent recently published introduction to Marx's thought is R. Heilbroner: *Marxism: For and Against,* Norton, 1980. A more advanced discussion is M. Dobb: *Political Economy and Capitalism,* Routledge, 1940. In the end, however, the only way to understand Marx is to read him. *Capital* consists of three volumes: Volume I presents the Labor Theory of Value and the associated doctrine of exploitation, culminating in the General Law of Capitalist Accumulation; Volume II examines the turnover of capital-monetary accumulation —analyzing the conditions for balance between the sectors in the process of (expanding) reproduction; Volume III moves from "values" and the "underlying" categories of Marxian analysis to the practical categories of the business world—prices, profits, interest, credit, and rent. In Volume III we are given Marx's version of the "transformation," the movement from value analysis to the categories of the real world.

Reading *Capital* is notoriously difficult. But a great deal of help is provided by comparing the argument of *Capital* with corresponding points in *Theories of Surplus Value,* Progress Publishers, 1971, where Marx contrasts his work with that of others, or in the *Grundrisse,* Vintage Books, 1973, where Marx sketches the overall plan of his life's work.

*

The four complaints raised against neoclassical economics are developed in the following works, among others:

M. Hollis and E. Nell: *Rational Economic Man,* Cambridge University Press, 1975.

M. Lutz and K. Lux: *Humanistic Economics: Fundamentals and Applications,* Benjamin-Cummins, 1979.

J. Robinson: *Economic Heresies: Some Old-Fashioned Questions in Economic Theory,* Basic Books, 1971.

V. C. Walsh and H. N. Gram: *Classical and Neo-Classical Theories of General Equilibrium: Historical Origins and Mathematical Structure,* Oxford University Press, 1980.

The most fundamental work providing the basis for a critique of modern economics is P. Sraffa: *Production of Commodities by Means of Commodities,* Cambridge University Press, 1960. That this work lays the groundwork for powerful—some would say decisive—criticism of marginalist theory is well known. An apparent paradox, however, is that these same foundations provide the basis for the critique of the Labor Theory of Value.

*

The text distinguished four positions on the Labor Theory of Value. The following representative works present the basic ideas of the different positions:

I. I. Steedman: *Marx After Sraffa,* New Left Books, 1977.

G. Hodgson: "Exploitation and Embodied Labor Time," *Bulletin of the Conference of Socialist Economists,* March 1976.

M. Morishima: *Marx's Economics: A Dual Theory of Value and Growth,* Cambridge University Press, 1973; and, with qualification, "Marx in the Light of Modern Economic Theory," *Econometrica,* 1974.

II. J. Roemer: "Marxian Models of Reproduction and Accumulation," *Cambridge Journal of Economics,* March 1978.

Wolfstetter: "Positive Profits with Negative Surplus Value: A Comment," *Economic Journal,* 1976.

Abraham-Frois and Berrebi: *Theory of Value, Prices and Accumulation: A Mathematical Integration of Marx, von Neumann and Sraffa,* Cambridge University Press, 1979.

W. J. Baumol: "The Transformation of Values: What Marx 'Really' Meant (an Interpretation)," *Journal of Economic Literature,* March 1974.

D. Laibman: "Values and Prices of Production: The Political Economy of the Transformation Problem," *Science and Society,* Winter 1973-74.

III. F. Roosevelt: "Cambridge Economics as Commodity Fetishism," *Review of Radical Political Economics,* Winter 1975. Reprinted in E. Nell, editor: *Growth, Profits and Property,* Cambridge University Press, 1980.

H. Ganssmann: *The Use Value of Marx's Theory of Value,* Unpublished Manuscript.

Armstrong, Glyn, and Harrison: "In Defense of Value—A Reply to Ian Steedman," *Capital and Class,* Summer 1978.

A. Shaikh: "Political Economy and Capitalism: Notes on Dobb's Theory of Crisis," *Cambridge Journal of Economics,* March 1978. Reprinted in *Political Economy in the New School,* New School for Social Research, 1980.

IV. D. Yaffe: "Value and Price in Marx's Capital," *Revolutionary Communist,* January 1975.

*

Other references mentioned in the text:

S. Amin: *The Law of Value and Historical Materialism,* Monthly Review Press, 1978.

Bowles and Gintis: "The Marxian Theory of Value and Heterogeneous Labor: A Critique and Reformulation," *Cambridge Journal of Economics,* June 1977.

D. G. Champernowne: "A Note on John von Neumann's Article on 'A Model of General Economic Equilibrium,'" *Review of Economic Studies,* 1945-46.

A. Lowe: *The Path to Economic Growth,* Cambridge University Press, 1976, and E. J. Nell: Appendix.

E. J. Nell: "Models of Behaviour with Special Reference to Certain Economic Theories," Ph.D. Thesis, 1964.

J. von Neumann: "A Model of General Economic Equilibrium," *Review of Economic Studies,* 1945-46.

Schefold: *Theorie der Kuppelproduction,* private print, 1971.

A. Shaikh: "The Transformation from Marx to Sraffa (Prelude to a Critique of the Neo-Ricardians)," Unpublished Paper.

11

Rationalism in economics

IRVING KRISTOL

It is widely conceded that something like a "crisis in economic theory" exists, but there is vehement disagreement about the extent and nature of this crisis. The more established and distinguished leaders of the so-called "neoclassical" school—the dominant school for almost half a century now—would assert that the "crisis" is nothing more than the kind of muddle that all scientific disciplines intermittently flounder in, as they try to probe more deeply into the mysteries of natural processes. Other critics assert that all of Keynesian macroeconomics—or even the very idea of macroeconomics itself, in any precise meaning of that term—is now being called seriously into question. Still others insist that we shall get nowhere in our understanding of either macro or microeconomics until we go back to the kind of fundamental conception of economics to be found in the marginalist school (circa 1870-1910), or in the writings of Karl Marx, or Ricardo, or Adam Smith. There are even some (and they are increasingly numerous) who would go further back and re-establish economics as a subordinate branch of political philosophy—though these, being economists by profession, are likely to describe their venture as the latest version of a "new economics."

What is most interesting and surely most revealing about these varieties of dissidence is the prevalence of what might be called the "reformationist" impulse—the impulse to "go back" to some original and purer source of economic understanding that has been obscured by the intellectual aberrations of later times. Now, we are familiar with this impulse in the history of religion, where the spirit of innovation almost always takes the form of a return to original truths that the existing religious establishment has perverted beyond recognition. But one does not usually find such an impulse in the sciences: Physicists do not try to cope with the riddles of subatomic particles by re-studying and re-interpreting the work of earlier scientists. Indeed, most scientists are extraordinarily and quite blissfully ignorant of the history of their disciplines—and, on the whole, properly so. For it is the distinctive characteristic of the modern scientist that he "stands on the shoulders" of his predecessors, and can therefore see further than they could. This is inevitably the case in any discipline where knowledge is, in some crucial sense, *cumulative,* and one might even say that it is only this feature of the discipline that gives it its standing as a *science,* as distinct from all other areas toward which the human mind directs the power of rational inquiry.

In the social sciences, it is now clear, the situation is radically different from that in the natural sciences. In sociology, for instance, after almost two centuries, there simply does not exist a body of knowledge that permits sociologists to talk with more authority about society than someone who may never have received sociological training. There have been great sociologists with most interesting *insights* into man's social life, and these insights are often embedded in a fertile conceptual schema. Anyone can read their works with profit. But these insights do not have the status of scientific truths, nor can they be assembled into a body of scientific knowledge, if only because they are (more often than not) in disagreement with one another. Today only Marxist sociologists still talk in grand terms of a "science of society," and that is because they are Marxists, not because they are sociologists.

Where does that leave economics, generally acknowledged to be the most "scientific" of all the social sciences? Well, economics is certainly in better shape than sociology, since the discipline does present a coherent body of theory about economic processes which, once mastered, does provide an "expertise" that a non-economist will not possess. On the other hand, the existence of a "crisis in economic theory" is attested to by the fact that this body of *undisputed* theory is shrinking before our very eyes, not growing. More and more of the intellectual energy of economists, these days, goes into the *dis*establishment of what our university textbooks still proclaim with serene confidence. Almost everything—almost every concept, every theorem, every methodology—in economics today has become fair game for controversy.

Where will it all end? Short of the dismantling of economic science altogether, one may fairly assume. But there can be little doubt that economics is on its way to becoming a much more modest science and will experience the loss of its more grandiose scientific pretensions. Indeed, the "reformationist" impulses at work strongly suggest that it was the luxuriant growth of these pretensions over many decades which is at the root of the present crisis. Those pretensions accumulated under the influence of a spirit of rationalism—a belief that a comprehensive understanding of all human affairs (i.e., of ourselves) can be achieved through the same methods, and with the same degree of success, as our understanding of physical processes in nature. It is what Hayek calls "scientism." In this sense, rationalism may be defined as a case of elephantiasis of the spirit of rational inquiry—a spirit that is in itself, of course, always unobjectionable in principle. Or, if one wishes to be theological about it, one might say that rationalism in the social sciences is a case of *hybris,* or *superbia,* of affliction with the sin of pride. To the extent that current "revisionist" critiques of economic science take hold, economics will not become less scientific. Indeed, as it sheds what are now seen to be its pseudo-scientific aspects, and its scope shrinks correspondingly, it will be more genuinely scientific. Only it will be more scientific about less of the human world.

What is economics?

What is economics about, anyway? That question is a lot less banal than it seems, for the ways in which we answer it will profoundly affect the methodologies thought to be appropriate for economists to use.

One famous answer to this question was provided by Sir Dennis H. Robertson who, responding to the query: "What do economists economize?," replied: "Love." This answer contains a terribly important truth, as well as some unfortunate ambiguities.

Economics, as an intellectual discipline, emerges in the course of the 17th and 18th centuries as an aspect of that philosophical revolution which created a distinctly "modern" world. It is, to put it bluntly, a world in which the economizing of Love is, in certain circumstances, morally permissible, instead of being—as the traditional teachings of Christianity would have it—morally reprehensible.[1] It is a world in which the injunction, "Thou shalt love thy neighbor as thyself," while never repudiated, is interpreted as being inapplicable to commercial activities. This liberation from theological contempt, of self-interest as a motive for human action, is a precondition, not only of a capitalist economy, but also of a liberal society and a liberal polity, as a reading of *The Federalist Papers* makes plain. It is *the* essential aspect of the process which sociologists call "modernization." Just how this process worked itself out, prior to the publication of *The Wealth of Nations*—how religion and the social ethos came to reconcile themselves to a commercial civilization—is still a matter of scholarly controversy (revolving mainly around Max Weber's conception of "the Protestant ethic"), but the results are clear enough: The Western world had ceased to be hostile—or at least had become much less hostile—to commercial transactions between consenting adults.

The significance and originality of Adam Smith's *Wealth of Nations* is that it offered a reasoned explanation of why the proliferation of such transactions was morally defensible. It was a very simple yet powerful explanation, its essential thesis being that the individual's pursuit of self-interest in the marketplace produces unintended consequences that are, on the whole and over time, beneficial to everyone. This is where the analogy of the "Invisible Hand" comes in—a literary analogy, not a kind of "mystical faith," as some critics claim. Smith perceived in the seeming chaos of the marketplace an always-emerging spontaneous order, an order generated through self-correcting actions (what we now call "feedbacks") by the participants. The net result of such action and reaction is that *everyone* ends up in a more "opulent" condition (to

[1] In this respect the traditional teachings of Judaism differ radically from those of Christianity. While emphasizing the importance of "fairness" and "just conduct" in all commercial relations, Judaism never perceived commercial relations as being, in and of themselves, inimical to the moral and spiritual life. Jews could never accept Carlyle's definition of economics as a "pig philosophy," since they have always regarded commerce and business as perfectly kosher activities. The famous Talmudic statement of Rabbi Hillel goes: "If I am not for myself, who will be for me? If I am only for myself, what am I?" Christianity tries to ignore the first question and directs its attention exclusively to the second, so that the "self-interest" which is a source of moral (or a least morally neutral) activity in Judaism, is never that for Christianity. It is reasonable to think that this initial predisposition in Judaism has something to do with the relative economic success of Jews in capitalist societies. It also helps explain why so many Christian thinkers have felt, intuitively, that there was something peculiarly "Jewish" about capitalism.

use Smith's own term). For the first time in the history of the human race it became possible to conceive of material progress, in which everyone improved his condition, however unequally or tardily, as a reality rather than a wish-fulfilling fantasy.

Smith's original insight that commercial relations are such that, as in the cosmos itself, the seemingly inchoate flux of phenomena and events can be explained in terms of an orderly disorder (so to speak)—that is the rock upon which economics is built. We might, without too much strain, call it the Law of the Conservation of Economic Energy. It is an easy principle to learn, much less easy to keep steadily in mind, as any teacher of economics—or an economic advisor to politicians—soon discovers. Most of the serious errors in economic policy committed by governments throughout the ages, and most of the layman's errors in thinking about economic affairs, flow from a failure (sometimes useful, often not) to consider the second-order or third-order effects of policies over time. (Wage, price, and rent controls are the most obvious examples.) Prior to Adam Smith, it was not at all clear that there were such effects, or that they could be discerned by coherent reasoning. The relations between such interacting phenomena as supply and demand can today quickly become the intellectual property of any high school student, and in this respect he does indeed stand on the shoulders of Adam Smith (and therefore need never read him). Without such intellectual guidance, our understanding of economic affairs would be overpowered by emotional anthropomorphism (e.g., blaming high prices on wicked merchants), as has been true throughout most of human history, and as is still true for some of us all of the time and most of us some of the time.

That there are some psychological assumptions beneath this analysis of human behavior in the marketplace, and of the rationality of economic phenomena, is clear enough. Smith took it for granted that the human beings he was talking about were at least as much (or almost as much) interested in improving their material condition as in saving their souls—and much more interested in improving their material condition than in saving other people's souls. He also assumed, not that these people were always and everywhere utterly rational, but merely that they were rational enough to adapt their economic behavior to what they learned from economic experience—e.g., to lower prices when demand falls, to raise them when demand increases. These are the distinguishing features of the so-called "Economic Man"—the kind of man who makes a market economy work. If you have a civilization where the people are convinced that it is hopeless to try to improve their material condition, or where the desire to improve their material condition is radically subordinated to other goals, or where the populace is coerced into such subordination, Adam Smith is of little use to you, since people's behavior in the marketplace will not then be "rational" in the sense that makes economic theory possible.

There are two important points to make about the Economic Man of capitalism, as Adam Smith conceived of him. First, he was never thought to be a whole man, only a man-in-the-marketplace. Smith never celebrated self-interest *per se* as a human motive, he merely pointed to its utility in a population that wished to improve its condition. (That he also believed this a normal and near-universal human desire, in all societies above the primitive level, is hardly to be taken as some kind of idiosyncracy on his part.) Smith's larger view of human nature, as expressed in *The Theory of Moral Sentiments,* was basically that of the 18th-century "Sentimental" school, a secularized version of the Christian outlook which rooted its perspective in psychology rather than theology, and which proclaimed "sympathy" to be as natural a human instinct as self-interest, and on the whole more powerful. Insofar as morality was concerned, he had little trouble with the received code of the Judaeo-Christian tradition.

The second point has to do with the relation of Economic Man to economic theory. Economic theory concerns itself with the interaction of Economic Men in a marketplace. *There is no non-capitalist economic theory.*[2] It is no accident that Aristotle did not write a book on classical economic theory, or St. Thomas on Christian economic theory, or Marx on socialist economic theory. In all of their ideal societies, there was surely a place for economic *wisdom*—the prudential management, based on experience, of economic affairs. But to have an economic theory, you need a market economy—just as, to have a scientific theory in physics, you need a universe in which order is always being created through action and reaction, not a universe where God prudentially manages all physical events.

It follows that people who, for whatever reason, dislike a commercial civilization will be utterly dissatisfied with what we now regard as traditional economic theory. And if such a person is an

[2] Socialism, in its ideal state, is a political community "in which, while no one is poor, no one desires to be richer" (John Stuart Mill). In such a community, what we have ever since Adam Smith called economic theory, is superfluous. One might even say that the goal of socialism is to make economic theory superfluous.

economist, he will invent a "new economics" that, while it may appeal to some economist forefathers (e.g., Marx or even Ricardo), frequently turns out to be in fact little more than a version of pre-capitalist thinking about economics, parading about in modern economic guise.

Economics after Smith

After Adam Smith, up to our day, the history of economic thought is the story of how economists went about making economics a more rigorously analytical science. Smith was a primitive Newtonian, one might say, in his conception of market phenomena as an aspect of human relations that possessed an inherent order, behind the apparent disorderliness. But he meant little more by this than that economic phenomena—i.e., man's economic activities—are interrelated in such a way that they can therefore be rationally explained. His successors, influenced by the success and prestige of the natural sciences, were understandably prompted to move on from there and try to structure such explanations as "objective laws" of the economic universe, laws most perfectly expressed when they could achieve a precise mathematical form.

In contrast to later economics, *The Wealth of Nations* is unabashedly "humanistic." Its vision of an economic universe is "Newtonian" only analogically and qualitatively, with no pretensions to quantitative precision. All of its economic causes and economic effects are purposive human actions and reactions that we, who are accustomed to self-interested activity in the marketplace, find utterly plausible. The aim of post-Smithian economics is gradually to rid the economic universe of purposive human activity altogether—to make this economic universe an abstract model of reality in the same way that physicists create an abstract model of physical reality, and from this model, based on the fewest possible axioms, deduce "laws" that "govern" the actual world we inhabit. One of the axioms of any such model is that economic *growth* is in principle no different from physical *change*. The economic perspective can now provide a series of static "snapshots" of a universe-in-change, not a discursive description of a dynamic marketplace in which men learn, innovate, and generate economic growth. Economic *states* becomes the focus of analysis as contrasted with the economic *process* that Smith rather casually (though brilliantly) analyzed. Inevitably, the question of the distribution of income among abstract "factors of production" achieves preeminence over the issue of economic growth, the ceaseless striving of human beings in the marketplace to "better their condition."

Along with this change in perspective, the whole climate of economic discussion moved from a buoyant optimism to a quite chilling pessimism. Malthus, of course, with his "law of population," took the first step in this direction, followed by Ricardo with his several "laws," so that by the mid-19th century, economics was generally perceived, by both economists and laymen alike, as that science which discovered the "iron laws" that ruled the economic universe. Smith's "open" economic universe—one vast marketplace—was now replaced by a closed universe in which human activity could no more affect the governing laws than the activity of an atom could affect the laws of physics. Economics, which had breathed an expansive spirit in *The Wealth of Nations,* now seemed eager to inform people that the economic universe was frigid, deterministic, indifferent to human aspirations. It was, in fact, the Newtonian universe without God as creator, sustainer, or redeemer—and just as a vision of such universe horrified Pascal, so economic science, up to and through John Stuart Mill, was perceived by people of religious or literary sensibility as a kind of enemy to humanity. There can be little doubt that this evolution of economic thought, under the influence of "scientism," did much to encourage socialist idealism, with its utopian goal of abolishing Economic Man altogether. By destroying the axioms of economic science, humanity would be liberated from its cold conclusions.

But it was not socialism that liberated humanity from "the dismal science"; it was the further evolution of that economic science itself. The "marginalist revolution" after 1870 directed attention away from the forbidding macro-model of the economic universe to a new complex model of the marketplace itself. The focus was now on satisfying the wants and desires of the individual-as-consumer—and this included producers as well, who "consumed" the factors of production—and on the way in which a utilitarian calculus, governing the individual's rational choices, caused a constant process of price adjustments, under circumstances of "perfect competition." This process pointed in turn to an ideal condition of "equilibrium," in which available resources are mobilized so as best to satisfy wants (expressed in money prices). What young European socialists today scornfully dismiss as the "pseudo-happiness" of "the consumption society" became the substance of economics.

Moreover, this utilitarian calculus, given a few additional, simple axioms about the rationality of Economic Man—e.g., transitivity of preferences, so that if you preferred A to B, and B to C, you then preferred A to C—permitted the economist to apply mathematics as both an analytic and descriptive tool in his work, so that economics achieved an intellectual rigor that soon made it the envy of the other social sciences. Moreover, this mathematicization of human choice, it became apparent, offered the possibility of explaining individual human behavior in general, not merely in the marketplace, so that "the economic point of view" was applied to all sorts of social and political processes or phenomena. The philosophy of this intellectual enterprise achieved its *summa* in the work of Lionel Robbins, *An Essay on the Nature and Significance of Economic Science* (1935). Economics is now defined as the rational allocation of scarce resources, and the economist is engaged in studying "the logic of choice" so as to come up with a "maximizing" strategy. It is this conception of economics that is today dominant in our textbooks.

The "Keynesian revolution" did not affect this basic conception of economics,[3] which is still today's orthodoxy in what is called "microeconomics." Keynes' originality lay in taking "wage stickiness" (the reluctance of the price of labor to fall when unemployment is widespread) as a permanent fact of a modern economy, and in further arguing that a money-and-credit economy was capable of giving false price signals to the businessman and the policy maker, resulting in a "general glut," or depression. This matter of a "general glut" had perplexed economists from the beginning, since in traditional economics—which gave no independent power to money or credit, and regarded all markets as essentially barter markets, "veiled over" by money prices—it was theoretically impossible. Keynes devised an explanation in terms of macro-aggregates which could interact in such a way as to achieve an "equilibrium" at a depressed level. The later incorporation of Keynesian insights into an elaborate, highly-mathematical econometrics, in which elaborate correlations were sought among the macroeconomic aggregates, might well have dismayed him. But as the "neo-

[3] Keynes himself, however, following Marshall, was highly skeptical of the mathematicization of economics:

"Unlike physics, for example, such parts of the bare bones of economics as are expressible in mathematical form are extremely easy compared with the economic interpretation of the complex and incompletely known facts of experience, and lead one but a very little way towards establishing useful results."

It is perhaps worth pointing out that some of the "mathematical economics" used by business management (e.g., linear programming for inventory control) represent instances of applied mathematics that have no organic connection with economic theory.

classical synthesis" emerged after World War II, this is the path that macroeconomics took, ending up in those "black boxes" attached to computers, which presumed to "model" the economy and predict its course. The very existence of an official governmental body, called the Council of Economic Advisors, would have been unthinkable and pointless without a high degree of faith in such a methodology.

Varieties of dissent

The evident inadequacies of economic theory, most glaringly revealed in the policies derived from such theory, over the past 15 years have given rise to much dissent within the profession. Three major dissenting movements have arisen. They are, reading from the ideological "right" to the ideological "left": (a) the "neo-Austrian" school; (b) the "post-Keynesian" school; and (c) "radical-humanistic" economics.[4]

These dissenting movements have quite a bit in common. To begin with, they all reject conventional Keynesian macroeconomics in its present form, and they do so on similar grounds. Essentially they argue that the prevalent econometric models of the economy are, in whole or in part, "scientistic" simplifications of economic reality that mislead rather than illuminate. Such "static" models are deficient in that their basic axiom of *ceteris paribus*—"other things being equal"—can never apply to the world of human action, human innovation, human willfulness, all of which can revise or upset previously established relationships and correlations that the economic theorist has come to take for granted. These models, so far from being truly scientific, are but a form of mathematical mimicry of the physical sciences, inappropriate for the understanding of human activity.

Emile Grunberg has made this point forcefully in his contrast between the subject matter of economics on the one hand, and the subject matter of the physical and biological sciences on the other.[5] Economics deals with "open systems," while the physical sciences deal with "closed systems." In an "open system" there are no real constants, no invariant relations, since everything is influenced, in

[4] It is fair in this connection to ignore the resurgence, among young economists, of an interest in Marxist economics. This belongs to the history of Marxism, not the history of economics. Its purpose is to validate Marxism as a world view, not to explain actual economic phenomena.

[5] Emile Grunberg, " 'Complexity' and 'Open Systems' in Economic Discourse," *Journal of Economic Issues*, September, 1978.

no clearly determinate way, by everything else. A "closed system" is one in which certain relations are so much stronger than others that these others can be pretty much ignored. The solar system is an example of such a "closed system," with the relations among the planets so much more powerful than relations between the solar system itself and the rest of the galaxy (or cosmos) that, whenever we analyze the solar system, we can dismiss these latter relations to the limbo where "other things are equal." Because the economic universe has no such "closed systems," precise predictions of future economic states are impossible. What economic analysis does allow us to forecast—and it is no small thing—are the *general* consequences of current economic processes and policies, but with no exact time-coefficient or exact measurement of those consequences attached to such forecasts.

Where "neo-Austrians" and "post-Keynesians" disagree sharply is in their attitudes toward economic aggregates *tout simple*. The "post-Keynesians" believe that "dynamic models" based on such aggregates are possible, and would be of sufficient theoretical power to permit the economy as a whole to be "planned" and "managed" by (the right kind of) political economists. The "neo-Austrians" are, at the very least, highly skeptical of the meaningfulness of macroeconomic aggregates altogether, since their perspective on economic activity ("radical subjectivism") is one that distrusts all economic statements that do not refer to something that is occurring in the minds of, and affecting the intentions and plans of, actual human actors.

Both "post-Keynesians" and "neo-Austrians" also reject, though in very different ways and again for very different reasons, the conventional, abstract models of the microeconomic universe—one in which there is "perfect competition" between profit-maximizing units which confront scare resources and make rational, allocative decisions. For the "post-Keynesians," the Smithian free market has been completely replaced by corporate and trade-union oligopolies, so that the textbook views of "competition" are little more than anachronistic myths, which constitute a form of capitalist ideology. They therefore see the need for economic planning—with wage and price controls, etc.—to give the market the coherence that economic teaching assumed it had (or still pretends it has).

The "neo-Austrian" critique of textbook microeconomics is more fundamental and more interesting. Its vision of the marketplace is not so much consumer-oriented as entrepreneur-oriented, and it gives the innovative entrepreneur a creative and dynamic role

—someone who takes advantage of generally unperceived opportunities, rather than someone who, by referring back to a utilitarian calculus, maximizes satisfaction by choosing among known alternatives. Those opportunities are found—it is inappropriate to say they "exist"—because competition is indeed always and inherently *imperfect*. The kind of "perfect" competition that permits of mathematical treatment assumes that something called "equilibrium" is achieved by virtue of every person in the market knowing every other person's intentions (and his own as well, of course), so that a complete coordination of these plans ensues. For the "neo-Austrians" the market is not a series of equations but an actual *marketplace*—where no one knows beforehand what goods are "scarce," or even what goods are "good"; only experience in the marketplace teaches us that. In the same way, it is only in the course of human participation in the marketplace that we can know what "capital" or "resources" are. To think of them existing outside human intention or human ingenuity is to commit the sin of what Marx (after Hegel) called "reification"—taking abstract concepts for real entities. It is only in the marketplace that we discover the meaning of such concepts, just as it is only *im*perfect competition and *dis*equilibrium that permits the marketplace to function at all. It functions, not as a *mechanism*, but more like a self-correcting, perpetually-learning *organism*. The order that emerges from the marketplace is part of a process of growth, not a state—a process of incessant adjustment and readjustment of plans, intentions, and expectations.

It should be noted, however, that though both "post-Keynesians" and "neo-Austrians" are highly critical of the "scientistic" pretensions of modern economics, each is in its own way thoroughly rationalist. The "post-Keynesians" might wish to replace the Newtonian-clockwork model by something they call a "cybernetic" model, which may be an improvement (if it could ever be devised), but a shift from mechanical statics to sophisticated mechanical dynamics is no radical conceptual revolution. Basically, "post-Keynesians" still see the economy as a system organized as natural systems are organized, one whose governing laws can be discerned by economists, who in turn therewith earn the credentials for operating this system in a rational (least-cost, most-benefit) way.

And "neo-Austrians," too, are wedded to a rationalist view of the economic universe—though, once again, it is a more interesting version of rationalism. Their rationalism is located within the individual himself, not within something called "the economy." Their "methodological individualism" in economic reasoning is based on "the self-evident proposition, fully, clearly, and necessarily present in every human mind" (von Mises) that man acts purposefully, learns from such action, and that any existential disparity between intent and result flows from an error of knowledge. These purposeful actions, of course, flow from "self-interest," defined as whatever it is the individual is interested in. To the objection, "And what if the individual is not interested in improving his condition in the marketplace?," the reply is that this is the nature of human nature, and only the mentally ill would think or believe otherwise.

The "neo-Austrians" really are so much the true heirs of the 18th-century Anglo-Scottish liberal enlightenment that one member of the school has actually written: ". . . Modern Austrian economists view capitalism as the only social system compatible with the nature of man." What this means for the history of the human race is left unexplained—but, then, "neo-Austrians" are not much interested in history (or religion, or politics). The critiques levelled by "neo-Austrians" against the "scientism" that began to envelop economic theory after Adam Smith are often very trenchant. Their great merit is that they perceive Economic Man to be a willing, striving, learning human being, not a manipulable mathematical abstraction. Their limitation derives from their tendency to reduce human beings to Economic Men.

The radical economists

No such limitation is to be found among dissident "radical economists," for whom Economic Man is a modern, monstrous invention, and whose post-modern economics can best be understood as an effort to re-establish the pre-modern sovereignty of political, moral, and religious values over economic life. Since most of these economists have never studied pre-modern thought, they are content to think of their efforts at "reformation" as being definitely "progressive."

A particularly interesting specimen of this genre, recently published, is a textbook called *The Challenge of Humanistic Economics,* by Mark A. Lutz and Kenneth Lux. It is in many ways a most attractive book—high-spirited, well-written, cogently argued. Its most important service is to bring to the fore some serious criticisms of conventional economic analysis which have been for the most part blandly ignored. Some of these criticisms overlap with both the "post-Keynesians'" and "neo-Austrians'"—e.g., the "tyranny of the correlation." This refers to all of these research efforts in which the most sophisticated mathematics "teases out" one correlation or another without ever attaining the kind of causal explanations that the physical sciences insist on. Thus, biochemists find a very strong correlation between smoking and lung cancer, so strong as to imply causality; but they will never rest until they have substituted a causal explanation for this correlation. In economics, the correlations are rarely so strong—they are, indeed, often merely the temporary fruits of research, soon subverted by further research—and anything resembling a satisfactory causal explanation is a rare event. Indeed, there are some economists who, misunderstanding the nature of the physical sciences, insist—in the name of something called "positive economics"—that correlations can substitute for causal explanations, so long as these correlations permit precise predictions of economic phenomena. But there are very, very few correlations—some scholars would say there are none—that permit any such predictions in economics.

But some of the criticisms of Lutz and Lux are far more radical in the sense of challenging prevailing economic concepts that most economists would regard as absolutely essential to their professional equipment. The transitivity of individual preferences in the marketplace, a sign of the "rationality" of individual choice, is one such concept. It is, the authors point out, a dubious concept when applied to commodities which, from a consumer's point of view, have more than one dimension of utility or satisfaction. Thus, homes and automobiles not only have use-value, they also have status-value. In a sense, therefore, these are all-in-one multiple commodities, and the "indifference curves" on which the economist tries to locate preferences for such commodities become quite meaningless—one never knows what the choice signifies, or what satisfactions are being maximized. True, this dilemma can be avoided by appealing to something called "revealed preference" theory, which asserts that any actual purchase, by definition, maximizes satisfaction and is therefore rational. But this is Hegelian metaphysics, or market research; it is not economic theory. It offers no intellectual guide to understanding, explanation, or prediction.

Similarly, they point out that the "Pareto optimum"—surely one of the key concepts in "welfare economics"—is a rather defective guide for anyone concerned with the general welfare, as this is commonly understood. That concept decrees that an economic condition is at its optimum if no change is possible which increases someone's welfare without decreasing someone (or everyone) else's. But this means that, if the rich get richer while the poor get no poorer, a Pareto improvement has occurred. In effect, as Messrs. Lutz and Lux emphasize, this also means that there is a different Pareto optimum for every initial distribution of income—this latter being a subject about which economists *qua* economists have nothing to say, since it is history, not economics, that determines any such initial distribution. But such a version of "welfare economics" profoundly violates our commonsense understanding of what "welfare economics" is supposed to be about. Some welfare economists do try to "correct" this situation by reverting to interpersonal comparisons of individual utility, according to which a marginal increase in the income of the rich represents less "satisfaction" than a comparable marginal increase to the income of the poor. This *does* correspond roughly to commonsense understanding—but all such interpersonal comparisons of utility have no scientific basis in economic theory, and we have to import a philosophical-egalitarian bias into economics to legitimate them. The sad truth is that economics today has become so rigorously "scientific" that the idea of "economic welfare," which Adam Smith thought we all understood well enough, has become vague, ambiguous, even protean.

But, having made a forceful critique of the efforts of contemporary economic theory to reduce human experience—collective and individual—to rationalist-utilitarian premises, Messrs. Lutz and Lux then proceed toward the opposite extreme, and try to base economic theory on rationalist-*utopian* premises. Theirs is a Platonic economics, but bereft of Platonic political wisdom. Plato (and Aristotle too, for that matter) would have agreed that ". . . economics as a science should promote human welfare by recognizing and integrating the full range of basic human values." But the inference to be drawn from that proposition would have been evident to them: Economics is a subordinate branch of political philosophy, not an autonomous intellectual discipline. For economics as a distinctive mode of intellectual inquiry into human affairs can exist only to the extent that it does *not* recognize and integrate the full range of basic human values.

There is a powerful moral impulse behind the new radical economics, and an equally powerful moral revulsion against contemporary capitalist society and the kind of economic theory it produces. The radical economists point out, for instance, that if one performed an economic analysis of a prison or a concentration camp, one would never know, from a reading of that analysis, that it *was* a prison or a concentration camp. In short, economics tells you nothing about the moral and human quality of the "universe" it knows how to explain. Most economists would agree that this is so, but would point out that there are other forms of human inquiry—political philosophy, moral philosophy, theology—whose task it is to deal with such "normative" issues. The trouble with this rejoinder is that political philosophy and even moral philosophy have themselves, as academic disciplines, in recent decades become transformed into positivistic, "value-free," sciences, while theology has practically ceased to be a respectable form of intellectual activity. So the young economist with moral passions, having nowhere to go, turns upon economics itself and proceeds to devour its substance.

Above all, what radical economics attacks is the basic idea that self-interest, the key human motive in economics, is an inexpungible aspect of human nature—not necessarily to be admired, but always to be respected and ultimately to be channelled into constructive (or at least harmless) activity. Once you deny this premise, it is easy to dissolve economics into moral and political philosophy. The tactic used by Lutz and Lux is derived from the psychological theories of the late Abraham Maslow, who posited a universal hierarchy of natural human needs—not subjective wants, but objective needs—and perceived human developments as a progressive process of "self-actualization," whereby human beings become "mature" and most "human" as they subordinate their particular selfish "wants" to deeper "needs" whose satisfaction produces a community of autonomous—but no longer self-regarding—persons.

Maslow's distinction between "wants" and "needs"—a distinction which no mere economist is in a position to make—frees economics from the tyranny of the consumer and gives it refuge under the benign sovereignty of the philosopher-king, now transmuted into a "humanistic economist." As Lutz and Lux put it:

> Humanistic economics is a scientific framework for the theoretical understanding of, *as well as the design of appropriate institutional arrangements pertaining to,* the processes of production, distribution, and consumption that will enable optimal satisfaction of the hierarchy of human needs. (Emphasis added.)

The Maslovian distinction between wants and needs is little more than a secularized and pseudo-scientific version of the ancient distinction between our "higher" and "lower" selves—a distinction that is at the core of both classical philosophy and the Judaeo-Christian moral tradition. It is a distinction that Adam Smith, author of *The Theory of Moral Sentiments,* would never have dreamed of repudiating. Nor would Ricardo, Malthus, Mill, Jevons, Walras, or

Keynes. What they would have said (and did say) is that such a distinction is outside the scope of economics, which deals only with the "wants" of our "lower selves." The assumption of those economists was that it was utterly utopian to think that these lower parts of ourselves could ever be successfully repressed, or completely transcended, or utterly nullified, and that the virtue of free commercial transactions between consenting adults was that it willy-nilly directed our self-interested impulses toward a simple (but limited) common good: the general improvement of humanity's material condition. As for the preservation and cultivation of our "higher selves," economics leaves that to philosophy and religion.

The vision of radical economics today is that of a democratic equalitarian community in which individual self-interest would be rendered a negligible force through education, peer-group pressure, community festivals, and a constant flow of elevating rhetoric. It is a romantic-utopian vision in its substance, though scrupulously secular-rationalist in its articulation. It is, in truth, utopian socialism in modern academic dress. That it should find expression within the economic profession itself, instead of inciting a mass exodus from that profession, is but one more testimonial to the intellectual confusion of our age.

The bedrock truths of economics

So economics today does seem to be at something like an impasse. The dominant "scientistic" model tends to drift ever further away from economic reality, so that inferences for economic policy are ever more ambiguous and baffling. But the three main schools of thought that have arisen through dissociation from this excessively rationalistic model are themselves infused with varieties of rationalism that lead to their own kinds of impasses. Their criticisms of the status quo in economic theory are often well-taken, but the alternatives they propose are unconvincing. There is not the slightest reason to think—and many reasons to doubt—that post-Keynesians, fiddling with their "cybernetic" model, can do any better than Keynesians with their "Newtonian-mechanical" model. The neo-Austrians end up insisting that the best of all possible worlds would be one populated by rationalist-utilitarian individuals whose pursuit of self-interest (as defined by the individuals themselves) would be left undisturbed by state or church or whatever—an anarchical (or libertarian) world that is, in its own way, a construct of a rationalist-utopian vision. And the radical economists have, as counterpart, their own rationalist-utopian dream of a world in which individuals have so transcended their self-interested inclinations that economics itself has vanished along with its detestable incarnation, the marketplace. It is a fair judgement that, common to all four of these ways of thought, is the impassioned hope (a) that economic theory can give us a more absolute understanding of reality than it possible can, and/or (b) that economic reality can give us more by way of human "fulfillment" and happiness than *it* possibly can.

And yet economic theory lives on, surviving all the unreasonable or supra-reasonable demands that are made on it. It survives because of that bedrock of truths about the human condition that were first comprehensively enunciated in *The Wealth of Nations*. Among these truths are: 1) the overwhelming majority of men and women are naturally and incorrigibly interested in improving their material conditions; 2) efforts to repress this natural desire lead only to coercive and impoverished polities; 3) when this natural desire is given sufficient latitude so that commercial transactions are not discouraged, economic growth does take place; 4) as a result of such growth, everyone does eventually indeed improve his condition, however unequally in extent or time; 5) such economic growth results in a huge expansion of the property-owning middle classes—a necessary (though not sufficient) condition for a liberal society in which individual rights are respected.

This is not all we need to know, but it is what we do know, and it is surely not asking too much of economic theory that in its passion for sophisticated methodology it not leave this knowledge behind.

INDEX